W9-BYV-193

ILLINOIS CENTRAL COLLEGE
JK1896.F76 1976
STACKS
From parlor to prison :

A12900 311865

JK
1896
.F76
1976

From parlor to
prison

DATE			

WITHDRAWN

© THE BAKER & TAYLOR CO.

FROM PARLOR
TO PRISON

FROM PARLOR TO PRISON

Five American Suffragists Talk about Their Lives

EDITED, WITH AN INTRODUCTION, BY

Sherna Gluck

FOREWORD BY KATHRYN KISH SKLAR

VINTAGE BOOKS
A Division of Random House
New York

I.C.C. LIBRARY   55976

FIRST EDITION April 1976
A Vintage Original

Copyright © 1976 by Sherna Gluck
Foreword Copyright © 1976 by Random House, Inc.
All rights reserved under International and Pan-American
Copyright Conventions. Published in the United States by
Random House, Inc., New York, and simultaneously in
Canada by Random House of Canada Limited, Toronto.

Library of Congress Cataloging in Publication Data
Main entry under title:

From parlor to prison.

Bibliography: p.
1. Women—Suffrage—United States—History.
I. Gluck, Sherna.
JK1896.F76 1976   324'.3'0922   76–2624
ISBN 0–394–71642–6

Grateful acknowledgment is made to *Ladies' Home Journal*
for permission to reprint from articles (pp. 9–12, 99–101,
153–54). Copyright 1907, 1908, 1911 by Curtis Publishing
Company; also to *The New York Times* for permission to
reprint from articles (pp. 19–20, 50, 66, 136–40, 191–95,
201, 237–39, 241, 246–47, 248, 272). Copyright 1910,
1911, 1912 by the New York Times Company.

*All royalties from this book will go to support the work
of the Feminist History Research Project, an independent,
non-profit, feminist organization.*

Manufactured in the United States of America

ACKNOWLEDGMENTS

The oral-history interviews on which this book is based were conducted as part of the work of the Feminist History Research Project. I wish to thank all those who supported the efforts of the project, particularly Ann Forfreedom and the individuals and groups who lent financial support to it. Without the assistance of Malca Chall and Willa Baum of the Regional Oral History of the Bancroft Library, the interviews would never have been transcribed and this book would not have been possible.

Grateful acknowledgment is also made to Mary Thygeson Shepardson and Ralda Sullivan for their assistance in the Sylvie Thygeson interviews.

The work of the Feminist History Research Project and the product which has resulted here could not have been sustained without the support of my sisters in the women's liberation movement in Los Angeles, and particularly without the encouragement, support and advice of my husband, Marvin Gluck.

Above all, I owe a great debt to the five women who shared their lives with me. The experience of meeting them has had a profound effect on me. They enabled me to discover my past as a woman and radically changed my feelings about old age.

—SG

FOREWORD

by
Kathryn Kish Sklar

These strikingly honest self-portraits allow us to view the early twentieth-century woman's suffrage movement from five different perspectives: those of a Greenwich Village radical, a Midwestern activist in the movement for birth control clinics, a politically committed newspaperwoman, a federal lobbyist, and an advertising executive and clubwoman. Looking back on their lives from the vantage point of today's feminist movement, they trace the influences that fostered their commitment to woman's suffrage, and they reveal the experiential complexity of their activism.

These five women, who reflect the social circumstances of their time so richly, represent suffragist experience in the movement's rank and file. Through their stories we can see the diverse motives and varying backgrounds of women who were drawn by the logic of their lives into a public affirmation of woman's suffrage. Their testimony resonates with themes frequently found in the two generations of suffragists that preceded them: a mother's example, political commitment, female support groups. Amid the press of daily decisions, including the need to make a living, we see these women devising suffragist strategy, implementing that strategy on street corners and in jails, and combining various strategies with various life styles.

The woman's suffrage movement already had a venerable

history by the time they joined it. Born in the social ferment preceding the Civil War with the first Woman's Rights Convention in Seneca Falls, New York, in 1848, and ending in the twilight years of Progressivism immediately after World War I with the passage of the Nineteenth Amendment in 1920, the cause of woman's suffrage was one of the most sustained and long-lived reform movements in American history.

The origins of the nineteenth-century woman's rights movement was similar to that of our own time. Like its twentieth-century successor, the nineteenth-century woman's rights movement was born inside other social movements. Just as the activism of women within the civil rights and anti-war movements prompted them to challenge accepted notions of gender relationships in the mid-twentieth century, so female participation in the anti-slavery and evangelical moral reform movements of the early nineteenth century caused women to oppose the gender restrictions that limited the extent of their social activism. Participation in each of these movements carried women beyond the perimeters of their own class and into a consideration of their rights and responsibilities as women and as human beings.[1]

By the 1830s, an autonomous female politics crystallized within the abolitionist movement as an answer to their exclusion from leadership roles. Angelina and Sarah Grimke, Quaker converts from a prominent slave-holding South Carolina family, were the most popular public speakers for the abolitionist movement. Opposition to "unnatural" women who assume "the place and tone of man as a public reformer" grew rapidly within the movement, and in response, the Grimke sisters published the first fully articulated theory of woman's rights in the United States. "All moral beings have essentially the same

[1] See Aileen Kraditor, *Means and Ends in American Abolitionism, Garrison and His Critics on Strategy and Tactics, 1834–1850,* Chapter 3, "The Women Question," for a discussion of women within the abolitionist movement, and Carroll Smith-Rosenberg, "Beauty, the Beast and the Militant Woman: A Case Study in Sex Roles and Social Stress in Jacksonian America," *American Quarterly* 23 (1971): 562–84, for a discussion of women in Evangelical Reform.

rights and duties, whether they be male or female," Angelina Grimke insisted in her 1837 *Appeal to the Women of the Nominally Free States.* "Men and women were CREATED EQUAL; they are both moral and accountable beings, and whatever is *right* for man to do, is *right* for woman," Sarah Grimke declared in her 1838 *Letters on the Equality of the Sexes and the Condition of Women.*[2]

Every reversal that female activism suffered within the abolitionist ranks increased the growth of an independent woman's rights movement. Elizabeth Buffum Chace, a leading abolitionist and suffragist, described in her memoirs in 1891 the process by which women abolitionists grew into suffragists:

> In the progress of the Anti-Slavery movement experience revealed the great injustice, the detriment to human welfare, of the subordinate, disenfranchised condition of woman. Every step in that great reform was impeded by the inequality that depressed and degraded her. And these experiences were to [women] Abolitionists, in this, as in other directions, a liberal education. So when the crime of slaveholding was overcome, they became the leaders in the Woman Suffrage cause, their children, as a rule, following in their footsteps.[3]

What began in the 1830s as an affirmation of the moral equality and equal rights of women grew gradually through the 1840s and 1850s into an affirmation of political equality. In both cases the demand was the same—that women be recognized as persons in their own right and not only as wives and mothers. Throughout the nineteenth century women who were generally involved in reform activity continued to be drawn into the cause of woman's rights. Like most American reformers, they tended to be middle-class and white, but as the five women in this volume demonstrate, political motivation, a strong

[2] Pastoral Letter from "The General Association of Massachusetts (Clergy) to the Churches Under Their Care," 1837. Quoted in *History of Woman Suffrage,* Vol. I, edited by Elizabeth Cady Stanton, Susan B. Anthony, and Matilda J. Gage (Rochester, N.Y.: Charles Mann, 1881).

[3] Elizabeth Buffum Chase and Lucy Buffum Lovell, *Two Quaker Sisters* (New York: Liveright, 1937).

sense of self and a willingness to work for change cut across ethnic, class and regional boundaries.

In these five lives we have an unusual opportunity to observe the different motivations behind the commitment to suffrage, the strategies implemented on the eve of the movement's success, and the effect of suffrage and other reform activity on the lives of individual women. Some, through their mothers, reached back to Elizabeth Cady Stanton's generation; others, through their active participation in the current women's movement, carry the history of American feminism to our own time. These five women represent a long history as well as a cross section of the early twentieth-century suffrage movement.

Kathryn Kish Sklar received her B.A. from Radcliffe College and her Ph.D. from the University of Michigan, where she was an assistant professor of history from 1969 to 1974. Now an associate professor of history at UCLA, she teaches social history related to women and the family. She is the author of Catherine Beecher: A Study in American Domesticity (1973), *which was nominated for a National Book Award in Biography and won the annual prize of the Berkshire Conference of Women Historians in 1974, and is currently a fellow of the National Humanities Institute at Yale.*

CONTENTS

FROM PARLOR
TO PRISON

INTRODUCTION

by Sherna Gluck

In these pages Sylvie Thygeson, at the age of a hundred and four, recalls the discussions of woman's suffrage that took place sixty years ago over tea in her parlor in St. Paul, Minnesota. Jessie Haver Butler, eighty-eight years old, remembers watching her mother stump for suffrage in a horse-drawn wagon in Colorado in 1893. Some years later the young Jessie Haver did the same thing by train. Miriam Allen deFord, at eighty-three, describes how she began her career in the movement in 1904 by stuffing envelopes at suffrage headquarters in Philadelphia. A few years later she was speaking to street-corner crowds from a soapbox. Laura Ellsworth Seiler, now eighty-three, spoke from soap-boxes and horseback. From the deck of a motorboat on the Hudson River, she shouted "Votes for women" at unreceptive longshoremen on the docks. Ernestine Hara Kettler, now seventy-nine, picketed in front of the White House in 1917. That militant action earned her the abuse of hostile onlookers and thirty days in the Occoquan Workhouse.

These five unheralded women who participated in the final decade of the suffrage struggle came from various economic, regional and social backgrounds. They reveal the feelings and aspirations that brought them into the suffrage movement and that shaped their lives afterwards. Their accounts make it possible to fashion a kind of history very different from the traditional one derived from official documents, movement manifestoes and the memoirs and biographies of movement leaders.

This traditional history is little more than a record of the experiences of the powerful and the prominent. As applied to women's history, it simply replaces heroes with heroines and leaves unnoted those millions of others who also played a part in shaping our past. Maintaining history as the exclusive province of the elite not only denies most women a sense of their past but inevitably diminishes the significance they attach to their own lives. Considered irrelevant as a force in history, they can only discount the importance of their own actions and experiences. Unrecorded, the history of the non-elite does not become part of our collective memory.

Sylvie Thygeson. Jessie Haver Butler. Miriam Allen deFord. Laura Ellsworth Seiler. Ernestine Hara Kettler. These are women who would not ordinarily publish their memoirs and whose biographies would not be written by others. They were not leaders of the suffrage movement. Nevertheless, through the oral history interview, it is possible for their voices to be heard, for the story of their lives to be known. Through them, the anonymous suffragists who populate the faded photographs acquire new dimensions, and show themselves to be complex and fascinating women with a wide range of attitudes. We can begin to share in both the exciting and ordinary moments of their lives. We can come to know them in ways that the history of headlines and speeches never makes possible.

On the other hand, this is not a "history of suffrage as revealed through the intimate accounts of five unsung heroines." Participation in the suffrage movement represented a moment, brief but important, in the lives of these five women. It is not an isolated moment: it was an inevitable product of their individual pasts and of the changing status of women in the late nineteenth and early twentieth century. They were among the many white, educated, middle-class women who, after the turn of the century, began to push at the boundaries that traditionally circumscribed woman's behavior. This phenomenon prompted the popular journals of the day to coin the phrase "the new woman."

These five personal accounts not only provide insight into

the suffrage movement and the lives of the women who participated in it, but they also give us some understanding of the forty-year hiatus in the women's movement that followed the passage of the Nineteenth Amendment in 1920. Six decades after their participation in the suffrage struggle, these women are staunch supporters of the women's liberation movement. Yet, in the intervening years, all of them made the individualistic choices that were both cause and effect of the suffrage movement's failure to become a continuing force for women's rights.

By the time Sylvie Thygeson was born, in 1868, twenty years had passed since the historic woman's rights convention at Seneca Falls, New York. It was there that the first demand for the redress of women's grievances, including their disenfranchisement, was formally made. In those twenty years many woman's rights conventions were held, and such early feminist leaders as Lucretia Mott and Elizabeth Cady Stanton were joined by others like Susan B. Anthony. Nevertheless, in 1868, the Fourteenth Amendment was ratified and, with it, the word "male" was first introduced into the United States Constitution as a criterion for representation. This was a bitter irony for the many feminists who had risked their lives and reputations in the abolition movement. In order to rectify this injustice, these women fought to have the word "sex" included in the Fifteenth Amendment along with "race, color or previous condition of servitude." The failure of many male abolitionists to support this effort on behalf of women led to a split among the woman's rights pioneers.

In 1869 Elizabeth Cady Stanton, Susan B. Anthony and other women who felt betrayed by the male abolitionists formed the exclusively female National Woman's Suffrage Association. This group had a broad interest in all issues that affected women, and in regard to woman's suffrage, felt that the appropriate tactic was to fight for an amendment to the federal Constitution. The more conservative women veterans of the abolition movement, led by Lucy Stone, formed the

American Woman's Suffrage Association a few months later. This organization included men and focused on state-by-state battles for suffrage. Suffrage was not only viewed as a natural, inalienable right, but was also seen as a means to change the many laws denying women's civil status. In the mid-nineteenth century, for example, few states granted married women the right to control their own property earnings or to retain custody of their children in the case of separation or divorce. Many of the early feminists were convinced that even these laws did not constitute the totality of women's oppression. Like Elizabeth Cady Stanton, they pointed to social institutions like marriage and religion as the underlying sources of this oppression.

By the late nineteenth century, when Jessie Haver, Miriam Allen deFord, Laura Ellsworth and Ernestine Hara were born, women's legal status had improved even though they still could not vote. The elimination of the most blatant civil inequities affecting women tended to make enfranchisement an end in itself. Reflecting this trend, the two suffrage organizations merged in 1890 to become the National American Woman Suffrage Association (NAWSA), which adopted the narrower view and the strategy of the more conservative American Woman Suffrage Association. This occurred despite the fact that *its* state-by-state effort was no more successful than the constitutional-amendment approach of the National Woman Suffrage Association.*

This growing conservatism soon became evident in the arguments that were used to support woman's suffrage. These often appealed to the racism, xenophoboia and class prejudices of the middle-class male electorate. Many suffragists assured the men that only middle-class women would vote and their vote would serve to counterbalance the much feared vote of the poor, the black and the immigrant. Even Lucy Stone and Elizabeth Cady Stanton, who were active abolitionists, used these expedient arguments.

* The proposed Sixteenth Amendment to grant woman's suffrage was defeated 2–1 on the Senate floor. By 1890, in no states and in only one territory, Wyoming, did women have the right to vote.

By the beginning of the twentieth century the pioneers of the woman's rights movements had either died or relinquished their positions to the next generation of suffragists, women like Carrie Chapman Catt. For these new leaders, the concentration on woman's suffrage did not represent the narrowing of a previously broad feminist vision. Since their matriculation into the woman's movement had occurred when suffrage was already the central issue, their feminism was very limited.

During the 1890s a reorganization plan introduced by Carrie Chapman Catt and adopted by the NAWSA resulted in a brief surge of suffrage activity. Three Western states granted women the right to vote (one, Utah, was merely reinstating suffrage after a lapse of nine years). By the end of the decade, however, the suffrage movement had gone into the doldrums. From 1896 to 1910 no new states had granted woman's suffrage. Susan B. Anthony and Elizabeth Cady Stanton died and Carrie Chapman Catt, due to ill health, resigned as president of the NAWSA.

During this period, even though the progress for women's enfranchisement was moving very slowly, American women were reshaping their lives in other ways. In the late 1860s, when Sylvie Thygeson was an infant, it was, for the most part, only lower-class women who worked outside the home. Even those few middle-class women who had jobs, such as schoolteachers, were expected to withdraw from nondomestic activities when they married. For these middle-class matrons, the first tentative steps into outside activity were usually related to either church organizations or literary clubs. Some of the church groups that concerned themselves with such issues as the plight of the female operatives in the textile mills could be considered the forerunners of later reform organizations.

The women's literary clubs, though mocked by influential magazines like *The Ladies' Home Journal,* offered the middle-class woman a taste of a different world, a refuge from the burdens of home and kitchen. Through participation in her club a woman might not experience a revolutionary change but she would for the first time become absorbed in intellectual activity. In a sense, the woman's club represented a middle ground between the narrow confines of family life and the proscribed world of gainful employment. The proliferation of these clubs around the country led to a convention in 1890 which launched the General Federation of Women's Clubs. Though the federation had no clear-cut purpose, the fact that it was founded was an indication that the participants were seeking new avenues of expression, new ways of relating to the society. A woman journalist at the turn of the century, writing in *Cosmopolitan,* observed, "My mountain of mail is often a volcano of seething unrest."

WOMAN'S MISSION AND WOMAN'S CLUBS

By Grover Cleveland, Ex-President of the United States

"I am Persuaded that There are Woman's Clubs Whose Objects and Intents are Not Only Harmful, But Harmful in a Way that Directly Menaces the Integrity of Our Homes"

THE SCOPE AND CHARACTER OF WOMAN'S MISSION

At first blush it would appear easy to deal with the topic we have in hand . . . It is a melancholy fact, however, that our subject is actually one of difficult approach; and it is a more melancholy fact that this approach is made difficult by a dislocation of ideas and by false prospectives on the part of women themselves . . .

THE QUESTION OF A WOMAN'S VOTE

The restlessness and discontent to which I have referred is most strongly manifested in a movement which has for a long time been on foot for securing to women the right to vote and otherwise participate in public affairs. Let it here be distinctly understood that no sensible man has fears of injury to the country on account of such participation. It is its dangerous, undermining effect on the character of the wives and mothers of our land that we fear. This particular movement is so aggressive, and so extreme in its insistence, that those whom it has fully enlisted may well be considered as incorrigible . . . It is a thousand pities that all the wives found in such company cannot sufficiently open their minds to see the complete fitness of the homely definition which describes a good wife as "a woman who loves her husband and her country with no desire to harm either"; and what a blessed thing it would be if every mother, and every woman, whether mother, wife, spinster or maid, who either violently demands or wildly desires for women a greater share in the direction of public affairs, could realize the everlasting truth that "the hand that rocks the cradle is the hand that rules the world."

... The real difficulty and delicacy of our topic becomes most apparent when we come to speak of the less virulent and differently directed club movements that have crossed the even tenor of the way of womanhood. . . .

WOMAN'S DANGER OF THE CLUB HABIT

To the honest-minded women who are inclined to look with favor upon such of these clubs as indicate beneficent purposes or harmless relaxation it is not amiss to suggest that these purposes and characteristics are naturally not only of themselves expansive, but that membership in one such organization is apt to create a club habit which, if it does not lead to other similar affiliations, induces toleration and defense of club ideas in general. It is in this way that many conscientious women, devoted to their home duties and resentful of any suspicion to the contrary, through apparently innocent club membership subordinate their household interests, and are lost to the ranks of the defenders of home against such club influences and consequences as the unbiased judgement of true womanhood would unhesitatingly condemn . . .

WOMAN'S CLUBS NOT ONLY HARMFUL, BUT A MENACE

I am persuaded that without exaggeration of statement we may assume that there are woman's clubs whose objects and intents are not only harmful, but harmful in a way that directly menaces the integrity of our homes and the benign disposition and character of our wifehood and motherhood . . . I believe that it should be boldly declared that the best and safest club for a woman to patronize is her home . . .

This magazine is writ in large and angry letters in the minds of many estimable women as being opposed to woman's clubs. And it is. But not in the way that many of these women think. It is not so much opposed to the club idea as to what that club idea usually stands for: what it strives to accomplish and fails.

THE SANE WOMAN'S CLUB

If the average woman's club were carried out along sane lines: along lines of actual benefit to the community in which its members live, it would be a factor for power and for good which this magazine would be the first to applaud. Just fancy, for a moment, a State Federation of Woman's Clubs offering a substantial prize for the prettiest, best-kept and most attractive town or village of a certain size within its State borders. Just calculate the valuable and attractive enterprises that such an offer would set in motion: what interesting expeditions, communions and acquaintanceships, and all on a sane, healthy basis, it would develop

and bring about. To make the young people of our small towns in love with their surroundings, an actual part of their village life, imbued with the spirit to make their homes more attractive—is there a finer spirit, a higher ambition to cultivate? Of what value are papers, copied from encyclopædias and ill-digested, on Egyptian art, mediæval literature and what-not, compared to such a community work that would make the face of the earth more beautiful and the people more content?

WHAT IS MORE IMPORTANT

The main trouble with the woman's club idea is that it is misdirected: it chases the mythical pot of gold at the end of the rainbow and sees not the beauty of the prismatic arch itself. When its members study the Filipino and Filipino history and life it misses a signal point—for instance, that the tiniest little Filipino village is far more beautiful than is the perky little railroad town in which the club members live. If the members saw that fact then their studies would be worth something to the community. The gathering would then break up, not with a confused notion of what it had been discussing, but with a concrete need in its mind of the beautification of the architecture of its town: of the cultivation of trees on its public highways and flowers in its home-plots: of the embowering of country roads: of the laying of village drives: of the uplifting of the community spirit. To inculcate the love of the beautiful and the pride of home in the mind of the young is far more important to us in the immediate present than what Cæsar did or Rameses stood for.

The social forces and technological developments that were releasing women from the home and affording them the leisure to participate in these clubs were gaining momentum. Domestic responsibilities were diminishing as a result of decreased family size and the reduced physical dimensions of living quarters. Industrialization meant that many household chores were assumed by outside establishments: commercial laundries, bakeries and ready-to-wear clothes manufacturing. Even child rearing was made slightly less demanding by the establishment of an increasing number of recreational facilities for children outside the home. Day nurseries, playgrounds and kindergartens were founded—all, appropriately enough, by women in various clubs.

By 1902 membership in the clubs constituting the General Federation of Women's Clubs had reached two hundred thousand. This remarkable growth occurred despite relentless ridicule and hostility from the press. Men were clearly aware of the threatening implications of women organizing, even in this most genteel way. Of even greater significance than the numerical growth of the club movement was its change in direction. No longer a mere resting place for the middle-class matron, the women's clubs were paying more and more attention to current events and to civic improvements in their communities. That this change was a self-conscious one was amply demonstrated at the biennial convention in 1904. Not only did a discussion of suffrage take place for the first time, but a woman voter, Sarah Platt Decker of Colorado, was elected president. On assuming office she told the assembled delegates:

"Ladies, you have chosen me your leader. Well, I have an importance piece of news to give you. Dante is dead. He has been dead for several centuries, and I think it is time that we dropped the study of his *Inferno* and turned our attention to our own."

The clubwomen did turn their attention to the inferno of their own society. What they found was corrupt local government, miserable working conditions, child labor, destruction of forests and a host of other ills. They not only found these social ills, but they organized to combat them. Major women's reform groups were established, such as the National Consumers League and the National Women's Trade Union League. These groups allied themselves directly, albeit maternalistically, to the cause of working-class women.

And so, concerned middle-class women—women like Sylvie Thygeson—began to participate through their organizations in that reform impulse which characterized the progressive era of the early twentieth century. They were, in fact, largely responsible for many of the social reforms of the period.

While the older middle-class woman was seeking new avenues of participation in society through organizational activity, her younger counterparts were entering the world of respectable gainful employment, a choice which gave them more flexibility and the freedom to live outside the family home. Women from the poorer classes had been working outside the home in increasing numbers since the advent of the power loom in 1814. Decade after decade, until 1920, the number of women working in manufacturing, like the total number of men, increased. Relatively few of these women, however, were found in skilled occupations. They worked as domestics or at manufacturing jobs which required little training and paid the lowest wages.

Normally, middle-class women simply moved from the parental home to the conjugal home. Those few who remained unmarried stayed in the parental home until they died, taking care of their parents as they aged. One of the few professions open to women outside the home was that of elementary or secondary school teaching. The first half of the nineteenth century saw a gradual feminizing of the teaching occupation, so that by the Civil War women constituted almost 90 percent of the teachers—at a much lower pay, of course, than what their male counterparts had received.

With the growing availability of public high school education and the continuing denial of access to most professions, women formed a ready labor pool for the new jobs being created by the rapid expansion of industry and commerce. By the end of the nineteenth century, they began streaming into the offices, so that in thirty years the proportion of female stenographers and typists jumped from 4.5 percent to 76.7 percent. During the same period, nursing, after centuries of being held in low esteem, was becoming more and more professionalized and respectable. From 1880 to 1900 the number of graduates from formal nursing schools increased from 157 to 3,500. In the next decade this figure more than doubled.

Although the office jobs provided much needed respectable employment for younger educated women, the implications of this trend alarmed many. Edward Bok, the editor of the influential *Ladies' Home Journal*, who had first railed at the clubwomen for overstepping traditional bounds, now found a new target in the women office workers. He used the pages of his magazine to decry the "unnatural position of women in business" and "the alarming tendency among business girls and women to nervous collapse." * Despite Bok's dire predictions, all of the women whose lives are described in this volume worked at one time or another in offices and seemed to have suffered no ill effects. Laura Ellsworth Seiler had a forty-year career as a successful business executive.

Though the advent of the middle-class woman worker and the organization woman was the most obvious indication of changing female expectations, there were other less obvious

---

* Sixteen years later the same magazine found certain feminine qualities were perfectly suited for office work. See Margery Davies, "Woman's Place Is at the Typewriter," *Radical America*, Vol. 8, 1974, pp. 1–28, for an excellent recent analysis.

signs. The declining birth rate began to affect not only the more educated and prosperous, but was also evident among second-generation immigrants and white-collar workers. Despite the influx of new immigrants, the rate of population increase steadily declined beginning in 1880. The small family was rapidly becoming the American ideal.

Many factors may have contributed to this decline in the birth rate, but one of the most important has been the changing attitudes and expectations of women. Although safe and effective birth control methods were not readily available, even to the most prosperous until several decades later, women for centuries have controlled their fertility by abortion, if not by other methods. The fact that the birth rate declined in this period, prior to the widespread dissemination of modern birth control information, suggests that more women were resorting to abortion, probably self-induced in painful and dangerous ways.*

Once again there were cries and alarms over the social trends created by the changing expectations of the "new woman." From his "bully pulpit" President Theodore Roosevelt urged larger families, denouncing family limitation as "race suicide."

The "new woman," in all her manifestations, was by no means an emancipated woman, nor was she a feminist. She did not deny her traditional role, but rather redefined some aspects of it. The clubwoman simply expanded the definition of home to include the community. Most young workingwomen expected to eventually leave their jobs and become wives and mothers. Even those who joined the suffrage struggle in the 1910s did not radically challenge their position in society, and few considered themselves feminists.

There were, of course, women who *did* seriously challenge their role in society, women who *were* feminists. They were usually involved in the bohemian life of Greenwich Village or the radical political groups of the period. The bohemian fem-

---

* Information obtained through oral-history interviews about this period indicates that abortion and other birth control techniques were very common among women of all classes.

inists were often preoccupied with the development of new life styles that would help to emancipate women.* They were concerned with communal living arrangements, rationalized housekeeping methods, nonmarital sexual relationships. Those bohemian feminists who became involved in the suffrage struggle in the 1910s had attitudes very different from those who were committed exclusively to woman's suffrage. They had few illusions about the fundamental changes the vote would bring and understood the need for basic structural transformations in the society, even though they lacked any clear notion of what these should be. On the other hand, the feminist radicals, those tied to the Socialist Party or the Industrial Workers of the World (IWW) or the anarchist circles of the period, were committed to an overthrow of the system and defined their activities primarily in economic terms. They shared the politics of the men in these groups who, despite abundant evidence of male chauvinism, were assumed to consider their woman comrades as equals. Feminist radicals, even those few from the upper and middle classes, considered the struggles of the clubwoman, the career woman and the bohemian feminists as irrelevant and bourgeois. Nevertheless, some, like Ernestine Hara, were moved more by their feminist indignation than by their radical scorn. Their anger at disenfranchisement as an almost personal insult led some to take part in the suffrage struggle in its last years.

The tide of change was rising in the first decade of the twentieth century, and by 1910 the time seemed ripe for the final triumph of the suffrage movement. There were now millions of clubwomen, workingwomen, and socially or politically unconventional women who felt that women should have the right to vote. Yet, despite the apparent ripeness of conditions, the resistance to woman's suffrage was so entrenched and so

---

* For a description of the Greenwich Village feminists, see June Sochen, *The New Woman in Greenwich Village,* 1910–1920 (New York: Quadrangle, 1972).

well financed that it took ten more years of bitter struggle before woman's suffrage was enacted.

During the fourteen-year lull that began in 1896 no progress had been made. In 1910, after six other state referenda had been lost, women won the right to vote in the State of Washington. This victory in the West, coupled with the earlier introduction of new strategy in the East, were prime factors in the resurgence of the suffrage movement. This strategy, much less ladylike, was imported by several American suffragists who had been inspired by the militant "suffragettes" in England.* The first of these returning suffragists was Harriet Stanton Blatch, daughter of Elizabeth Cady Stanton, who founded the Women's Political Union,† patterned after its English counterpart, the Women's Social and Political Union.

The Women's Political Union represented the first major effort by an American suffrage group to seek the support of workingwomen in general and women in the labor unions. Taking to the streets, and through soapbox oratory and massive parades, the Women's Political Union brought a new militancy to the suffrage campaign. In 1910 they sponsored the first of a series of major suffrage parades in New York City. Hundreds of women, including Miram Allen deFord, participated despite the strong objections of the more conservative suffrage leaders who expressed grave doubts about the necessity of "so radical a demonstration" and who were convinced that the parade would set suffrage back fifty years. The conservative suffragists who did not absent themselves for reasons of "ill health" reluctantly joined the marchers in a contingent of automobiles. Many women, too timid to openly join the still unpopular cause, lined the sidewalks. Along the route the houses of sympathizers were decorated with flags and bunting.

The new tone set by the Women's Political Union inspired

---

* This diminutive term was used in England largely because the women involved in the struggle there were relatively young. The American suffragist, generally older, considered the term an insult when applied to them by most of the American press. They referred to themselves as "suffragists."

† Originally called the Equality League of Self-Supporting Women.

dramatic and unorthodox activity all around the country. The suffrage campaign in California, which saw the use of huge billboards, electric signs, pageants, plays and essay contests, culminated in victory in 1911. The next year the women of Oregon, Arizona and Kansas became voters. Clearly, a new era had dawned, and by 1912 even the conservative organization NAWSA, then under the leadership of Dr. Anna Howard Shaw, organized a major parade in New York City, in which both Laura Ellsworth and Ernestine Hara marched.

Though it was attracting more and more women, the suffrage movement was still dedicated to the tedious state-by-state method of winning the vote. It was not until Alice Paul and Lucy Burns returned from England that the American suffrage movement again turned its attention and energy to the goal of a constitutional amendment. In November 1912 they approached NAWSA, offering to launch a renewed campaign for a federal amendment beginning with a parade in Washington, D.C., to coincide with the presidential inauguration in 1913. Alice Paul was made chairman (sic) of the Congressional Committee of NAWSA and given their blessings. Raising the necessary money herself, she opened offices in the nation's capital. The day before Woodrow Wilson's inauguration, a parade of eight to ten thousand marched down Pennsylvania Avenue. Denied police protection the procession was attacked by mobs and the Secretary of War was finally forced to call out troops from Fort Meyer.

5,000 WOMEN MARCH, BESET BY CROWDS

Demonstration at Capital Badly Hampered and Congress is Asked to Investigate

CAVALRY TO THEIR AID

Authorities Denounced by Dr. Shaw— Wonderful Allegory Tells Story of the Ages

Special to The New York Times

WASHINGTON, March 3.— In a woman's suffrage demonstration to-day the capital saw the greatest parade of women in its history. In the allegory presented on the Treasury steps it saw a wonderful series of dramatic pictures. In the parade over 5,000 women passed down Pennsylvania Avenue. Some were riding, more were afoot. Floats throughout the procession illustrated the progress the woman's suffrage cause has made in the last seventy-five years. Scattered throughout the parade were the standards of nearly every State in the Union. It was an astonishing demonstration.

It was estimated by Gen. John A. Johnson, a Commissioner of the District of Columbia, that 500,000 persons watched the women march for their cause.

Imagine a Broadway election night crowd, with half the shouting and all of the noise-making novelties lacking; imagine that crowd surging forward constantly, without proper police restraint, and one gains some idea of the conditions that existed along Pennsylvania Avenue from the Capitol to the Treasury Department this afternoon. Ropes stretched to keep back the crowds were broken in many places and for most of the distance the marchers had to walk as best they could through a narrow line of shouting spectators. It was necessary many times to call a halt while the mounted escort and the policemen pushed the crowd back. . . .

It was when the head of the procession turned by the great Peace Monument and started down Pennsylvania Avenue that the first indication of trouble came. Hearing the bands strike up, the crowds on both sides of the avenue pushed into the roadway. At once the police authorities knew that they had not made proper plans for keeping the spectators in restraint.

Looking down the avenue the paraders saw an almost solid mass of spectators. With the greatest of difficulty the police were keeping open a narrow way.

As far as the eye could see, Pennsylvania Avenue, from building line to building line, was packed. No such crowd has been seen there in sixteen years. . . .

Through all the confusion and turmoil the women paraders marched calmly, keeping a military formation as best they could. The bands played and hundreds of yellow banners fluttered in the wind.

The outrageous attacks on the marchers, some of whom were congressmen and their wives, led to an investigation and the eventual removal of the chief of police. The effect of the entire affair was to make woman's suffrage a prominent topic around the country and in the corridors of the Senate and House.

Alice Paul's relationship with NAWSA was short-lived. In 1913 she founded the Congressional Union, renamed the National Woman's Party in 1916. Adopting the English women's attitude of "holding the party in power responsible," Alice Paul petitioned the Democrats to caucus on the subject of a standing House Committee on Woman's Suffrage. The caucus not only voted against the standing committee, but they declared that suffrage was a state issue. When Wilson feebly claimed that he had no choice but to follow his party, the Congressional Union held him personally accountable and thus laid the groundwork for future anti-Wilson demonstrations.

A woman's suffrage amendment was passed in the Senate in 1914 by a narrow margin, but was defeated in the House the following year. Nonetheless Alice Paul's National Woman's Party (NWP) and Carrie Chapman Catt's NAWSA* both

* Carrie Chapman Catt reassumed leadership of NAWSA in 1915, when Anna Howard Shaw resigned. She proposed a "winning plan" which involved combining the "states" route and the federal route.

continued to press for a federal amendment using very different tactics. NAWSA used personal lobbying and pressure from home state constituents, while the NWP actively campaigned against the party in power, particularly in the Western states in which women voted. Even though their differences in approach made it impossible for them to work together, both groups descended on the Republican convention in 1916. They succeeded in getting woman's suffrage adopted as part of the Republican platform and in getting Charles Evans Hughes, the party's presidential candidate, to come out in favor of a constitutional amendment.

When the Democratic party's convention resulted in the nomination of incumbent Woodrow Wilson, and a platform that would go no further than to endorse suffrage action by individual states, the NWP opened a militant attack against Wilson which continued for two years. The campaign began on January 10, 1917, after Wilson's reelection, when suffragist pickets appeared outside the White House gate. These "sentinels of liberty" were changed hourly, marching out of and returning to the NWP headquarters, which was located on Lafayette Park, across from the gates of the White House. For three months the picketing proceeded without incident. Then, when the United States entered World War I in April 1917, the mood of both the police and passers-by became ugly. The NWP openly opposed the war and on their banners they reminded Wilson that "Democracy Should Begin at Home." Obscene insults were hurled at the "brave sentinels" by the gallant men who had always proclaimed their desire to keep women on a pedestal. They threw tomatoes at the very women they were protecting from the ugly world of politics by denying them the vote.

With the number of hostile onlookers growing and becoming more unruly, the police began arresting the women pickets in June 1917.* Initially the women were given short sentences

* An appellate court decision nine months later ruled that the arrests of the women, eventually reaching a total of 218, had been illegal.

for obstructing traffic, but by the time Ernestine Hara joined their ranks in the fall, thirty-day sentences were being meted out. The arrested women declared themselves to be political prisoners and demanded to be treated as such. They refused to work at the workhouse and many eventually went on hunger strikes. After nine days, the hunger strikers were brutally force-fed three times a day for three weeks, not intravenously as is the practice today, but with tubes forced into their stomachs. To further humiliate and intimidate them they were threatened with transfers to an insane asylum. Once the plight of these women was publicized, the resulting national outrage became an added pressure on Congress.

While the NWP was engaged in dramatic, militant actions, the NAWSA continued its quiet maneuvering and campaigning at both the state and federal level. In 1917 eight more states granted women the right to vote. Unlike the NWP, the NAWSA firmly backed the President and pledged its members to the war effort. Both the flamboyant militancy and the conservative respectability of these two groups were necessary in the eventual achievement of the woman's suffrage amendment.

In January 1918, one day before a House vote on the issue, Woodrow Wilson finally declared his support for woman's suffrage. Although the amendment passed the House by exactly the two-thirds majority needed (272–136), parliamentary maneuvering kept it from coming to a vote in the Senate. Without diminishing its pressure on the President, the NWP moved its pickets to the Senate. Wilson finally appeared on the Senate floor in October 1918 to appeal for immediate passage of the suffrage amendment as a "war measure." His effort was too little, too late, and the amendment fell two votes short of the two-thirds majority required for passage.

Ending its eight-month moratorium on demonstrations against President Wilson, the NWP in January 1919 lit a "perpetual fire of freedom" in front of the White House. Seeking to embarrass the President, who was traveling around the world preaching democracy but was unwilling to use his influence to ensure it at home, the women burned copies of his speeches.

As a bell tolled at the NWP headquarters, Mr. Wilson's pious words were consumed in the flames of the demonstrators. The women stood guard over the "perpetual fire of freedom" all night long. When their flaming urn was broken by hostile observers, the demonstrators would replace it and rebuild the fire. They were eventually arrested for violating an obscure law that prohibited outdoor fires between sunset and sunrise.

These public manifestations, combined with the more private efforts of conservative suffrage groups, forced President Wilson to exert pressure on the Democratic members of the Senate. On June 4, 1919, forty-one years after it was first introduced, the Susan B. Anthony amendment granting women the right to vote was passed by the U.S. Senate.

The struggle was still not over. It took more than one year and a well-planned campaign by women all over the country to gain the ratification of thirty-six states. In this drive for ratification, the lobbying skills developed by Carrie Chapman Catt and members of NAWSA were extremely important. Finally, on August 26, 1920, the Nineteenth Amendment became part of the U.S. Constitution. All across the country women celebrated and breathed a sigh of relief. They, unfortunately, seemed to feel that the suffrage victory meant the end of their struggle.

Without the efforts of millions of women using different tactics and working on different fronts, the battle to enfranchise the American woman might easily have been lost or endlessly prolonged. Women with widely divergent views laid aside their differences to work together, and though this détente may have been necessary for the success of achieving woman's suffrage, it carried within it the seeds of the destruction of the women's movement. Because suffrage had become *the* goal, there was little to hold the movement together after the goal was achieved. Feminists who had a deeper understanding of women's position in society suspended their analysis while they worked for the immediate goal of suffrage. Consequently, they had developed no long-range program for a women's movement.

Those suffragists who saw the vote as a means to achieve

progressive legislation did, initially, join forces to form a women's lobby, the short-lived Women's Joint Congressional Committee. Various of the women's reform and special-interest organizations did have some initial success in obtaining enlightened legislation relating to women and children. Generally, however, the power of organized women, as demonstrated by the suffrage victory, was not translated into political power. The largest suffrage organization, the NAWSA, dissolved itself in 1920 and was reconstituted as the National League of Women Voters. Instead of seeking to elect women to office or to organize a women's bloc, this organization dedicated itself to local civic matters and to education of the new women voters. By 1925 it had become obvious to most politicians that there was no effective women's voting bloc. It became increasingly difficult to enact progressive legislation that would benefit women.

Progressive ideals also suffered from a change in the mood and temper of the country. By the end of the 1910s a period of reaction set in. In November 1919 a period of repression was ushered in by Attorney General A. Mitchell Palmer and his zealous assistant, J. Edgar Hoover. Major radical groups of the day were subjected to the notorious Palmer raids, in which records were seized and members beaten. Native-born radicals, particularly in the IWW and the Communist Labor Party, were imprisoned on charges of criminal syndicalism, and foreign-born radicals were deported. The ranks of the radical movement, from which many feminists had come, were thinned. In the face of the ascendancy of anti-labor forces, the American labor movement was barely able to cling to the gains of the previous decade.

Exhausted and drained by the Great War, most people became preoccupied with their private lives. The country experienced a superficial "revolution in manners and morals." New ideas and attitudes about sex had been gradually appearing in the literature of the early twentieth century. These changing values were reflected in the life styles of bohemian women. With the importation of Freudian psychology and its emphasis on sexual impulses, and with the changing role of the family, these new ideas gained wider currency. However, though women could now more openly express their sexuality, the "revolution" had little effect on their basic role in society. The portrayal of the seductive, fun-loving, youthful woman in film and literature, and the exploitation of this image by the advertising industry, served to reinforce women's role as a sexual object. She had no identity or value apart from that of fulfilling the needs of men. Even more pernicious was the promotion of the idea, again greatly aided by advertising, that a woman's primary function was to serve as a consumer of goods and services. The seeds of the "feminine mystique" were planted.

The many women's reform groups and professional organizations of the period were never able to coalesce into a sustained women-centered movement. Those groups that remained committed to woman's rights were unable to overcome the class barriers that the suffrage movement had successfully bridged. Never attracting large numbers of working-class women, the suffrage movement was viewed by them at most as being irrelevant to their needs. When the NWP made the passage of the equal rights amendment its next major goal, it was confronted by the opposition of those women in the labor movement and reform organizations who had worked so hard for protective labor legislation for women.* This kind of legislation was extremely important because so few women workers were shielded from gross exploitation by union membership. The fear that their hard-earned protective legislation would be jeopardized by an equal rights amendment was obviously heightened by the anti-labor climate of the period.

Fearful of both the implications of the equal rights amendment and the split it was creating in the women's movement so soon after the suffrage victory, the National Women's Trade Union League, the National Consumers League, the National

---

* These laws varied among states, but generally they placed limitation on working hours and conditions, e.g., a maximum ten-hour day, elimination of night work, minimum wage standards, protected machinery and sanitary workshops.

League of Women Voters, and even representatives from the General Federation of Women's Clubs and the YWCA met with Alice Paul and the National Woman's Party in 1921 to try to hammer out a compromise. After some vacillation on the part of Alice Paul, the compromise efforts collapsed, and the NWP declared that the protective laws only served to hold women back and limit their opportunities. The lines were clearly drawn when, in 1923, the courts ruled against the minimum wage law for women (the very law for which Jessie Haver had so assiduously lobbied in 1918), and the NWP hailed as a triumph what other women saw as a stunning defeat.

It was at this point that Florence Kelley, long a champion of the rights of women workers, broke with the NWP of which she had been a board member and became a principal opponent of the equal rights amendment. Many other former supporters of the militant suffragists joined her. At the same time, an increasing number of business and professional women endorsed the equal rights amendment because it was in their own self-interest to do so. The cleavage along class lines became irreconcilable. The NWP and its allies continued to work for the passage of the amendment. The other side consisted largely of women affiliated with labor unions. Their position was articulated for several decades by the Women's Bureau, an agency of the Department of Labor which was created through the efforts of union women and the reform organizations allied with them.

Birth control was potentially the cause around which former suffragists could have united. It was clearly an issue that cut across class lines. The initial impetus of the birth control movement came from radical women like Emma Goldman and Margaret Sanger who also strongly identified themselves as feminists. Concerned with the condition of women, they wanted to provide them, especially those of the working class, with control over their own reproductive processes. During the 1910s the illegality of the distribution of birth control information virtually guaranteed that those involved in its dissemina-

tion would be on the radical fringe of the women's movement.*
Women reformers and suffragists did not openly espouse birth
control, even though some, like Sylvie Thygeson, worked cov-
ertly for the cause. Those organizations that were devoted to
the legalization of contraception were usually run by feminists.

With the dissolution of the suffrage forces and the weakening of left-wing groups, it would have required a conscious,
deliberate program to reorganize a woman's movement around
a feminist issue like birth control. Crystal Eastman, a Greenwich Village feminist who was on the board of the National
Woman's Party, tried to do this at their annual meeting in
1921 when she proposed a program "to make an end to the
subjection of women in all its remaining forms." She felt that
among other tasks they should devote themselves to the removal of all laws whch denied women access to birth control
information. The NWP did not accept her proposal and instead pledged itself to another single-issue fight: for the equal
rights amendment. Since the more conservative women's groups
were even less likely to rally to such a cause, it was clear that
birth control and other feminist issues would not be used to
ressurrect the women's movement.

The failure of feminists to become involved in the birth control issue also had an impact on the orientation of the birth
control movement.† Without feminist support, Margaret San-

* In addition to the Comstock law which prohibited the dissemination
of information on birth control through the U.S. mails, there were twenty-
four states that had laws specifically penalizing contraceptive knowledge.
The other twenty-four states did not specifically mention contraceptive
knowledge in their obscenity laws, but by using federal precedent they
were able to suppress this information as obscene. The laws suppressing
contraceptive knowledge ranged from prohibiting bringing any information into the state (Colorado) to telling anyone where or how contraceptive knowledge could be acquired (fourteen states, including New York,
Washington, Pennsylvania, Minnesota, Massachusetts). Even physicians
were not exempt until a judicial decision was handed down in New York
in 1918 and legislative changes were made in the 1920s in some other
states.

† For a more detailed analysis along these lines, see Linda Gordon,
"The Politics of Population: Birth Control and the Eugenics Movement,"
Radical America, Vol. 8, 1974, pp. 61–98.

ger increasingly had to turn to the eugenics movement for support, using its arguments in her own propaganda and de-emphasizing the earlier feminist ones. In other words, rather than stressing the need for women to control their own repro-ductive processes, the argument became focused on the need for society to control undesirable genetic characteristics. By the mid-1920s the die was cast, and by the end of the 1930s the birth control movement had shed almost all of its feminism and radicalism.

During the 1920s, the women who had taken part in the suffrage struggle seemed to choose individual paths devoid of any feminist cohesion. Those who pursued professional careers devoted all their attention to those careers and belonged only to organizations directly tied to their professional interests. There was a large exodus, usually permanent, from self-support-ing independence to the life of home and family.* A few de-voted their political energies to radical movements which they felt would bring about structural changes in society that would necessarily mean freedom for women. The full range of choices made by former suffragists is represented in the lives of Sylvie Thygeson, Jessie Haver Butler, Miriam Allen deFord, Laura Ellsworth Seiler and Ernestine Hara Kettler.

In the 1930s social, economic and political forces combined to stop the progress made by women in the first three decades of the century. Ironically the avenues that had earlier created new options for women now reinforced their subordinate role in society. The office jobs which originally offered middle-class women the chance for economic independence now froze them into underpaid work with little chance for advancement. The nurses who had finally achieved a sense of independent profes-sionalism now found themselves merely ill-paid doctors' assis-tants. The club movement, which had expanded the horizon of so many women, contracted once again to a concern pri-marily with women's traditional activities and interests. Only

---

* A 1920s study of college graduates revealed that only 11 percent re-turned to work after marriage.

among those groups representing working-class women and professional women was there any effort to concentrate on what might be called "women's issues."

Although there was a brief flurry of feminist expectation in the 1940s, when millions of new women joined the work force and hundreds of thousands of others moved into more responsible, higher-paying jobs, it was not until the 1960s that anything like a feminist revival occurred. Their participation in the liberal and radical activities of the 1960s led many women to examine their *own* status in American society. The result was a rebirth, almost one hundred and twenty years after the Seneca Falls Convention, of an autonomous women's movement, a movement which, for the first time is beginning to transcend class, race and ethnic divisions.

Even though the women who participated in the suffrage struggle were not able to sustain a women's movement, even though they did not accomplish for women what many had hoped, and even though they were predominantly middle-class, their contribution to the cause of women's rights cannot be denied. No matter how limited the direct effects of the Nineteenth Amendment might have been, it *did* mean the removal of an institutional insult to women, a removal accomplished *by* women. It *did* mean that women banded together to struggle against the established forces of society. That shared effort, that defiance of entrenched male authority, that glimpse of possible triumph, could and should become part of the consciousness of all women.

The oral-history interviews with five unknown suffragists presented here will, I hope, contribute to that consciousness.

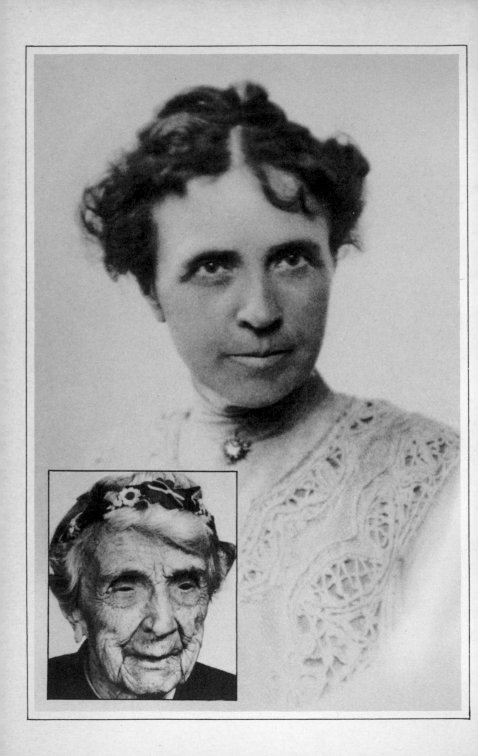

SYLVIE THYGESON

In the Parlor

Sylvie Thygeson sat in the lounge of a convalescent hospital in Palo Alto, California, in 1972 and, at the age of a hundred and four, reminisced about her life and her experiences in the suffrage and birth control movements in the first two decades of the twentieth century. I had come to the hospital with little more information than the fact that Sylvie, known as "Mother T," had been active in the suffrage struggle. Her daughter, Mary Thygeson Shepardson, herself a rather remarkable woman of seventy, accompanied me and assisted in the interview.

I was unprepared for my first sight of Sylvie, having never before come face-to-face with anyone a hundred and four years old. She was very frail and stooped; her sunken eyes, glazed by cataracts, looked like dark pools in her deeply lined face. As she sat down next to me on the sofa, I couldn't help but wonder how much mind and memory were left in this ancient woman.

After Mary established for her mother what my interests were and my questioning began, it became readily apparent that Sylvie Thygeson was not only quite lucid but that she still had a remarkable command of language. She also displayed, at one point in the interview, a steadfast loyalty to two of her long-dead friends that was extraordinarily touching: she stubbornly refused to give the names of two women with whom she had been involved in an illegal birth control clinic almost sixty years earlier.

There was a striking contrast between this hundred-and-four-year-old woman, discoursing on her world view, and the surrounding environment. As Sylvie Thygeson recounted her experiences in a manner that was both articulate and sophisticated, there could be heard in the background the voice of the hospital recreation leader calling out numbers as she diverted the other residents, all considerably younger than Sylvie, with a game of bingo.

A CENTURY AGO:
CHILDHOOD AND YOUTH

I was born in the little town of Forreston, Illinois, in 1868. It was a beautiful little town with white painted buildings and green roofs and green shutters, and very beautiful elm trees. People loved flowers; everybody had flowers.

I was named after this little slave girl from Louisiana. My grandfather was a Presbyterian minister and worked with the underground railroad. He wasn't in charge of a station, but he stopped at these stations. My grandparents were coming along the Mason-Dixon Line, and at this one spot where they stopped they were entertained along with this fleeing Negro family: husband and wife and two or three children. My father was a little boy at the time, and he got well acquainted, during the two or three days they were held over there, with this little Negro girl. So, years afterwards, when I came along, they were thinking about a name and wondering. I was the fourth child in the family and they had no special name for me. My father suggested, "Call her after that little girl from Louisiana." This particular set of Negroes was from Louisiana and the little girl had a French name. Since they didn't have any other name in view, I was named that—Sylvie.

My grandparents stopped and settled in Fayette, Iowa. My grandfather had a congregation there. He was a real pioneer. But he was burned to death in a prairie fire. He'd been out ministering to a sick patient, a patient who was dying, in fact. He had taken his little boy with him, his five-year-old son, and coming back cross-country they were caught in this prairie fire and burned to death. That's the way my grandfather met his death. He was on this errand of mercy and was coming back. So I never in the world could have had any religion after that, after hearing that story.

My father, of course, was in the Civil War. He served with Grant; he was with Grant at Vicksburg. He was wounded in the head, and had to have a silver plate. He did his share. They put up a special tomb over his grave in Illinois where he was buried because he had served in the Civil War.

He was born with a high temper. He got quickly angry at things. My mother was more placid. It was difficult for her to get angry. My father could be angry and he could denounce, and so forth. But he did value education, had ideas that were good. I never considered him as well-balanced a person as I considered my mother. She was only fifteen years old when she married. She was just a child and he was twenty-seven years old. He had been to what they thought of as college in those days. It had the same kind of standing as a college has today. It was only a seminary, but he had the advantage of that. That was considered one of the higher institutions in those days.

My father was a small-town lawyer. It amounted more to what today would be a justice of the peace, because no one went to law in those days to work out any cases, but in real estate deals and all kinds of things my father settled matters. He earned his living in a white-collar way, but we often had a precarious living. We never went hungry because we always had a big garden in summertime. There was a lot of land and everything was cheap. We had plenty of space to grow things. We raised chickens and everything. You had a lot of opportunity to earn one's living. So we never went hungry, though we often didn't have much money to spend.

Being poor in this little town where I lived was a very different matter from being poor in a big city. For instance, one of the things we were never without was milk. There was plenty of land and pasture for anybody to have a cow who wanted it. There was always milk, always milk to be given away. So all we would ever have to do would be to go after milk.

My mother was very thrifty. She knew how to fashion things and sew. We were all girls for so many years except for the one boy. This beautiful material we call calico was only five cents a yard, so in the summertime, at least, we always had what we thought were very pretty dresses. In the wintertime you always had one or two very heavy woolen suits. Our winter coats my mother made. They were lined with blanket material, the kind we used on our beds. They were very warm. We lived in a cold climate, in middle Illinois.

When my mother married at fifteen she had her whole life and education, at least in the higher ranks, to be lived, and it was very important the way she lived it. She went through the Civil War as a young woman with her children. She had her children early, but we were not any of us born close together; we were at least two years apart, and there were eight of us that grew up. I had two sisters older than I was, and a brother. The next to the oldest in the family was a boy and also the youngest. But the youngest was born long after the oldest members of the family; they were away and married before my youngest brother was born.

As we were numerous children, it was highly to my mother's credit that she never deviated from the intellectual side of life. She read all the finest books and had the finest literature and did everything right, from the beginning, with us children as we went along. And she never fell back at any time on her lack of comprehension on what our aims in life should be. No, my mother was very advanced in her ideas. She always was ahead of her time. When she died at a hundred and one (in 1946) she was a highly intelligent woman. She knew what was going on all over the world. I asked her on her deathbed (those last days she had were spent at the hospital because of a broken hip) what she thought of the world and the way it was going, because I valued her opinion. She hadn't the good eyesight that I have; she listened a great deal to the radio, to all kinds of opinions. She said that we were going on to worse things. We were in no position where we were going to right some of the wrongs in the world. There was going to be this upheaval. And, of course, we've gone into the wars since then.

The only sad thing I remember about my mother was that she was an inveterate reader, and if she got a book to read maybe we had to wait around for meals in a very sad kind of way while our mother was absorbed in this book. One time we did the terrible thing—we bought a set of Dickens. It was six volumes, I remember so well—green-bound with three columns on the page. We paid fifteen cents a month to buy this set of Dickens, and when we got that set, oh, how we suffered! Because our mother just sat there reading Dickens. She was an inveterate reader. She read all of George Eliot, The Scottish Tales, everything. They were the books we brought in from the school library. And we had many German translations of fine authors that we got from the Lutheran Church library.

My father was what you would call an intellectual in the town where we lived, and we were brought up to love good books and everything. He talked a lot about politics. We took the *Chicago Inter-Ocean*. In our most poverty-stricken days, we took the Chicago daily paper. We were a hundred and thirty miles from Chicago, and the paper came out every morning on the morning train that was going down south. My father got it, and he used to read that paper walking the floor. We might still be sitting at the breakfast table. We always kept abreast of the news.

Once, a wonderful thing happened in our house. We became the owners of a secondhand, old-fashioned square rosewood piano. I don't know where we acquired it. My father acquired it in some business deal. There were only three or four pianos in the town where I lived, so it was a wonderful distinction to own a piano. My older sisters learned to play some simple pieces. None of us were musicians. We didn't take to music.

Even though my grandfather Thompson was a Presbyterian minister, and my mother's family was religious, too, my mother and father were not. We were brought up with no religion. In the whole town we were the only family that were atheists. That was a problem, socially, but we overcame that by standing the highest in school.

We would have been ostracized in that little town where we lived if we hadn't been children as progressive as we were. We never had failures in school, my family. We were a large family and there were probably five or six of us functioning in school at any one time. We were always on top. We always carried away all the honors. When we had a literary contest between our town and the next town, which was a little larger than ours, my brother and I were both on the program. They couldn't leave either one of us off. I recited a wonderful poem that I still remember today. It was called "The Knight and the Page." I think it has a large number of verses, six lines in every verse. So two of us out of our family were on that special competing team.

No, they never could leave us out intellectually, because we were always there, all of us. There was not one of our family that fell behind scholastically. We never took a back seat, as you would have to if you were what we called in those days "dumb"; we never were "dumb" in my family. We were always high in high school. I went into high school when I was twelve years old. We were all progressive, advanced in our studies. We were advanced when we graduated from high school. They had good schools in this little town where I lived. We had some of the finest teachers because we had young men who just came out of college. The principal, the man who was head of the high school where I graduated, was a graduate of one of the big Eastern colleges, Princeton, I think. He was a very wonderful high school teacher. He gave us all advanced ideas.

But I never would have been as far in advance in my way of thinking and viewing of life if it hadn't been for my mother—and my father, too, of course. We took it for granted because he was the best-educated man in this little town where I was born. We just took it for granted about my father and his family, because they were all students.

My childhood was a happy one. Whatever were the vicissitudes of childhood, it was always interesting. We were always interested in what each other was doing. We had our quarrels and strife and all the things that belong to childhood, possibly our little jealousies and things. I don't remember about that. I only know that I look back on a very happy childhood.

When I graduated from high school I taught. My country school where I taught began a month before I graduated, but they gave me a certificate. My father died that fall (1884) that

I graduated high school and taught that school. I was sixteen. My uncle came down to the funeral and took me back to St. Louis with him. While I was down there I had a wonderful time. It was a wonderful time of mental and spiritual awakening. My uncle was a judge of the appellate court in St. Louis, Seymour D. Thompson.

They lived in a great big three-story white stone-front house on one of the most beautiful streets in St. Louis. We had three servants in the house doing the work, with a man outside cleaning the front steps and doing the work around. I became one of my uncle's helpers. He was one of the editors of *The American Law Review*. My uncle was a traveler. He went abroad after his duties were over, and I worked verifying the cases that he cited. I wrote the opinions of the court and of all the things that were interesting.

My aunt was away at school with my two girl cousins. She went away to where her sister was living in Elton, Illinois. It was a semipreparatory college school. I don't remember any more just what the name was. They went off to school and their mother went with them. She was away quite a bit of the time.

My cousin George, who was nineteen years old, was a medical student. The Missouri Medical School was located in St. Louis. I went all over when I had any time in the evening. I worked many evenings, but when I did have time George and I went to all these different lectures on theosophy, spiritualism, and all kinds of things. We went to seances where people materialized in spiritualism. One time we went we had to link little fingers with everybody around the table; the lights were out. There was supposed to be a three-year-old boy that died years ago who belonged to one of the people at our table; he was materialized and floated in space. It was a very noted spiritualist who conducted these. They don't allow them anymore.

We went to everything and had all that experience. My cousin George, of course, was open to that. He was a medical student and he went later to Leipzig, Germany, to study medicine before he became a doctor. We had a wonderful time, and it had a great deal to do with my education and my whole outlook. I was there two years. It was a wonderful experience. Progress and awakening and opening up of the mind. My whole desire while I was there was a great desire to acquire knowledge, to learn and to do something. I couldn't have had any other kind, living with the people I was living with.

My uncle had all the volumes of illustrated Shakespeare. They had a little table where, when you wanted to read one of these wonderful books that were quite, quite huge, you put it out on this table and there was a chair by that. You sat at that table and you read this Shakespeare. And that was the way I read Shakespeare, quite a bit of it. I became very familar with *Othello* and all the different ones.

My uncle valued learning. He was born back in the wilds of Iowa. His father was a Presbyterian minister, and when he was burned to death in that prairie fire, my uncle and my own father had to make their own way. But their jobs were all on the intellectual order. They didn't work by hand or anything. But my uncle was the one who succeeded more, of course. His house was very beautifully furnished with the mohair carpets in the great salons they had. They had these beautiful gold-framed pictures hanging on the sides of the large living room. I was living in great luxury; I was living in a kind of a luxury there and in an atmosphere that I had never lived in—I had come out of this little town in Illinois.

There had been this boy. I was just this young girl at that time, only sixteen years old. He was one of the boys that came out when I was teaching school out in the country. I met him in this small town where I lived in Illinois. He was very dear and nice. I really did care a lot about him. He was a very nice boy. He came from a nice family. His mother had been a nice person. He was going out to Broken Bone, Nebraska, to establish a restaurant out there first of all. I had been engaged to him. Yes, he was in my life.

My uncle interfered with that. He said "No" right away, and sent him back. He said I wasn't fitted for that life. I wasn't, being this cripple, having this bad ankle and never brought up to anything like that, never brought up to hard work. [My bad ankle happened one day when] I was hastening along to school. I was going to have my examinations for high school. I was only twelve years old when I went into high school. I just kind of twisted my ankle, sprained it. We didn't have proper doctors. Afterwards, I fell over on it and broke a bone in it. I had a lot of trouble. On account of that I had never been brought up doing housework. My older sisters did that.

Oh yes, I cared a lot for that young man. He was very nice. But, of course, I was totally unfitted for that type of life and it would have turned out disastrously. I don't know, though—I often think about it because out in this section of Nebraska where he was going to locate, gold mines were developed afterwards and people became very wealthy. This man I was engaged to became very wealthy.

But I wasn't upset about my uncle doing that. I was going into a new and very wonderful life. Because my life down at my uncle's in St. Louis was like a dream world to me. I was living in luxury in what was a palace to me. It would be pretty nearly a palace today, not anything I'd ever lived in, with all the beautiful gold-framed mirrors, the carpets, the large rooms. It was very dramatic, all the way, what I went through. It was just a wonderful spiritual and, in a way, intellectual and cultural kind of relationship. I was just at that age, sixteen and seventeen, where I was open to it all.

Of course, that was a very great loss to me when I was young, coming out, that I couldn't go to college. But I never had the hope that I could go. Because we were never able financially to have ever financed anything like going to college. So it was never a part of my life. But I had unusual experiences during my two-year session, my two years of life in St. Louis.

MARRIAGE AND FAMILY

After my father died, my mother had gone to St. Paul from where she was living in our little town. She wanted me to come to St. Paul and live there at home. She wanted me to get a job there in St. Paul and have the family united. I had one little brother and two little sisters. I was homesick, too. I was devoted to my little brother and sisters and to my mother. So I went there. It wasn't too hard to leave where I was, though it was entirely different.

I came and got a job. I had learned stenography and typewriting at my uncle's in order to work for him. I was quite proficient because I had done the opinions of the court. I took them from dictation, the opinions of the appellate court. They were quite interesting, every one of them. All my work was interesting. I was always alive to it, but I wanted to come home. I was very homesick.

So I was there with my mother in St. Paul until my mother left to go down to where my sister was living, where she had established a kind of business. I didn't go with her. I had a job at a hundred dollars a month, which was a fabulous sum of money. It wasn't long after my mother left that I met my husband. We were only engaged five weeks when we were married. There wasn't any reason in the world why we shouldn't marry. He was without a home and I was without a home. There was every reason when we fell in love why we should marry and establish a home. It would have been strange to have gone on being engaged for a long time.

I first saw my husband, Marcus, in an elevator. I was going out to a lecture. It was a lecture on Shakespeare. Ingersoll was lecturing, Robert G. Ingersoll. I had come from my friends, and I had forgotten something, so we had to go back up. She had told us about this very nice man. As we went up, this young man stepped into the elevator. I whispered to Mrs. Burns, "That's Mr. Thygeson." He was going to take out this very intimate friend of mine who was engaged and whose lover was away. They had tickets, and so she had asked him to fill in and use Bob's tickets. They were going to the same lecture.

He heard me saying, "That's Mr. Thygeson." He heard me whispering this. He looked at me and he says—I don't know how true it was—that when he looked at me he said to himself

that that was the girl he was going to marry. He always asserted
that was really true. I discounted it when he was telling me this.

That's where I saw him. I met him later on. I met him in his
own office. I went in there on some errand for the people I
was working for. He was with a firm of lawyers, Munn, Boyesen
and Thygeson. He was already established in his profession. He
had his own private office.

I think he was twenty-five or twenty-six. I was twenty-three
at the time I was married. I wasn't married young. But as far
as attention was concerned, I had the usual amount of attention. I was reasonably interesting as a person. I had a number
of friends I was more or less intimate with.

But I was terribly fortunate, because I got about the finest
man in the world when I married. It was through no virtue of
mine or anything. He just fell in love with me, and it all worked
out. He was just everything that you wanted in a man. I look
back and I think that although I felt I did appreciate him to a
large extent, I didn't know enough to appreciate him enough.
He had to come from a farm and work his own way through
college and up into his profession, and then in his profession
up in the upper ranks where he stood in that. He was young
when he died (in 1917), so he could have gone on to greater
things.

He was just this boy off the farm. He came from Wisconsin,
not far from St. Paul. His father was a Norwegian farmer. He
went to normal school and he had to walk miles. There was
another boy in the next farm, and these two boys hobnobbed;
they were friends all their lives. They worked together and
they both graduated from this normal school and then went
on to the University of Wisconsin. Harold Harris was his name.

They were Damon and Pythias, those two boys, all their lives.
They loved each other. They had associated ever since they
knew anything about friendship of any kind. I look back on
that, and one of the things that I bless myself for—and sometimes get scared when I think about it—was that I never interfered with it. And I could have interfered with it, because they
used to go off every Sunday. They went off on a shooting tour.

They never shot a rabbit. My husband couldn't have killed a fly. He wouldn't have thought of killing anyone, an animal or anything. I never interfered with that, with their going off on Sundays, although sometimes I had wanted him to stay at home. But they were inseparable since earliest boyhood.

Of all the people in the world, there never was a nicer, kinder or more capable man than my husband. He had graduated in engineering as well as in legal work and was highly efficient. He was too busy a man to be out doing any saving of the world. He was too busy in his law practice. They were a very noted firm, a very busy firm. But he stood for everything that was good; he stood for woman's suffrage and birth control and all these things that were good.

I limited my own family. We were married four years before I had a child, and then my children were three years apart.* I wasn't plunging into a large family. We limited our family, and I believed in that limited birth control for every family. I went along with Margaret Sanger. I didn't have any children that I didn't want. We wanted all the children we had. My husband was very fond of children, and he would have been the most disappointed man in the world if I had not wanted children. I wouldn't have dared to live my married life without children, though I don't know if I lived it over again if I would have had four children. But at that time we thought we were amply able to support four children. We thought it was very nice to have them. They were not close together. Some of them were five years apart. I think maybe the only one of the children who was what you might call an accident was Mary. But Mary was born out of a great affection. Her birth was inevitable, in a way, I think.

Because I had four children, my time was limited in a way. But I was quite free because I had good help with the children, which left me the free time to do the things I did do. So, instead of devoting myself to the children at that particular time

* The children are Ruth Adelaide, born 1895; Elling, born 1896; Phillips, born 1903; Mary, born 1906.

when they were small, I gave it to the suffrage and birth control movements, of which I really was a part. It's not anything to be regretted. It was a part of the larger movement.

That's the way I want my children to regard it, as part of participating in the larger movements of the world. I could have devoted more time to family. They were all well looked after and well taken care of and beautifully tended in every way, so I wasn't neglecting them. And I gained a great deal of prominence—more prominence than I would have had. Except that I had four children that were all thriving and they never had any problems in school or any troubles. They did me credit all along the line.

"PARTICIPATING IN THE LARGER MOVEMENTS": WOMAN'S SUFFRAGE AND BIRTH CONTROL

I think I was always interested in suffrage and birth control. My mother was always interested in woman's suffrage. Way, way back, when my mother was a young woman, there were women working for suffrage. They talked about it. They gave some lectures and did things and took part in some things that required women. My mother never had the time to take part in those things because she had too many children, but she was interested.

It was just one of those things. If children are brought up in an open-minded family where you discuss everything, it isn't that you instill special principles in them: you give them a large outlook. You give them anything that comes along, everything they are able to investigate, look into, read about, study— one of those open-minded sorts of atmospheres, intellectual atmospheres, where people are not limited.

Of course, when I met my husband he was a progressive man. He liked me and he liked the way I did things. He was interested in my society and what I had to say and the things we talked about. We always had very interesting subjects to discuss at the table. He discussed things and I discussed things. I brought things to talk about and he brought things to talk about. Just one of those things where people who think they're intelligent, at least, sit at a table and converse.

So I was interested in every kind of social problem that came my way. Perhaps I stood out. I was a little more aggressive than some of the people that I was associated with. I belonged to certain groups. We were working hard for the suffrage movement. The part that I played in suffrage, was, I think, a really good one. You had these little afternoon gatherings of women, maybe six or eight women. You had a cup of tea. A little social gathering. While we were drinking tea, I gave a little talk and they asked questions about what was going on.

They asked all kinds of questions. I don't remember exactly, but they were usually quite intelligent questions as to what was being done, who was doing it, who was prominent at the time, things like that. I was, of course, enthusiastic, so I answered. I didn't think of putting over anything. I had no feeling that I was important in any way. We just met. It was a very nice, interesting social time for meeting people and enjoying ourselves.

I don't remember anything but being very happy about it and feeling that when I went out and spent an afternoon that it was worthwhile. It was a lot better, I thought at the time, than to have a lecture. Because a lot of them wouldn't go to a lecture. And it was what I could do. I took my own neighborhood when I went out and did that talking. I couldn't have gone out on the lecture stage. Of course, one of the big things we did was the Woman's Welfare League. It was incorporated. It was large enough to be incorporated and we gave a luncheon in downtown St. Paul every Saturday at noon to over a hundred women. We had a very beautiful place to have this dinner, the second floor of this place that had glass on two sides. We had twenty-five tables. We served a luncheon for twenty-five cents every week on Saturday.

We didn't have to pay any of our helpers. There was no expense to it. The women on the staff brought the things for the luncheon. The woman that did my washing and ironing, when it came my turn to furnish the luncheon, she did it for me. She was very capable. We took turns, the women on the staff. We had very prominent women on the staff, very nice, intelligent, some of the women of the highest intelligence.

Our main purpose was education. We were educating for suffrage. Suffrage was not established at that time. We not only lectured for suffrage, but we also lectured for birth control and any of the things that belonged to women. We had someone who came through St. Paul to lecture. It was never any special person lecturing. These were people who came through St. Paul. St. Paul is halfway on the traveling circuit.

One time it was David Starr Jordan.* Sarah Bard Field † would come from the East, where she had gone off to Erskine Scott Wood, the man she married later on. She was living with him in sin at that time because his wife wouldn't divorce him. But we welcomed her. She was very beautiful. She dressed very beautifully. She came to this group of very interesting, fine women. She talked on suffrage and the woman questions. I toted her around with these other women that came from the East in my seven-passenger Cadillac car, different places where she wanted to go. She lectured sometimes in more than one place. I toted all the suffrage people around from one place to another. I never intruded myself as a personality, never. I was the chauffeur when I was driving her around.

We also had the wife of a professor at the college in Indiana, the State University. We had her lecturing in St. Paul and other places. I paid her expenses for a month's suffrage work in Iowa. She gave a whole month up to that and I paid her expenses. She was a fluent speaker and very attractive.

We had a lot of people who came to those lectures. We allowed everyone to come in and speak for and against. They

* President of Stanford University and outspoken advocate of civil liberties and woman's suffrage.

† Western poet and suffragist who first assisted in the Oregon and Nevada campaigns for woman's suffrage in 1912 and 1914 and later became a national figure and speaker for the National Woman's Party.

came and listened. There was never any bad reaction. The people who came to those lectures were intelligent people who wanted to know what was going on in the world. It was all a part, in our lives, of education. Just as I think it probably is today when our young people go out among these things. Only there aren't these special questions that come up like woman's suffrage and birth control. Those have all been settled.

We had our big banquets when some of these lecturers from abroad came to St. Paul. I remember one time, at one banquet especially, how inordinately proud of my husband I was when he looked so wonderful and intellectual that night. It was a time when the women brought their husbands, and my husband was called upon to speak. I never will forget that night. I was so overwhelmingly proud of him. He got up and gave a very fine, sensible talk. He spoke forcefully. He spoke about the suffrage movement. He said they should long have had suffrage. They should never have been without it. Although he was not a handsome man at all, he seemed very handsome to me that night. He was distinguished-looking. The way he spoke and the subject he spoke on, he was one to be highly proud of. I remember that great thrill I had. That remained with me a long, long time. I was so proud for all the things he stood for; they were so fine and good. He was just as free and open-minded a man as you can think of. I'm sorry that my sons, neither of them, are that large and open-minded like their father and I were. It's one of the queerer things of life.

The Woman's Welfare League went on for several years. I was the first vice president. We had a president, Mrs. C. P. Noyes, who was not at the meetings. Her husband was a wholesale druggist in St. Paul. She was a very wealthy woman and went away with her husband every year. They went to Europe. In the summer they went down South. So I was always there presiding.

Mrs. Noyes was a very beautiful, high-minded woman. She came over to my house one morning—I didn't live in the high-grade section that she lived in, I lived in the middle section of St. Paul—and begged me to come over to Summit Avenue, where the elite lived. She wanted me to be her guest for a certain time and go to these social affairs that were being given; go where I could meet these people in this higher social circle and talk to them. She wanted me to be her house guest, and mingle in the social life and in my talks, to talk to these women about the larger views I had on suffrage and the woman question and the various things which were not too far advanced in those days.

She thought I was greatly fitted for taking part in that social atmosphere. I declined. I told her I wasn't at all fitted for that. I told her I would be making faux pas on every occasion. I told her that in that life in society you have to be born to it. You're not fitted, whatever you may think you can do; you're going to be gauche on many occasions. Like the miner's daughter who married the Rockefeller and had his child.

Another of our group was Mrs. Leonora Hamlin. We called her Norah Hamlin. Her father had been governor of Minnesota at one time. He was a very prominent man. Mrs. Hamlin was a very highly educated woman. I think she graduated from some Eastern college. She was highly intelligent. She was responsible for many of the programs of the Woman's Welfare League. She worked with us heart and soul. I was very glad to be intimately associated with her. I was happy to be associated with all those women.

Most of the women who were very prominent in the suffrage movement were also prominent in the birth control movement. Some of the wealthy women of the city. We were very active and did a lot. We didn't draw the line too strictly about things. Woman's suffrage was not declared at that time. Woman's suffrage was not established and birth control was not established. So we had both of these things to establish and work with. In my life the two were so closely identified. I mean, we were working at the same time on both movements. They were part of our lives. The Woman's Welfare League couldn't be identified with the birth control movement because that was illegal, but the women who belonged to the Welfare League and were officers in it all supported the Birth Control League.

So we were closely identified—not as an organization, but the people were closely identified with the movement.

It was the most natural thing in the world to go into birth control. I guess I was kind of born into it. I know that when Margaret Sanger and some of the women that came out publicly worked for it on a large scale, it was the most natural thing in the world for me to join it and to go along with it as I did with what I thought were the progressive things at the time.

We three women—there were two connected with me—organized this birth control clinic that we had. I wouldn't want to mention the names of the other two women, because it was illegal.* I don't know that they would want me to be mentioning their names. It had to be secret because it was against the law. It was against the law at that time to buy any contraceptive material, anything that prevented conception. And certainly it was against the law to print anything or to advertise in any way, shape, or manner any kind of thing you were doing in the line of birth control.†

* Sylvie Thygeson was initially adamant about not mentioning the names of the other women involved and a lengthy exchange ensued. Later in the interview, however, she does reveal their names.

† Under Minnesota obscenity laws, it was illegal to publish or advertise contraception information, to have any instruction for contraception in one's possession, and even to tell anyone where or how contraceptive knowledge could be acquired. Although some states exempted medical colleges, medical books and/or physicians from penalties, Minnesota did not.

THE NEW YORK TIMES, FRIDAY, JANUARY 5, 1917

BIRTH CONTROLLERS UP EARLY FOR TRIAL

Women Give Mrs. Sanger a Breakfast, Then Go to Brooklyn to Wait All Day in Court

MRS. BYRNE'S CASE BEGUN

Fifteen Mothers Held for Hours Away from Their Babies to Give Evidence for the State

One of the cases growing out of Mrs. Margaret Sanger's "birth control" fight reached the courts yesterday when Mrs. Ethel Byrne, sister of Mrs. Sanger, was put on trial in Special Sessions, Brooklyn. The charge against Mrs. Byrne was that she had sold articles the sale of which was prohibited under Section 1,142 of the Penal Law. The sales, it was charged, took place at the "birth control clinic" opened by Mrs. Sanger at 46 Amboy Street, Brownsville, twice raided and closed by the police.

THE NEW YORK TIMES, TUESDAY, JANUARY 23, 1917

MRS. BYRNE MUST GO TO WORKHOUSE

Sister of Mrs. Sanger Sentenced for Use of Birth Control Literature.

THREATENS HUNGER STRIKE

Followers Hoped Court Would Suspend Sentence Instead of Giving Her 30-Day Term.

We women, women of standing in the community—that is, whose husbands had some kind of standing—established the Birth Control Clinic. It functuated [sic] in St. Paul. Margaret Sanger came and lectured to us. We accepted her ideas and believed in it. We worked very strictly [sic] with her, of course, because she was organizing the movement all over the country. Of the three of us that established the clinic, one of these women had only one child; Mrs. Alice Bacon, one of my friends, had four children; and I had four.

The other two women went out and rented the room and did everything. They took over and did all that part of it, the part that was necessary, like setting up the work, the cleaning, and having the doctors come. I didn't know the doctors before that. We got these doctors to associate with us. You couldn't do anything without the doctors. We had two very fine, wonderful, high-spirited men: one from Minneapolis and the other from St. Paul. They sanctioned the birth control movement and said they would work with us. One of these men, we never knew if he was a bachelor, or what he was. He was not married. Just what he had gone into, or what it was, we never knew. The other man had a wife and four children. He was very much in favor of having birth control. So he gave out information at the clinic without any fanfare or difficulty at all.

The clinic wasn't designated a birth control clinic. It was just an office, a room where we met and had lectures. We lectured on the desirability of birth control, tried to educate people to the idea of having too many people in the world. But what we were doing was very active work. It was not only advocating what we were doing, but it was helping people that couldn't otherwise have done anything about it. Women had no access to the information that would help them limit their families. Women didn't know, in those earlier days, anything about family limitation, and the only way they could practice family limitation was by abstention. You know that many people aren't capable of abstention. I can't blame them or anything like that, because they're just born that way. I think it's especially difficult, in a way, for men, who shouldn't be too much blamed about things. So I thought it was necessary, and Margaret Sanger thought it was, to give women the information where they could limit this on their own. After all, if you don't have the cooperation of your husband, you have to have mechanical means to limit birth.

We advocated and we circulated the birth control contrivance that Margaret Sanger had invented for the prevention of pregnancy.* It was a very ingenious sort of one. (Since then they have found easier methods than that.) It cost a certain amount, but they always paid for it. I don't think it was very much, maybe one dollar and twenty-five cents, something like that. Of course, you didn't talk much about what people paid for it because it was illegal; it was illegal to disseminate birth control, so we weren't out peddling instruments.

I don't remember that we ever had any money troubles. I don't remember that we ever had to go out to get money or that we were hampered for lack of money. It came from all kinds of sources, from anyone and everyone who wanted to make a contribution. It was a volunteer movement and whoever felt interested in it or wanted it to continue made a contribution. But we didn't advertise. We were entirely secret, and had no name.

I remember one time when a young man, a very nice young man, came up from the country. He had just been newly married and he had heard about birth control and he wanted to get the information. He didn't want to get his wife pregnant right away. Yet he didn't want to do things, do what they have to do. So he came one morning to my house. We had this very heart-to-heart conversation about family, raising families and so forth, and then I sent him, of course, to the clinic, where they gave him the very definite information and fitted him out.

It's very difficult to imagine that you couldn't legally limit the size of your family. This would have been way back. You see, I'm one hundred and four now and I think this was in my early days when I was in my forties. So it would be sixty years back. I can't remember special years, though.† Because I have never formulated it. It was never published, except just as anyone made a little sketch of it; a little notice or something might have been published in one of the papers. Because it was so strictly against the law, we weren't printing it nor advertising

* She is probably referring to the so-called dutch pessary introduced first by Emma Goldman, from Europe, and later by Margaret Sanger. It was similar to the modern diaphragm.
† The date was probably around 1916–17.

it nor doing anything public about it. You don't do something that is against the ordinances of your city and the laws of your state. You don't do anything in the open.

They would have thought a long time before arresting me, though, on birth control, with my husband in the position he was in. I was written up, though. My two co-partners, they would have been written up as much as I was if their husbands had been as prominent as mine. One's husband was a doctor, and the other was divorced from her husband. I was written up editorially in our principal paper, *The Pioneer Press*. I wasn't exactly denounced, but I wasn't commended. I was written up editorially, written up detrimentally as being the head of the birth control movement.

As long as my husband didn't mind it, I didn't mind it. They couldn't say anything really bad. They wouldn't have done it on account of my husband's prominence. I didn't have anything to fear. I went along in a terribly interested and happy way because I had a very happy family, a very wonderful husband. I was enjoying my life to the fullest extent. I don't know how many of my social friends knew what I was doing. I wasn't out lecturing to the general public. My name wasn't prominent in that way at all. We were just doing sort of underground work, working with Margaret Sanger, principally. We didn't make a social affair of it at any time.

We were just working along, just as I would be doing now if I were working among people. I wouldn't be out having a meeting and a place to meet and all that kind of thing. I'd be doing probably the same thing, meeting around at houses, educating women who were either newly married or going to be married, giving them the information. I was as active in the suffrage movement as I was in the birth control movement.

I came out to California in 1917 and always in some way or other was connected with the [birth control] movement. I never lost out in connection with it. I'm still connected with it today. I'm still a member of the organization of San Jose, Planned Parenthood. I have contributed.

Ruthie * and I worked together. I contributed money to things and she did the work. She gave her time and her experience and her knowledge as a doctor. She belonged to a special clinic, but I don't know too much about that. That was not to promote the movement or anything like that; it was given as a genuine service in showing how to work the birth control contrivance that was used. In other words, how to use what knowledge was available, how to make it practical and use it.

I did other kinds of work in California, too. I don't know that I could tell [about specific activities] because I was always very active in whatever was going on. I was active just as I had been up until this time. One of my greatest interests at the present time is the ACLU, the free speech movement. I think it is terribly important that we keep that alive. I belonged to that since its inception, way back there when it was first organized by Roger Baldwin. I consider that one of the most valuable organizations that we have in this country. I wish my family felt the same. I don't urge anything on them because they are highly intelligent, each one of them, and they know what they want and what they consider valuable.

I belonged to the NAACP since it was founded, too. I couldn't swear to it, but I think there's no question because I can't remember when I didn't belong. I wouldn't like to be put on the stand and have to certify, though, because I wouldn't remember.

I do remember going to the Soviet Union. It was something very special, something way out of this world. Mary and I were there. We went along with a very interesting group. It was a time not long after the Revolution.† I felt that history was being played there. The Soviet Union was writing history. They were in the forces of evolution as much as anyone. They could only play the part that was possible for them. You can't go out and make over something. You have to deal with people. The people couldn't go any faster than they can go along certain

---

* Ruth Thygeson, Sylvie's eldest daughter.
† It was in 1929.

lines. The women had complete freedom. What more could they have? They had birth control, they had everything! There were no restrictions on them, so I don't know what more they could have had. Oh yes, when they had the Revolution, they had complete freedom, as much as any of the women would take. The women were very ignorant, a great many of them. They never had had any opportunities for any kind of education or knowledge or anything. But they had every kind of freedom that they could possibly take and absorb. It was a question of getting them to accept the freedom and to measure up to it. They came along very rapidly, the Soviet Union did. They did go along, and they have gone along with the process, what I would call the evolutionary process.

Yes, I always tried to work along progressive lines. Each one, no matter how simple that can be, or in what a simple way that can be, can always make a contribution to the larger expanse of knowledge. That's the way I feel. Any one of us can make that their larger contribution to the world of knowledge, wherever that is made, and in however small or large a way it can be made.

LOOKING BACK: THE EVOLUTIONARY PROCESS

All of these little things like suffrage and birth control and everything are just parts of a great movement of evolution. That's all the way I can explain it. Just as we're going on and on. We're going on to greater and greater evolutionary processes all through. The only thing is that things then that were just evoluting [*sic.*], that we were just coming out of, are just taken so completely for granted that we don't even stop to think about it. No one thinks for a moment, or stops to think, that it's uncommon or unusual for women to go to the polls and vote. We don't even think of that. It's so common now. We don't think of the fight that was made for it. We just accept it. And that's the way with all these processes. To my mind, the whole process is a process of evolution.

I never had any illusions about what women would do. I was never that foolish. No, I think women are responsible for a great deal of backwardness of the world. I never had any feeling at all that the world would be better and go on to happier and wiser things. I thought women were just as corrupt in every way as men were and just as lacking in any kind of judgment. In other words, I never had any illusions about women. I think we tried to have a myth, you know, that women were superior; that if the world had suffrage that was advocated, then the whole world would be better and all these things that were evil would disappear. All of which was perfect nonsense, because women were just people like men were; good and bad, enlightened and not, the same as men were. I never had the illusions. My husband had a lot of illusions about what women would do, but I never had any of those illusions.

I looked at it intelligently. I didn't look at it in the light that women, as women, were going to change. They would change as a group of people, as a product coming along in the evolution of society and the world, not as men or women. I couldn't read the history of the world from Neanderthal man up to the present time without knowing there'd be a great many changes.

Suffrage was part of the movement, like these movements going on today. Each little thing helps the large movement until it comes out and can really accomplish something. It educates and it works. It's part of the education of the world, these small movements are. They can't on their own accomplish anything. It has to be in the larger effort as they put that forth. So it was all a great part, as I looked at it, a part of an educational process.

Of course, I thought that suffrage would be of direct benefit to women. I think it was not only of benefit to them, but I think it was part of the educational process. It was inevitable that women were to vote. They were human beings endowed with certain, as we say the old words, "inalienable rights." They had the creation of things, the same process that men had, and had to be a part of it. I thought that as the world progressed and went on further, that men and women would come to have absolutely equal rights. They'd be human beings, not sexes. They'd be human beings and have certain inalienable rights, both sexes.

I thought it was ridiculous, when you stop to think of it, in a world composed of women and men, and where the women had the most influence because they brought up the children, that they should be the ones restricted in what was the larger field for progress. That was in the voting process and in the participation in municipal affairs and state affairs.

I don't think we've gone very far because we are far away yet from anyone thinking of a woman being President of the United States. There isn't any reason in the world why some women aren't just as capable as some men to become head of the government. But we're a long way from that, I think. Of course, I might be surprised if I were to live on and see that it would be possible much sooner than I am looking for it. But women will run for President of the United States. Of course, there have been many other changes that have happened and much broadening out since the amendment was passed, the woman's suffrage amendment. I think that women have every chance now for higher education. There isn't any restriction at all on women now.

I think these things are bound to come along as the world progresses. It is inevitable; there's no way in which you can stop them, but you can always help by going along with an intelligent process. It might not be made as rapidly nor as efficiently and some things might not be accomplished as quickly if there weren't these ardent workers who fully believed in things. Perhaps if I hadn't done what I did, somebody else would have come along and done it. Who can say? I think I just worked along with the evolution of my time.

And I want my family to go along with the intelligent process. Mary has and she's gone along—and her sister did, too—highly intelligent progressive lines. In every line she has been working in she has gone along progressive lines. She has made a great contribution to the world advancement of knowledge and enterprise and looking at things—an intelligent way of grasping. I think she has made very great progress in what she has done. She is carrying on in a very fine way in her teaching of anthropology, the story of man and man's place in the world. I wish she had a little more of the evolutionary point about it, as I think I have.*

Kowinsky, an engineer from Poland, wrote a book called *The Manhood of Humanity*. He said that in this world we were all evolutionists or space binders. He said the great masses of people in the world are just space binders, that all they really contribute to the world is to fill up space living; that there is only a certain percent of them that are evolutionists, that want to project something into the future that's worthwhile. I thought Kowinsky's idea was one that illustrated more than anything what I thought about life. Are we evolutionists that have helped forward the world? By the children we've produced or by what we've done, have we made a definite contribution or are we just sitting there in space and existing?

Sylvie Thygeson died, at the age of almost a hundred and seven, on May 13, 1975. Like her mother, with whom she spoke about world events on her deathbed at the age of a hundred and one, Sylvie Thygeson remained interested in current affairs. Several months before her death, she inquired of her family where Nixon was, asking, "Did he have a disgraceful departure?"

Sylvie Thygeson told her children that she was dying and asked them to please not interfere. In the end, she took matters into her own hands and refused to eat. The process took six weeks.

She remained lucid and remarkably sensitive to the feelings of her family. About three days before she died she informed her daughter that she would "exonerate" her if she no longer came to see her.

---

* Sylvie is referring to her daughter, Mary Thygeson Shepardson, who, at the age of fifty, received her doctorate in anthropology and was teaching at San Francisco State University.

JESSIE HAVER BUTLER

On the Platform

Jessie Haver Butler is active in the current women's movement and is a well-known "old-timer" among feminists in the Los Angeles area. At eighty-nine she displays the physical vitality of someone half her age. Recently, on the occasion of the fifty-fifth anniversary of woman's suffrage, she spent two days on a round of speaking engagements, relaxing between them by swimming ten lengths of a hotel pool. Jessie is an imposing woman who pays close attention to both her physical condition and her appearance. Her manner is direct and she uses her loud, clear voice with great effect.

My interviews with Jessie were conducted in her small housekeeping apartment in a retirement community in Claremont, California. She lives there by herself now that her husband of fifty-five years is permanently hospitalized. The move ten years ago to the retirement community, with its central dining room and available housekeeping services, was motivated largely by Jessie's disdain for domestic chores. The contents of her apartment reflect her ongoing commitments and interests. Her desk is piled high with papers, feminist publications and popular health magazines. Photographs of her grandchildren share wall space with a picture of her 1909 Smith College graduating class. Her bookshelves are crammed with feminist writings, old and new, books written by her spiritual teachers, and copies of her own book on public speaking for women, Time to Speak Up.

In the eleven hours of interviews from which the following material was edited, Jessie was most cooperative and candid about her life. She spoke with the careful deliberation that comes from long experience in public speaking and revealed in great detail the forces which shaped her life. At the age of eighty-nine she is still open to new experiences and breaking new ground.

PIONEER STOCK

The background of both my parents is amazing, really. It's an example of what fine and talented people helped to build America, though handicapped because of the primitive environment. We must never forget that the United States was built from the Atlantic to the Pacific in just two hundred years. What's two hundred years to build a great nation! A lot of the people who helped build up the West, like my mother and father, were rare people. Had they lived fifty years later, they'd have been leaders in any community.

My mother's father was a graduate of Berlin University and was also a trained Lutheran minister. He wanted to get out of Germany because that was the era in which Bismarck was launching his great Prussian campaign. He was inspired to come to America to Christianize the Indians. Siegmund Rehwaldt was a short little man who wore chin whiskers like Oom Paul * in Africa did. He traveled to Iowa and later to Nebraska, where he founded all the Lutheran churches and a great many private Lutheran schools that are still in existence. Evidently, he was a man of great drive and energy.

In Nebraska he had six children. During the birth of the last child, there was an Indian raid and his wife died in childbirth. He put all the smallest children into the hands of different farmers in the area, but my mother, who was ten years old, and her sister, who was eight, were put in an orphanage. What an orphanage in Nebraska must have been like is hard to imagine. I later learned through analysis in London that my mother was raped in that orphanage, which accounted for the fact that there was a tremendous emotional situation between her and me. This is just the kind of thing that happened in those early days.

When she was sixteen years old, my mother wanted to get

* Paul Kruger, late nineteenth-century South African Transvaal statesman, known as Oom Paul.

educated, evidently having inherited the kind of mind her father had. He let her go to Colorado, which, in those days even
before the women had the vote, had the best school system of
the West. She went to Pueblo and became a maid for one of
the leading families of that city while she went to high school.
Being a German girl, she was a good cook and good housekeeper, and a pretty woman. She was short with blue eyes and
a gay and happy character. In her job she met my father, who
was the first dairyman of Pueblo. He had started a dairy a mile
and a half west of Pueblo. He built his own house out of adobe
bricks which he made himself on the ground—formed them,
baked them and then built his home. Then he brought his
wife, my mother, to this house already built.

Just before they were married, she decided that she wanted to
go back to visit her German relatives in Nebraska. To their
horror and astonishment, she pasted a notice on the door of
her father's church that on a certain night she was going to give
a lecture on socialism. She and my father, just like myself and
my husband, were very much interested in public questions. In
those days, instead of reading about communism if you were
radical, you read about socialism. Their favorite book was
Looking Backward, by Edward Bellamy, and my mother decided to lecture on it to this farm community.

You can imagine that in a typical German farm community,
where the girls were supposed to be housewives for life, what
a shock it was to have a young girl like that, about to be married, lecturing on socialism. Everybody went to hear what she
said, but disapproved thoroughly, as I later learned. I stopped
there once on my way home from Smith College. My mother's
younger sister told me this story with great reluctance, saying,
"You know, your mother was really peculiar. We never quite
understood her." I asked how was she peculiar, and then she
told me this story about her lecture on socialism. I said, "Did
people go?" "Yes, the church was filled. It was such a sensation.
But they felt very sorry for her future husband, that he was
marrying such a strange and peculiar woman."

I was the first child, and when I was born, in 1886, there was no one there but my father to help with the process. In that valley of the Arkansas River and the farm area where my father had his ranch, there wasn't a single family whose mother brought up the children. They all died early. There were no doctors, there were no sinks in the kitchens, there were no bathrooms, no telephones, and there were no cars.

But my mother was very smart. She had a great big health book with which she was thoroughly familiar. She was also a faddist, so it's natural that I've been somewhat of a faddist all my life. She had all the books of a man named Dr. Jackson, who started a whole new system of eating. He had some strange ideas that didn't fit with farm life very well. One of them was that there was to be no supper. Of course, this was difficult for my father. He had the largest milk barn in all of Colorado and had five hired men who were fed by my mother in our home. To go without supper until breakfast, from the dinner meal until breakfast, must have been a great strain.

My brother and I took care of the situation. We swiped turnips and celery and watermelon and corn from all the neighboring fields, and apples, too. So even though there was no supper in the kitchen, we were well fed. In fact, we became such thorough thieves when it came to finding food at night that our mother had to hide everything that was edible in the kitchen. She was unable to cope with the thievery.

Just think of it, she had four children in the end, and no sink, just a cistern out in the backyard. My father had a highly organized dairy with hired men whom she had to feed, as well as her children. Yet, I remember vividly when the campaign for woman's suffrage was going on in Colorado, how she climbed into that spring wagon. I can see her yet doing it. She toured that valley to get the men to vote for woman's suffrage. And this wasn't something that a good little housewife, even in Colorado, in those days was supposed to do.

Of course, this is when that great woman's suffrage leader, Susan B. Anthony, had been all over the state for months. She walked, she rode donkeys, and do you know what she did when she got to a mining town? There was no place to speak but the saloons. So she walked into the saloons, cold, where she made her speeches. The men were so grateful and happy to see that lovely Quaker woman who would take such an interest in them that she was a sensation. Women were scarce in Colorado in those days and terribly valuable, and Susan B. Anthony was such a sweet and gracious person. That she would take the trouble to go into the saloons and talk to the men, that's one way that Colorado got the vote.

THE NEW YORK TIMES, MONDAY, DECEMBER 4, 1893

Women May Vote in Colorado

DENVER, Col., Dec. 3.—The State Canvassing Board completed its work yesterday. The count shows that woman's suffrage was carried by 6,347 majority. Gov. Waite has issued a proclamation giving women the right to vote at all elections in this State.

My mother didn't go along with Susan B. Anthony. As far as I know, she never met her. She just did her little thing all on her own in that valley where we lived. Why she didn't take me along, I don't know. That would have been a good thing to do, but I think I was baby-sitting at this point. My job there was to baby-sit—a job which I loathed.

I loved animals. I didn't like dolls, but I loved animals. I had a lamb for a plaything and I also had a cat named old "Three Legs." She was called that because early in her career, when she was going through the big alfalfa field near our place, one leg was cut by the mowing machine, right at the ankle. That didn't stop her. Every year she produced a nice litter of ten or twelve kittens. Finally, one of her children had kittens and we found all the kittens in the barn crying for food. Their mother had been killed by the mowing machine. My brother had said he was going to take the starving kittens and put them in a bag with a rock and take them over and dump them in the river. I told him that if he did that he'd never live to tell the tale. I would punish him in such a way, he'd never forget. I knew "Three Legs" had a set of kittens, so I thought maybe

55976

she'd give the other litter some milk. This sort of undertaking interested me intensely, rather than that of dolls. So I took "Three Legs" to the screaming kittens and she lay down at once and gave them a big meal. The next thing I saw, she was moving them one by one down with her litter of kittens.

We went to Carlisle School, an excellent school, on the edge of Pueblo. We were two miles from the school, out of the valley, up over the hills and across the prairies. As we got a little older, our father bought us a little Shetland pony and cart to drive to school. That little Shetland pony and cart that we had was a sensation at the Carlisle School.

It was a regular public school. The principal was a very strong, domineering woman, an excellent teacher. I never liked her because in her class she said that her life was getting very difficult because she never could get Jessie to stop talking—in class or out. So I didn't get on too well with her. Her name was Miss Chase. But it was in that school that I had a gifted teacher of rhetoric in the fourth grade, a teaching that has stayed with me all my life. She was a humpback, a homely little woman, but a great teacher. I loved English rhetoric even at that age.

It was when I was in the fourth grade, when I was getting these fine lessons in rhetoric, that I invited the whole grade to come out one Saturday in the summer for a picnic. Somehow or other, the parents let them come. They brought some lunches and we had a lot of things to eat and we had a big picnic. Then I asked them would they like to go wading in the river. Oh, yes, they'd like to wade in the river! So we ran over to the river.

I didn't know it was full of holes. Pretty soon, first one little skirt and then another began getting wet. So I said, "Let's take everything off; that's the way the boys do. Why shouldn't we?" Well, they were in doubt as to whether that was a nice thing to do or not. They were in great doubt. But they were getting all wet. I led the procession. My cousin, who was a very religious little girl and very particular, refused, but everybody else stripped.

We hung the clothes on the shrubbery by the side of the river, and we had a swim! Nothing feels so good as water on the body without a costume on it. So we just had a gorgeous time, the whole crowd. Then everybody began putting clothes on and looking very ashamed to think they'd done it. Finally they all went home and told their mothers. I found out later that every girl was told that never again could she come to our ranch and visit me, a naughty girl like me that would get them to go swimming without clothes on.

When I was ten years old, my mother died a very tragic death. The youngest child was drowned in the irrigating ditch. Four days later my mother died. I was with her when she died and she told me that I was to get educated, that I was a bright child. This was news to me. She had never talked to me up till this point as if I were an intelligent, understanding person. She had never even let me help her in the kitchen, which was a mistake. She was so busy and under such pressure, I suspect she felt she didn't have the time.

After my mother died, my father took on Maude Fitch, who had been my mother's intimate friend and had been a schoolteacher. She came with her mother and was the housekeeper, and in the end, my father married her. She was a marvelous woman and an excellent disciplinarian. I went haywire after my mother died! I really took it terribly hard. I was almost impossible to handle, but Maude Fitch could do it. She had me ride my pony across the prairie to get calmed down.

My father sold the dairy then, and we moved down onto the other side of Pueblo and he went into the cattle-raising business. He had thousands of acres of land and cattle. There was no other way to get me into town into the school there except to live in somebody's home. He didn't have the money to pay for that, but if I was working in somebody's home, then I was properly sheltered and all the rest of it. So for two years during the school term I lived with a family in Pueblo and did the housework. I was a horrible household worker. I broke dishes. I dropped everything. I didn't seem to have my heart in it from the beginning. Anyway, I hadn't been trained by my mother.

It became evident that I was not a successful household assistant. My father saw I needed to be in the public schools in the city instead of the horrid little schools out in the country where we were living. So after two years, he sold his ranch and moved into the edge of town and went into the real estate business. I had a bicycle and rode to school. I was now in high school.

EARLY DETERMINATION:
THE SEEDS OF THE FUTURE

When I was fourteen years old, in a very mediocre geometry class suddenly there walked into the room the first modern woman I had ever seen. Up to that point my knowledge of women was of Mexican housewives and ranch women done up in calico dresses. I assumed that's the way everybody would look when they got older. This woman was beautiful. She was tall and stylishly dressed. She was from Ohio and was a very gifted teacher. My problem was, How could I get her to know I was around?

I was at this point having a very bad time with my stepmother who'd gone into the menopause period. She had had a child and was in a terrible emotional and mental condition and should never have been left in our family at all. She would threaten, day after day, to burn the house down—and she meant it! So I was going through this frightful situation, helping with the housework and everything, when this new teacher walked into the room.

I thought, Maybe I can get her to help me. But how? She couldn't see me at all. I was badly dressed. Honestly, I looked older than I do now. I was all round-shouldered and an unhappy child. There were all these pretty little girls with nice dresses that their mothers made, so she didn't know I was there. Then she began giving an original problem in geometry that the students were to work out at home. Every day she would ask, "Who has the answer to the original problem?" Nobody ever had the answer. One night I was sitting in our kitchen doing the homework and thought, If I could get that original problem, she'd know that I was there. But it was just Greek. I wasn't interested in mathematics, I was interested in getting help. I sat at the kitchen table and said, "I *must get that* problem."

I went to bed and what do you think happened? I dreamed the answer! I saw it on the blackboard. I woke up at once and memorized it, and that morning I went downstairs at five and wrote it down and proved it. That day the teacher asked, "Who has the original problem?" My hand shot up in the air and she said, "Why, Jessie, have you got it?" I said, "Yes, I have." She told me to put it up on the board.

I don't think modesty at that point was my great asset. I *strutted* up to the board. And the answer was right. Well, wasn't I astonished! After that, for five days in succession, I had the answer. I had found how it worked. At the end of the week the teacher called me to the desk and said, "Now Jessie, I want you to tell me who's helping you with your original problems." I said, "Miss Mumford! I did them myself. I'm not that kind of a girl!" From then on, I knew that she knew I was there. And it was she, in the end, who got me off to Smith College.

It was that very year that I met this beautiful teacher that I called on the principal one night. If ever a man looked like Abraham Lincoln, that was the man. He was a very great teacher and a very wise man. Remembering that my mother had said to get educated, I called on him to ask what was the best women's college in America. I did not want to go to a college where there were men, where I would be distracted from getting an education. I felt that was a job in itself and it was better to put off the companionship with men until after education was absorbed.

The principal said Vassar was one of the best colleges but that it was for rich girls. I said, "Well, I won't be rich. I don't want to go there." Then he said that though Wellesley was a pretty good college it never interested him especially, but that

Smith College was one of the most alert and modern colleges. He thought that was one of the best. I said, "Thank you very much. I will go there." He was somewhat surprised. I didn't exactly look like a Smith College possibility. I was ill and badly dressed.

I wrote to Smith to find out what you had to do, and they said you had to send ten dollars to get enrolled. I dragged ten dollars out of my father on some excuse—ten dollars to him in those days was a lot of money—and got myself enrolled in Smith College at the age of fourteen, but nobody knew it. They were admitting girls, if they had high enough marks, without taking an examination. I wasn't what they call an all-A kind of student, so I figured that I was really going to have to slug like I'd done in geometry in order to secure high enough marks for entrance.

For the next two years I got up every morning at four o'clock to do homework so that no children or anybody would bother me. Then I began staying at the high school and getting homework done in the library, where it was quiet and peaceful. I ended up with very high marks. But, oh, it was a terrible strain. In the end Mr. Barrett, the principal, put me on the graduating program, and I recited Van Dyke's essay "The Lost Word."

By this time my stepmother was so ill and so unaffiliated to her family life, that I had to get all my own clothes. I got a dressmaker myself and was getting a dress made to wear for graduation. I would walk from our house across the prairie a mile and a half to get on a streetcar to get to the dressmaker's. Saturday morning it was always my job to clean the house from top to toe. It was about three weeks before graduation, and I had to go down on this particular Saturday and have my dress fitted. I told my stepmother and she said, "If you go out of that door this morning, you need never come back." I went upstairs and said, "What do you know about that! I'm all through here. I am kicked out."

I was delighted. I was a typical eighteen. I put on my hat and coat, got my purse and, without a word, walked out the back door and got on the streetcar. One of my best friends,

Lorena Underhill, lived in her mother's boarding house. I beat it there to ask if she'd take me in. Sixteen dollars a week, it was. She said, "Why, Jessie, we'd love to have you here." I went down to the office and told my father what had happened. I was a wreck, physically, from the housework I'd had to do, the nervous strain I had been under, and the studying I was doing. So I holed up there for the summer and got rested. It was wonderful.

But suddenly I developed a terrible ulcer on my right eye, and there was no eye doctor in Pueblo. Then, the first of two miracles happened. I believe in miracles. The first was in the middle of that summer when the first eye doctor that Pueblo ever had arrived from Philadelphia. He was one of the great eye specialists and was in the last stages of tuberculosis and had come to Colorado to be cured. I beat it down to the office the minute I heard he was there. He said that it was a terrible eye, but if I would come to his office every day and sit there all morning so that he could treat it every half-hour, he thought he could save my eye. So I did, and he saved my eye. That's the first miracle.

Three weeks before I was to leave for Smith College, my step-mother committed suicide. My father came for me at the boarding house and brought me home. By this time the news had got out that I was going to Smith. The minister of the church called and said that it was my duty to stay home and take care of the family, my brother and sister. Whereupon the darling teacher arrived back for the fall session, and hearing of the tragedy in our home, called on my father. She told him that if he didn't get me out of there at once I'd be dead in a year. When she got through with him, he had nothing more to say. He said to her, "What will I do?" and she told him, "That's your problem, not hers."

Then, the second miracle happened. About ten days before I was to leave, a letter arrived from a fourth cousin of my father's from Illinois. She was in Colorado and wanted to come to visit. Our house was hectic and the whole situation was awful, but my father said, "I always liked Emily Bonham and

I'd love to see her." We went down to the train one afternoon and the sweetest little woman I ever laid eyes on got off. She was five feet two, had lovely soft brown eyes, was beautifully dressed and was just a darling.

The next morning I explained I had to leave to go to the oculist. That afternoon, when I came home, there was the smell of food in the air. The kitchen floor was waxed, the old kitchen stove was blacked, there was a white tablecloth and the silver was cleaned. We sat down to the first really decent meal we'd had in months. At the meal I said, "What have you been doing all your life?" "Well, I stayed home with my father and mother on their farm. First my mother died, then last month my father died. I don't know what to do. I have to have a home," she said with tears in her eyes. I said, "Well, there's a home here needs somebody like that." The next morning we had a new housekeeper. She helped me buy some clothes and a trunk and got me off to Smith College. That was miracle number two.

In those days there was maybe just one other girl in the town who went to college. Neither my brother nor sister had a college education. My brother went awhile to Dartmouth, but he was not a scholar and not interested in studying. In the end, he married a girl with a lot of ranch money and had a big ranch near Boone, Colorado. My sister was the sweetest and least ambitious member of the whole family, and very domestic. A very beautiful child. She must have inherited her looks from our mother. She had blue eyes and was just a beautiful little girl and very sweet and gracious. Later, when I was in Boston, she came and went to Massachusetts General Hospital as a nurse and became a great success. When I was in England, she came over, and on the boat met a brilliant Harvard professor and she married him, lived at Harvard and had a very wonderful life.

My father hadn't taken my college plans very seriously. He made fun of me when I kept talking about it in high school. He said that most girls he'd known would say, "I'm going to get educated, get married and have babies. But not Jessie! She's

going to get educated in high school and go to Smith College."
He didn't see why I couldn't go to school in Colorado instead
of Northampton, Massachusetts. He didn't see that importance.
But after I'd graduated from Smith, I can remember walking
along the street with him one day when he met one of his business associates. This man said, "Well, is this the daughter who
graduated from Smith College?" My father said, "Yes," and the
man asked, "Well, how did you happen to send her to Smith
College?" "Well, I thought the best was none too good for
her," my father said. So that was that.

SMITH COLLEGE, 1906

Of course, to go to Smith College and get into that beautiful
New England culture atmosphere just completely altered my
life. It took me out of that pioneer environment that I'd come
from and got me into the cultural world of America. I took philosophy, aesthetics, ethics, logic, history, and another year
of Latin and Greek. I also took a course in Bible study that
was very interesting. I didn't understand philosophy very well
but I adored it and took every course in that department. In
my junior year I enrolled in the first class in psychology that
was taught in America, the very first class, I think. I went crazy
over it and, in the end, it became a tremendous part of my life.
When I was in London later, I attended the Tavistock Clinic,
which was conducted by Dr. Jones, the Freudian, and Dr. James
Hadfield, the first Jungian psychotherapist. Four years of study
with Dr. Hadfield followed, a study that changed my life and
character. So that psychology course at Smith was partly responsible for helping me to find my identity.

I did also want to learn to write, so I took a writing course.
But we had a teacher whose special interests were poetry and
fiction. I wasn't that type of student. Once or twice I wrote
something that she said had possibility, but I didn't get very
far with it. I was also dying for a speech course, but there were
none. All they did was test you. If you didn't stutter, then you

didn't need speech. I went into the only speech class they offered; it concentrated entirely on enunciation and diction. I had
a voice you could hear a mile. What I wanted to learn was how
to reach an audience: how to get material over, how to communicate, how to express it, how to organize ideas. There was
no such class there. There is none at Smith, yet.

Frankly, I was disappointed in my teachers. In my opinion
they weren't very interesting. My greatest teacher was the one
who taught psychology. He was simply great. I didn't fall for
many of the others. They didn't even touch my high school
teacher. What I longed for were women teachers who would
give me a plan for my span of life. We sat around our rooms for
hours at a time: "How are we going to carry on with this intellectual life and yet have a home and children?"

My mother had said, "Get educated." She didn't say, "Be a
housekeeper." I had no image of being a housekeeper except
inside me I wanted to have a baby. How could I coordinate this?
From all I knew of married life, you spent your life having
babies, washing "daidies" and cooking. Therefore, how were
you going to keep up with your intellectual life? No one had
the answer, and they haven't found it yet. There was nobody
there who had done it, and nobody there interested in homes
and children, so there was no guidance.

As a matter of fact, it was not a healthy environment, in a
way. There was a great deal of homosexual relations going on
there, and we had a terrible tragedy in our class that nobody
had coped with. There was a girl who was a very masculine
type of girl, head of the basketball program, and another who
was a very beautiful, sweet, delicate, typically feminine girl. The
two of them lived together. The one girl loved boyfriends and
dancing, and she went up to Dartmouth a great deal. A boy in
Dartmouth fell in love with her, but her roommate was determined to break that up. That summer during our junior
year the roommate persuaded her to cancel the engagement;
she had found out that the mother of this perfectly brilliant,
gifted young boy had been in a mental institution.

When they came back to college that fall, he wrote frantic

letters, and the roommate got her to send his letters back un-
opened. The whole campus was rocked with this love affair because the young man had come to town and was hanging
around, trying to see his fiancée. She was sneaking out the back
door, dodging him. We all thought it was terribly exciting and a
great love affair. Nobody else took any interest in it or knew
what to do or tried to do anything.

One day, as we were all looking out our windows, we saw her
coming along when he met her. She was swinging along as gay
as a lark. He had his hat pulled down over his eyes. They walked
across from our building into the center of the campus where he
shot her and himself, before our eyes. I was very critical of that
affair. I said, "That's what's the matter with this college. There's
no humanity in it. There's no guidance for women, the guidance that we need." There still isn't.

I wouldn't make any dates at Smith. Amherst boys go up
there and boys from Yale and Harvard and Dartmouth. Many
students had dates for weekends, but I wasn't going to get
sidetracked with dates. During those years the girls would want
me to go to dances and parties, but I said, "No. I'm getting
education. I haven't the time." While they were out dating, I
was in the library. That Smith library was so beautiful and
filled with great literature. I read all of Bernard Shaw and all
of H. G. Wells.

I never had a date until junior year, when we had our junior
prom. One of my best friends from Great Neck, Long Island,
said her boyfriend was coming up to Northampton and wanted
to bring his boyfriend. So she roped me in on the junior prom.
His name was Horace Lyon of Lyon's tooth powder. He was a
very fine young man and later came to Colorado to marry me,
but I was too busy getting educated and then getting a career
started, so I didn't want to get married until later on.

I am dead set against coeducation during college years for my
type of student. Being immature, as many college sudents my
age were, mentally and physically, such students are not ready
to struggle with a lively social life as well as with the kind of
intense study that goes with a college education. Besides, in a

women's college like Smith, the entire emphasis of the curriculum and environment is adjusted to the characteristics of the single sex, the only important sex there. Had there been men students in that college, the women would have become a second sex down the line.

That would have altered my life and my development, as I am sure it would have done for many others. I needed to be in an environment where studies and interests were primary. This fact in later life gave me the courage and the desire to take positions that were vital and important. I have often noticed how few women have the courage to speak up when it's necessary. They have never learned nor have they found out how important it is for them to stand up and speak.

THE BEGINNING OF A CAREER

While I was at Smith I didn't have any idea of what it was I wanted to do, but something happened that guided me. I have been blessed all my life with running into marvelous guidance. In Colorado, out on a ranch, there was an Englishman, a graduate of Oxford University. He was the younger son of a titled family, and in England in those days the older son inherited the title and the estate and the younger son had to be either a minister or a soldier. Cholmondeley Thornton didn't want to be a minister or a soldier, so he came to America to be what he wanted to be.

He had a red-haired daughter that he himself had entirely educated until she entered the senior year in Central High School. He had the philosophy that a girl should be herself, do what she wanted to do. Typical English people are a lot more liberal about women, incidentally, than we are in our country. We're still held down by the pioneer image that the men had to have a woman run a home or they couldn't have homes. The British have all kinds of ways of running homes; they don't depend on one woman to do the whole thing.

Well, Mary Thornton, who was a brilliant, beautiful girl,

went into high school just for the senior year in order to graduate because she wanted to go East and be trained as a nurse.
The one girl she picked out for a friend was me. She began in-
viting me out to their ranch for weekends in senior year and I
began telling them what my home problems were. Of course,
he had okayed my getting to Smith.

When I was a sophomore in college, I went out to his ranch
for the weekend. He asked what I was going to do when I got
through. I said that most of the Smith girls teach. He said,
"You aren't going to be any good as a teacher, a typical teacher
fitting into the machinery of teaching. But your father is a
brilliant businessman and you've probably inherited a lot of his
ability. Why don't you spend your summers learning shorthand-
typewriting?"

"Well," I said, "I've never heard of a Smith girl learning
shorthand-typing." I was beginning to be very top-lofty, you
see. But when I got back after my junior year, my father and
stepmother decided that as I was having this vast sum of money
spent on me, twelve hundred a year, that in the summer I
could come home and take the place of a weekly cleaning lady;
clean the house, do all the washing and ironing. At that point,
I felt called upon to learn shorthand and typewriting—*right
away!*

I beat it down to the little school there, and the minute I
hit the typewriter I found I didn't know how to spell, so I
began getting a little respectful. Finally, I worked like a dog
on it. The next summer I went back again. When I went back
to Smith and told my friends who were just off of their summer beaches what I was doing, they asked, "Why did I want
to learn shorthand-typewriting and just be an office secretary?"
I mean, really, a Smith girl a secretary! By this time, though,
I'd gotten very respectful of the whole thing.

So, after I graduated from Smith I went back to Pueblo and
suggested that I work in my father's office. He'd never had a
secretary. I also took in shorthand-typewriting from the lawyers
in the building and earned extra money. I earned a lot of money,
quite a lot. There was no typist there, certainly none that had

a college education. At the end of my second summer there, I told my father that I wanted to go back to the Smith reunion. I made him pay me, too. He didn't like that very well, and neither did my stepmother. I lived at home and ate at home but I didn't do very much work.

I went back to the reunion, and while I was there I heard that one of the English teachers had opened an employment bureau for those Smith graduates that weren't teachers. I beat it to her office. She asked, "What can you do, Jessie?" I told her, "I'm a legal secretary." "*What*?" she said. "You're the first girl to enter that room with a business training! I've got a hundred jobs, all over the place, and I haven't got anybody to fill them."

One of them was with the Macmillan Publishing Company in New York as an assistant to the head of the college textbook department. By September of that year, 1911, I started work on Fifth Avenue—with a secretary and file clerk. I never touched a typewriter myself, but he wouldn't have anyone there who didn't know how to typewrite because that was considered a business training.

My job was to find courses that would fit each new college book that was published. I had, in back of my desk, four hundred college catalogues, and I would write to the man that had the course and tell him about the book, and "Would he like a sample copy?" Of course, if he liked the sample copy, four hundred or however many books would go to that school. It was fascinating. And, of course, it turned out to be a great experience to get that inside look into one of the biggest publishing firms in New York—and a British firm.

When I started, I didn't even know how to write a letter. Here I'd taken this English course, but I couldn't write a simple letter. My boss had to teach me. He was quite happy, though, with the way I did it. My salary was fourteen dollars a week, and I had to punch a time clock like all the low-paid employees. I told him, "Fourteen dollars a week is going to be difficult for me to live on in New York City. When do I make more money?" He said, "At Christmas," if I made good.

At Christmas my envelope had another dollar in it. I took

it in to him and said, "Is this my increase?" as I held it up. He said, "Well, Miss Haver, I think you take a very unfortunate attitude. I came here for ten dollars a week." I said, "I'm told that now you're getting twenty-four hundred a year. How soon will I get that?" He replied, "Well, really, Miss Haver, we have Jessie Ried here and she's a Wellesley graduate and has edited a whole series of books. She's been here twenty-five years and she gets twenty-five dollars a week." Twenty-five dollars a week after twenty-five years was the status.

I met Jessie Ried in the rest room later and said, with my knees knocking, "Miss Ried, do you know what you're doing to the women in this firm? Every time we want more money, we're told about you and how you've been here twenty-five years and are getting twenty-five dollars a week and have edited a whole series of books." "*What?*" she said. "What do you mean?" I said, "I'm telling you what happens and what you're doing to us." She said, "Why, Miss Haver, I have a little apartment around the corner. I have no family. I love this sort of work. I was born for it. I never dreamed I was setting a standard for this whole firm. That's terrible." She promptly went to the president and told him that she wanted more money and royalties for the books she'd edited. He answered, "Miss Ried! Have you lost your mind?" "No," she said, "I've just found it." Well, she was fired, and the next Monday there were five publishers in the office after her. What I did was to get Jessie Ried a good salary, and then I prepared myself to be moved out as a result of my efforts.

I walked up Fifth Avenue to where the five women's colleges had started an employment service for non-teacher college graduates. I told them about the situation and they said, "Oh, goody! We knew this was going on there at that company and we're tickled to death to see you. We have another gorgeous job for you." The new job was to be the first secretary of the Pulitzer School of Journalism at Columbia University. Instead of fourteen dollars a week, I was to get eighty-five dollars a month. I was to be allowed to live in Whittier Hall, the lovely Columbia dormitory—quite a change from the horrible cheap boarding house that I was inhabiting near the Macmillan Company. I stayed there for two years, until 1913. Again, there was a very bad employment situation, from the feminist point of view. I didn't know I was a feminist in those days, but I knew what was endurable and I didn't intend to die on the job.

I went again to the employment office on Fifth Avenue. They had a job in Boston to be a statistician and an investigator for the Massachusetts Minimum Wage Commission at a salary of $1,300 a year. Amy Hewes, executive secretary of the commission and a professor at Mt. Holyoke College, interviewed me and I was invited to come to Boston the next month. I was working to help bring about a minimum wage for women. This was the era when women were beginning to work outside the home. They were the most exploited workers that ever existed. They were getting around four dollars a week in candy factories, in laundries and in five-and-dime stores. The Massachusetts Consumer's League had secured passage of a law that allowed employees of the Minimum Wage Commission to copy payrolls. I was sent out to big factories and industries to copy payrolls and was taught how to put them into statistical tables. It was a very great education and training era for me.

I wanted more than anything else to help women. I became dedicated, in a way, to the woman's world and the woman's needs. That dedication was really backed by the tragedy of my own family life and my mother's death when I was ten. I had lived in that valley where no woman in any family who gave birth to children lived to bring them up. I didn't think it was justice for women to suffer like that. Now I was finding women suffering outside the home, working in industry at starvation wages!

I saw how they had to try to survive. Most of them stayed with their families, but, of course, they were not paying for their keep with these wages. Or they had men friends that they lived with. They had to do one or the other. Neither one was justice because they were not carrying their own weight. They couldn't earn enough to survive without help from either their families or their boyfriends. I didn't think that was just. All down the line, it seemed to me it was a rough world for women. I wanted to find out why and to help change it. You see, I'm a Libra, and a Libra person's keynote is balance and justice.

By the time I left Boston the minimum wage became an accepted fact. Quite a number of boards were at work setting up new standards. When Edward Filene built the most beautiful women's store in Boston, all this shouting about a minimum wage had reached his ear. From the beginning he paid the highest minimum wage that was ever paid, $8 a week, and so the finest saleswomen came to his store. The store was beautiful; they had a big organ that played music all the time, and all these beautiful, attractive skilled saleswomen. The store thrived! And on good minimum wages!

I left Boston after four years to become an employee of the U.S. Bureau of Labor Statistics. World War I was on, and I heard that they were looking for statisticians to do a survey of the cost of living in Washington, D.C. Federal employment is always valuable. Opportunities to grow are everywhere, and I needed a higher salary. I wrote out my experience and was immediately invited down for an interview. The experience in Boston had been invaluable.

WASHINGTON, D.C.:
NEW PATHS TO BREAK

I landed the job and found myself in Washington, D.C., at $1,500 a year. It was a fascinating job. We had to go all over Washington to where the civil servants lived. Nearly a million workers were living there in the sort of small, brick, row houses which are so common to that part of the world. We had to go out and ring doorbells to get the families' budget—what their income was and how it was spent. We were trying to determine if the civil service people were getting enough to live on. I knew now how to make statistical tables and how to interview people. I just adored it. It was a great experience to be involved in that kind of statistical survey.

At the end of two years I had become very friendly with the secretary of the Consumers League of Washington, Mrs. Zold. I knew the Consumers League background from Boston and I admired them. This woman, for some reason, couldn't carry on anymore and they offered me the job. I earned a good salary, better than I'd been getting all along, but it was dependent on my raising money to pay it, and that was a little awkward. But I loved the job because I was my own boss and could run the whole show. I had an office in the Munsey Building, and at times I had secretaries to help me run the office. I set up meetings and lectures. I didn't do too much lecturing myself because I hadn't been trained to speak and didn't know how, but I did speak. In other words, it was a one-woman operation and I was the woman.

I had an executive committee, like all such organizations, but I was the only paid employee. There were very talented women on the executive committee of the Consumers League, brilliant Washington women that otherwise I would not have known at all. One can live in Washington one's whole life and not meet such women. Among them were the two sisters-in-law of Justice Brandeis, the Goldmark sisters. They were prominent in the New York League as well. And Florence Kelley, of course, kept coming down to Washington.*

I've forgotten what the issues were then besides the minimum wage law for women in the District of Columbia. The men were organized, but there were no women's organizations. Although the number of nongovernmental employees in Washington was not large and there weren't any great factories and industries there, the women were being exploited all right! In laundries, stores and restaurants. In order to get the minimum wage for the District of Columbia, the U.S. Congress had to pass a law. It is they who govern Washington, D.C. A minimum wage law that was passed by the U.S. Congress would set an important precedent for the rest of the country. To get a minimum wage law through Congress was a little different from getting it through the Massachusetts legislature. The Goldmarks worked with Justice Brandeis to draft the bill, and I was asked to present it as soon as possible to a legislator who was sympathetic to the issue. Justice Brandeis thought it would take two years to get it through, but it went through in months —to the astonishment of everybody. As it happened, the man we invited to introduce the bill into the lower house was Congressman Edward Keating from Pueblo, Colorado, my hometown. He was a very broad-minded legislator, one of the very rare men at that time who had a social conscience and understood the background of the Minimum Wage Law. He knew my father but I had never met him before. He jumped at the chance to introduce the bill into the lower house. Then we secured Senator Harry Hollis of New Hampshire to introduce the bill to the Senate. He was very close to Woodrow Wilson, the President at the time.

So there we were with our little bill now safely introduced into the Congress. My next job was to go up to the Capitol to learn how to be a lobbyist. I found out that the first man to be consulted was Congressman Ben Johnson of Kentucky. He was

* Florence Kelley, a social reformer with particular interest in child labor and the welfare of industrial women workers, was executive secretary of the National Consumers League.

chairman of the House District Committee, the committee that governed Washington. He was considered an old bear where women were concerned. He loathed having women clattering down the marble corridors of the House Office Building. He loathed advanced human ideas about things like minimum wages and women getting a living wage. Besides, women had no rights in the House Office Building because they were not voters. He was the heartbreak of the city because no decent, enlightened legislation for Washington could get through Ben Johnson. He seemed just impossible. I remember the day that Pauline Goldmark asked me, "What are you going to do about Ben Johnson? How are you going to get around him?" They seemed to think that somehow I'd find a way, but they weren't sure.

I will never forget the day I first called on him in his office. He had women working quietly in the rear of his office, but any woman with the status of a lobbyist was just like a red flag to a bull. This I knew. I had a cute little cotton dress with little red and white fine checks. We used to always wear those checked dresses. It had a ruffle right down the front, all starched and looking gay and fresh.

The door was open and I walked into Congressman Ben Johnson's back office. There he sat at his huge desk, looking very important. "Congressman," I said, "may I please speak to you for a few minutes?" I was very courteous. Looking up, he growled, "What are you doing here?! Why aren't you home having babies, where you belong?!"

I knew the fate of our minimum wage bill hung on my answer. "Well, Congressman," I answered in a soft tone, "you see, it's an awkward situation. You're supposed to have a husband before you have a baby and I haven't got a husband."

"Well, why don't you get one?"

"Well, Congressman, I would like one, but so far all the good ones are married." Of course he was already married, too.

"Oh, that's tough," he said. The tone of his voice changed and he said, "Well, come on and sit down and tell me what I can do for you. I'll have to help you, I can see that." I said,

"Yes, Congressman, I do need help." I started talking to him about the minimum wage bill and the women in the five-and-ten-cent store downtown who were getting four dollars a week and having to either live on their families or with a man. I explained how we wanted to change that. He asked what he could do and I told him, "Well, Congressman, if you'll just set the date for a hearing, I will see to it that all the leading employers of all the stores are there. I happen to know Edward Filene from Boston and he's now in town. He's widely known and was the president of the National Businessmen's Association. If I can get him to appear at your hearing, you'd be on the front page of every newspaper in Washington. How would you like that?"

"Well," he said, "that would be all right. When do you want your date?" I walked right downtown in this gay mood I was in at this point and there was Edward Filene. He said that he would be honored to speak at the hearing. So I walked back to Ben Johnson and told him. "Well," he said, "this begins to look interesting." We had the hearing and it was jammed with the leading employers of Washington. Edward Filene made the first speech and it was gorgeous. He told them how it paid to pay women well. A well-paid, happy, gay, well-cared-for, well-fed clerk in your store brings in business, and that's what you're after—*business*. They saw the point.

I've forgotten how long it was, but it was no time before he had the bill through the House. Florence Kelley, of course, came down and spoke, and neither she nor any of the women could believe that this thing they had fought and struggled for for years with such anguish would just fly through the U.S. Congress with no opposition. I went up to Congressman Johnson afterwards to thank him. "Well," he said, "I have a lot of influence around here and if there's ever anything you want around here, just let me know. I'm at your service." With that I bade him good-bye and beat it over to the Senate.

Senator Hollis told me, "We can't get that bill through our committee unless you can get Senator Reed Smoot to okay it." Reed Smoot was one of the most difficult men in the U.S.

Senate. He was head of the Rules Committee and he sat right down on the center aisle so that not a single bill could go anywhere unless he okayed it. So the thing to do was to call on Senator Reed Smoot. The Consumers League decided that the president, Mrs. Edward Costigan, whose husband was head of the Tariff Commission, had better go with me to call on Senator Reed Smoot. I don't know whether they thought he was going to chop my head off, or what. I knew he wouldn't because he was from Salt Lake City and was one of the leading Mormons—a very brilliant, clever legislator, a tall handsome man, a gentleman.

Mrs. Costigan, who was a lovely, sweet, gracious woman, and I descended on Senator Reed Smoot's office. We had an appointment. As we came in he rose graciously from his desk. He had a seat at one side of his desk for me and one for Mrs. Costigan. I said, "Senator, we have come to talk to you about this minimum wage bill. It's now gone through the House and so, of course, we look forward to your help to get it through the Senate." Whereupon he rose suddenly and began to pound on his desk so that everything on it danced. He said, "You women, with all this socialistic legislation! You know what? I'd like to be President of the United States when all this legislation gets in there. I'd just like to be President. I could be the greatest dictator you ever saw with this kind of legislation coming up!"

Mrs. Costigan commenced to tremble; she looked at the Senator with horror, as the desk was dancing with objects on it. But I just looked at him and smiled sweetly as I said, "You know, Senator, I wish you could be President of the United States." "Well!" he said, as he sat down with a bump. "Why would you like to see me as President?" I knew he was dying to be President, and he was capable of being President. He was a very great legislator, but he was a Mormon. At that time our country was a little stuffy about appointing people with such a strong religious background as that. "You see, Senator, if you were President and issues like this came up, you'd just have to look at both sides of the question and you're not used to doing that. Besides, this would make you a greater leader than you

are now." "Well," he said, "what do you want me to do?"
I said, "When that bill comes in, would you just pick up your
things and leave your seat until we can get it into Senator Hollis's committee?" He agreed, and we shook hands and left.

Mrs. Costigan could hardly walk out of the room, she was
so frightened at what had happened. But everything was all
right. As the bill reached the Senator's desk, I saw him gather up
his papers and walk out. In no time Senator Hollis had a hearing that was equally impressive, and we didn't have to work
so hard for it. He was a very generous and enlightened man and
one of the great leaders of the United States Senate. The bill
went flying through and the President signed it.

In the process of lobbying you must almost live up at that
Capitol. I was there in the Senate gallery for weeks watching
the men and studying the process. At the time there were very
few other women lobbyists. Just the suffrage lobbyists. Alice
Paul was carrying on her picketing of the White House, in
violation of the laws of the city. Mrs. Carrie Chapman Catt was
living in the big hotel down on Pennsylvania Avenue while her
cohorts were calling on Senator [William] Borah, who was
stalling the bill after all these years.

While the minimum wage bill was still hanging fire, I discovered the meat-packers hearing. I was clicking along the cor-
ridor one day and looked into a room where there was a hearing. I knew instantly that it was a meat-packers hearing because they had been publishing huge ads in the papers. It was
the most brazen advertising I'd ever seen for a big industry.
It was obvious they had a lot at stake. I was surely aroused.
Remember, my father had gone into the business of cattle raising and so I knew what it cost to raise cattle on the range.

It happened that was one of the days that Armour Packing
cornered rice and made a huge fortune. Because the war was on
and the potatoes were needed for the men in the army, women
shoppers were told to buy rice instead. I went into the hearing.
There were no newspaper people there, so when I caught this
story of the rice, I sent it down to one of the women editors of
the *Christian Science Monitor*. "Look," I said, "you must re-

port this hearing. This is hot stuff." She took the story and sent it in, and soon it came out on the front page as her story, of course.

I had called up the women on the board of the D.C. Consumers League, including Mrs. Edward Costigan, and told them that this was a consumers story and had to do with women. The next day ten women were at the hearing with nice little pencils and notebooks. When they filed in, you ought to have seen the expression on the men's faces, especially the man who was the district attorney back in Chicago who had been brought there to protect these men and their companies. The expressions on the faces of all of them, when they saw these women with their pencils taking notes, were just cataclysmic.

There was then a meeting of the D.C. Consumers League where the women reported what was happening, and after that women began filling the hearing room. Finally, Mrs. Kelley was persuaded to come down and testify, though she was very unwilling to do so because it was really not their field. Their field was women in industry, women's wages. To get off into this great monopoly of the meat packers was just something she didn't want to do. It's a wonder she ever came. But, as it turned out, she didn't carry too much weight.

A lot of publicity followed these hearings and the whole thing broke open. I attended the hearing every day, writing up what went on. My two years as a secretary at the School of Journalism paid off. I had absorbed valuable journalistic techniques, and my reports were being sent out through UP all over the country. The advertising stopped. It was a failure because the thing had broken loose and was being publicized.

So I was really at the head of the procession of women working outside their homes and with the U.S. government. I was running into all the problems headlong. Being of pioneer stock from Colorado, I was a pioneer up there as well. It was great. I never had so much fun and never loved anything in my life like that. I was completely fulfilled, as a woman even. After all, I was helping women. I seemed to be using, and using effectively, everything I had in me. I don't know where it came from, but there it was.

JOINING THE SUFFRAGE STRUGGLE DURING THE FINAL PHASE

Of course, immediately upon getting to Washington, I became interested in the woman's suffrage movement, which, at that time, was working to get a resolution through the U.S. Senate. In Boston I had gone to a lot of meetings on suffrage and on birth control. Margaret Sanger was always coming up to Boston and lecturing because they had a very bad law in Massachusetts and no information on birth control. I also went several times to hear Mrs. Pankhurst when she came from England. Even though I went to all the big suffrage meetings, I couldn't do much about it at that time because I was busy earning a living.

In Washington I began going to Alice Paul's place. Alice Paul, the leader of the National Woman's Party, had been given a lot of money by Mrs. O. H. P. Belmont and had a lovely house as her headquarters right on the edge of Lafayette Park, across from the White House. There was a big dining room, and I took a great many of my luncheons there, even while I was working in the U.S. Bureau of Labor Statistics, and that's where I met all those women. They were my intimate friends. One of the leading pickets, Mrs. Harvey Wiley, was one of the women who were in my first class in public speaking when I came back to Washington after eight years in London. Then there was Mrs. Kent, the wife of William Kent, who later gave me the money to take the trip with Carrie Chapman Catt. They all went to prison for picketing the White House and they fasted and had food pushed down their stomachs with a hose. It was a terrible story.

I remember one talented girl, young, beautiful, brilliant, and a recent graduate from Vassar, Hazel Hunkins. Alice Paul sent her all over the country to speak on woman's suffrage. I became acquainted with her personally and found that she had not only become radical about woman's suffrage but, along with others, she thought that it was all right for anyone to have a baby if she wanted and to pick the right person to be the father of the baby, to have a eugenic baby. She intended to do this. She went home to Montana to visit her family and told them her plans. Her mother cried night and day and holidays and Sundays, but this reformer couldn't be stopped.

In the end, she did finally get pregnant, whereupon she was fired. Alice Paul wasn't out to create a new family life for people. She was just interested in getting the vote for women. So the future mother secured a job and departed for London. She had four children and has since become a feminist leader in London. She eventually married the man who was the father of her children, a man who became a well-known journalist in England. So this was also an era when women were struggling for more freedom and made decisions they thought were sound.

I was very close to all that. I always went there and they worked hard to get me lined up with their more radical group, but I couldn't. For one thing, I was still a lobbyist at the Capitol for the Consumers League. Besides, they all had husbands, so they ate. Anyway, I was not inclined to go in for as rugged a program as they followed. I liked Mrs. Catt's legislative system better, but I believe they'd never have got woman's suffrage if they had depended only on Mrs. Catt! She had spent twenty years working for this and was very much of a statistician and a parliamentarian. Alice Paul had been taught by Mrs. Pankhurst in London, and Mrs. Pankhurst was a militant. Alice Paul followed her way of fighting and, in the end, took the position that if any man in the Democratic Party should vote against woman's suffrage, she would then condemn the whole party. This Mrs. Catt violently disagreed with, and that's why they separated.

There is another explanation to this fierce antagonism between these two women reformers. They were within two days of each other in their birthdays. Alice Paul was born January

11, 1885, and Mrs. Catt's birthday was January 9, 1859. To have two Capricorns latched together in a violent historical struggle could hardly be more trying. Each stood for the truth as she saw it, and each in her way has brought about and is bringing about lasting freedom for women equal to that for men.

I don't remember much about the National Woman's Party picketing or marching because, of course, I was earning my own living and having to work at the time. We used to go over to the restaurant, though, and hear the latest news of what was going on. It was very exciting, really. Finally, Alice Paul and her group began burning the words of the President in Lafayette Park and I also seem to remember that they burned him in effigy. I remember thinking at the time how bold it was and yet how disrespectful. He hadn't done a thing to help the women get the vote, although World War I was going on and he was giving out noble statements to the world about the rights of freedom of all people. But he didn't include women's rights in his statements. He finally became irritated about all this, and after this drastic attack, decided he would personally appear before the Senate. It was a history-making occasion, and my boyfriend, whom I later married, and I received tickets and sat in the balcony of the U.S. Senate the day he appeared and asked the Senate to vote for woman's suffrage. It was a very thrilling experience to be there when that happened.

The suffrage amendment went through, at last, while the meat-packers hearings were still going on. The news came out that Carrie Chapman Catt, with her party of speakers, was going to start through the Far West to hurry up the ratification of the amendment. They felt that in the West, where a lot of the states already had woman's suffrage and where they were sympathetic to it, ratification could be pressured easily. Mrs. Catt's hotel was just across the street from the Munsey Building, where I had my office. I barged into her office one evening about five o'clock, congratulating her on her victory, and said that I had heard she was going West. I told her what I'd been doing on getting the story on the meat-packing industry and explained why I was interested in her trip. "I wish I could go with you on this tour and, instead of talking about suffrage, tell the story about the meat-packing industry, as one of the great industries women are concerned with as buyers of food."

Of course, Mrs. Catt's first reaction was against it. She felt that if the big industries thought that the women voters were going to stick their noses into something like these monopolies, they'd see to it that the women still didn't get the vote. Being a great diplomat, she said, "Well, Jessie, it would be fun to have you go with us but we couldn't afford to take you." I asked her how much it would cost and she told me five hundred dollars. "If I can get the five hundred dollars, can I go?" She replied that I could, probably thinking that I would never get the five hundred dollars and that she need not worry about the danger.

I went over to Congressman William Kent's office on New York Avenue. I knew that he was the cattle man from California who had been responsible for those hearings. I told him about her trip through six states in the West and that I'd speak from the same platform with her and tell this meat-packing story. "But she says I have to have five hundred dollars to go along." He just pulled out his checkbook, put it on the desk, and wrote out the check for the full amount.

In half an hour I was back with the five hundred dollars. Mrs. Catt said, "Well, Jessie, I promised you could go if you could get the money, so I guess we'd better take you along." We started out before Christmas and were on tour over the Christmas holiday. I remember vividly how we stayed at the great hotel in San Bernardino, the Huntington-Sheraton, for the whole Christmas period. One of the famous women of California who really started the woman's suffrage movement there was our hostess.

The trip, of course, was a very thrilling experience for me. I had never gone on a trip like that or experienced those crowds at railway stations as we went along. At every station where we stopped to speak, there were huge crowds there to greet Mrs. Catt. You never saw such adoration and such admiration and faithfulness that the women gave to that great seasoned leader. I think that possibly she had the most influence with women and had the greatest effect in joining women to a cause than any other woman I've ever heard of. There was a magnetism about her character that attracted women and made them forget that women through the ages have always fought each other and been jealous. There was no jealousy in her program, just the selfless dedication to a great issue.

In those towns where we stopped there was lots of money. Many of the women were well-off, so there was plenty of money around. They always met her at the train and escorted her to the hotel, and all of us were there with her. Everything was so well thought out. Always they had these beautiful big meetings.

I sat back of Mrs. Catt as she spoke. In fact, she gave me my first lessons on how to speak on those platforms. I often noticed that she was wringing her hands behind her when she was speaking and so one day I asked her, "Why do you wring your hands behind you?" "Because," she said, "I suffer so when I am speaking. I'm in agony." I was astonished when I realized that she was really a shy woman. She really did not want to be out in front of an audience. When I asked her why she then chose that kind of career, her answer was, "I didn't choose it. It chose me and wouldn't let me go."

But her speeches were oratorical. They were profound speeches, they weren't just superficial. They were tied in with the history of government and the theory of democracy and what it all means. It wasn't just a superficial speech about the needs of women, but was a whole philosophy of the right of individuals to govern themselves. She had to fire up the women to go after their state legislators to endorse the amendment. All the big meetings and big luncheons were held at noon, and, of course, most of the audience were women. In California, I remember, the state legislature was in recess, so they gained permission to have this meeting in the Senate room of the State of California. We sat on the platform and made our speeches from there.

The other women usually gave the regular woman's suffrage talk they'd been doing for years. Mine was the only one that didn't. I think, in a way, I was kind of refreshing. It was a different talk and it looked to the future and how this was the kind of issue that the women should be interested in as consumers. The title of my speech was "The Government and the Market Basket." My future husband is the one who gave me that title, and it was right. It made for excellent publicity. Mrs. Catt wasn't too comfortable about it, though, because she didn't want them to kill woman's suffrage after all these years. At every state where we were, there was a row of meat-packers' lawyers listening. If I had made one slip of the tongue that was not on the record, they would have sued Mrs. Catt for misrepresentation. But, of course, I just spoke from the point of view of the public record that I'd received at the hearings in Washington.

We went to Colorado, California and Nevada, I recall. In Las Vegas a fascinating incident occurred. As we were leaving the hotel one morning to go to the high school where Mrs. Catt was to speak, there was one of my intimate friends from Washington. We had all been very enthusiastic about this girl because she had a fine boyfriend and they had finally decided to get married. What was so exciting was that he was perfectly willing to have her carry on with her job. That was the era when you just automatically stopped working as soon as you married. But she'd found a man who wanted her to go on with her job—a man who thought it was a great idea. We all thought so, too. But to date, such a plan was unheard of.

Here she was in Las Vegas. "What are you doing out here?" I asked, astonished. "I'm getting a divorce." "*What!* What's the matter?" I asked. "Well, we got along fine, but then I had a baby and I decided I didn't want to work anymore. I wanted to stay home and take care of the baby. I found it was rather nice not to have to crawl out of bed every morning on cold days and go down on the buses and the streetcars to a job. It was nicer staying home. But, you know, he wouldn't put up with it. He said that we had married on the theory that I was to continue work and that as soon as the baby got a little older,

I was to get a baby-sitter and get back to my job. He said he had no intentions of supporting me and the baby. That was the agreement when we were married."

So it occurred to me, at that point in Las Vegas, that we women were getting into hot water on some subjects about the future and some of the women were getting into hot water, too. Another incident happened down in San Diego that made me wonder. On the train, across the aisle from me, was a woman who cried all night. The next morning I took a step over to her seat and saw that it was a young girl. I asked her what the trouble was. She was still in college, and so was the young man that I saw saying good-bye to her with much apparent sorrow. He had decided that she was to give up her college and get a job so that he could get his legal degree. That didn't seem to be her idea of marriage, giving up college and earning the money so that he could get his degree. She had written her mother about it back East, and her mother told her to leave him at once and come back East and that she'd take her on a European trip. So she was leaving him to go on the European trip.

So, on the side, as we were having the trip, I was picking up some very interesting incidents. I'm a philosopher by nature and I like to see what's going on and then try to understand it. I came back from the trip thinking that there was a lot more study we were going to have to make of the perfect world into which we were not entering as soon as we got woman's suffrage.

Shortly after we returned from that trip, Mrs. Catt had a meeting of all her following and her officers to wind up the work of the National Woman's Suffrage Association. She invited me to go with her and sit on the platform. They wound up their organization and put it to bed, and then they created the National League of Women Voters. It was not a controversial issue. It had all been thought out, as Mrs. Catt always did. She was a stateswoman. She had all the plans made and Maude Wood Park of Boston was appointed the president of the National League of Women Voters.

The whole meeting was very peaceful and very happy because they were through with suffrage and now could go on to prepare women for the new program ahead. Mrs. Catt had that gift of dramatizing things in a human way that was beautiful and noble. There was a nobility about her and a high spiritual thinking that she put back of everything she did. That was the feeling of that meeting. It was uplifting. The big battle they'd fought for so many years was over, and now a new world was coming and they were going to help create it. She put a beautiful spirit of spirituality and idealism into the meeting.

They had a business meeting right afterwards and I was appointed the first legislative advocate, as they called it. It was a paid position, with the highest salary any woman was getting in Washington at the time, thirty-five hundred dollars. It was almost double what I was getting with the Consumers League— and I didn't have to raise the money, either, as I did with the Consumers League. So we went back to Washington and I was off the Consumers League and into a big new job for the National League of Women Voters. We spent all that summer laying the groundwork for the work of the League with the Congress for the next fall. My work, by this time, became somewhat confused because this whole question of marriage had come up. You can't think about getting married and still be completely sunk in the work of a reform movement like the National League of Women Voters. So I don't think I did so good a job that summer. By December, Hugh and I were married, and off to London.

I don't know what Mrs. Catt would have liked the League of Women Voters to have done, but maybe it was to have it concentrate less on the processes of government and more on getting freedom for women. I think she was very disappointed with the league for that reason. She felt that it lost its meaning by just limiting itself to government issues. Not many people agree with that, though, because the league has done great work in this country in getting women better trained in dealing with government and how it works. They've been very successful, though conservative, before city councils and state governments. They've taught their members how government works, how to influence government.

I didn't know what to think! As soon as the women had the vote, they just quit. It's one of the tragedies of the whole era that a slump took place. Women stopped seeking higher degrees in college, they stopped trying to be better educated. Many young women left school for marriage and many went to work to help husbands secure degrees. Over the years this custom has become commonplace—a strange reaction to the fire and the drama of the fight for woman's suffrage.

Maybe we needed new isues. Alice Paul was right. She began immediately to plan to introduce to the Congress the equal rights amendment. Although she had helped to secure woman's suffrage, she still believed that woman's suffrage alone was not going to give women everything they wanted and needed. They had only secured the right to vote. Even now the U.S. Supreme Court has stated that the only status women have in our government is as voters. Any state today can still pass any law they'd like against women, and they have no recourse except perhaps to vote against them. There are now a thousand very bad laws on the records of state legislatures against women. This is added proof that Alice Paul is a woman with a profound mind. Getting woman's suffrage was not enough, it was just the first step.

SUFFRAGE, FEMINISM AND ATTITUDES TOWARD MEN

Everything completely changed when I left Boston. Frankly, I was worried because I wasn't meeting any men. I had had a rigid rule in college that I would make no dates because I was getting educated, as my mother told me to do. But now I was twenty-five years old. At this point, I was beginning to wonder if I was ever going to marry. I hadn't yet made up my mind to that, so I began to be a little soft on red-hot suffragists. I mean, girls who were trying to get married at that time didn't shout their heads off about woman's suffrage, as yet not very popular with men. When I first arrived in Boston, woman's suffrage was a very *unpopular* subject. Even the president of Harvard came out against it during one of Mrs. Catt's visits there.

THE LADIES' HOME JOURNAL, JANUARY 1911

DO YOU, AS A WOMAN, WANT TO VOTE?

Some Prominent Women of America Answer the Question

It is supposed in some quarters that the agitation for woman suffrage which has been so industriously stirred up has won over to its side a majority of the thinking women of this country. The names of well-known women are juggled with in the newspapers until it is not strange that some should ask: How do the women whose works place them in positions of vantage think on this question?

To ascertain the opinions of some of the most prominent women this page was sent out with the request that each would, in a single sentence, answer the question given at the head:

"Do you, as an American woman, want to vote?"

The answers speak for themselves, and are, to say the least, illuminative.

THE EDITORS OF THE LADIES' HOME JOURNAL

WHERE THE REAL NEW YORK WOMEN STAND

The impression is sometimes conveyed that the best part of New York womanhood is in favor of the ballot for woman. But the other side of that impression is reflected by the Committees and Boards governing the two New York organizations that stand as against woman suffrage. Thus there appear as Honorary Vice-Presidents, Directors and members of the Executive Committee of THE NATIONAL LEAGUE FOR THE CIVIC EDUCATION OF WOMEN the following women, representative of the oldest and foremost families of New York:

MRS. GROVER CLEVELAND
  Wife of the Former President of the United States
MRS. ANDREW CARNEGIE
MRS. GEORGE R. SHELDON
MRS. HENRY SELIGMAN
MRS. LIVINGSTON SCHUYLER
MRS. JAMES TERRY GARDINER
MRS. WILLIAM PERRY NORTHRUP
MRS. WILLIAM HAYNES
                    TRUESDALE
MRS. DAVID H. GREER
  Wife of the Bishop of the Diocese of New York
MRS. SCHUYLER VAN RENSSELAER
MRS. CHARLES H. PARKHURST

MRS. ROSSITER JOHNSON
MRS. MABEL DEAN KALBFLEISCH
MRS. WILLIAM PERKINS DRAPER
MRS. DUNLAP HOPKINS
MRS. HIRAM W. SIBLEY

While on the Boards and Committees and member lists of THE NEW YORK STATE ASSOCIATION OPPOSED TO WOMAN SUFFRAGE there appear the names of women equally representative of the foremost New York families:

MRS. ELIHU ROOT
MRS. FRANCIS S. BANGS
MRS. FRANCIS M. SCOTT
MRS. CLEVELAND H. DODGE
MRS. C. GRANT LAFARGE
MRS. HERBERT L. SATTERLEE
MRS. HENRY A. STIMSON
MRS. GEORGE DOUGLAS MILLER
MISS ALICE HILL CHITTENDEN
MRS. JOHN G. MILBURN
MRS. WILLIAM M. POLK
MRS. LOCKWOOD DEFOREST

Those who call themselves suffragettes are making such a noise that I fear there is danger that the public may forget that opposed to these few is the great majority of womankind, proud of being women, and who glory in doing well those things which an All-Wise Creator assigned as woman's part in life.

LOUISE HOMER

I cannot interest myself in the subject in the slightest degree.

MRS. BENJAMIN HARRISON
Wife of the Former President
of the United States

No.

CAROLINE HAZARD
Former President of Wellesley
College

No. The active participation of women in politics would be a great and perhaps a hazardous experiment in government. I am opposed to trying it.

AGNES IRWIN
Former Dean of Radcliffe College

The whole suffrage movement seems to me unintelligent, unintelligible and uninteresting. The achievement of universal suffrage would multiply our clubs and divide our homes.

CAROLYN WELLS

AN AUTHORITATIVE VOICE FROM
COLORADO

I have voted since 1893: I have been a delegate to the city and State conventions, and a member of the Republican State Committee from my county: I have been a deputy sheriff and a watcher at the polls: for twenty-three years I have been in the midst of the woman-suffrage movement in Colorado. For years I believed in woman suffrage and have worked day in and day out for it —I now see my mistake and would abolish it tomorrow if I could.

No law has been put on the statute book of Colorado for the benefit of women and children that has been put there by the women. The Child Labor Law went through independently of the woman's vote. The hours of working-women have not been shortened; the wages of school-teachers have not been raised: the type of men that got into office has not improved a bit.

As for the effect of the vote on women personally, I have known scores of women who worked for the Republican party one year and worked for the Democratic party next year, telling me frankly that "the Democrats gave us more money."

Frankly, the experiment is a failure. It has done Colorado no good: it has done woman no good. The best thing for both would be if tomorrow the ballot for women could be abolished.

MRS. FRANCIS W. GODDARD
President of the Colonial Dames
of Colorado

I did go hear Mrs. Pankhurst speak in Boston and I went to the meetings, but I did not work for them. I was ashamed of myself because I wasn't getting out and helping, but of course, I was working for women in my job. Besides, at that point in my life, I felt I had something else I had to do: to learn how to get along with men. Underneath everything else, what I really wanted was to have a baby. And that meant I had to get married.

I had never taken any interest in boys, except for my brother who was my pal. For some reason I felt superior to them intellectually. I finally did have a boy invite me to the junior prom in high school. My high school teacher got him to do it, I think. He sent me some red carnations. By that time I was seventeen years old. I didn't know how to talk to boys. I was awkward and ill at ease. That's why I wanted to go to a college where there were no men, where I would learn to communicate with ease.

Of course, when I was at Smith there was Horace Lyon. He came to Colorado to get me to marry him after I graduated. He was just a perfect darling, very good-looking and very faithful, fine young man. The trouble was I did not love him. I tried, but it was no good. Within half an hour, I couldn't think of anything to talk about. Imagine that! Well, you can't marry somebody without love—at least I couldn't. I knew I'd never get a chance like that again. My family had a fit at the way I treated him.

In Boston I began to see that I was in an environment where I'd never meet any attractive men, the kind of men I'd like. In boarding houses and places like that, you don't. I was lonely. I had no home and I needed companionship. I liked this Portuguese at a boarding house. He was a handsome fellow. He was the one that aroused me sexually. I was twenty-four years old then. He was very interested in me, really, and is the one who taught me how to swim, but he was never with me for weekends. He would go back down to southern Massachusetts, where his family lived. He said that his father was a drunkard and would come home and beat up his mother, and so he had to be there to protect her. That was the story he told. He hadn't asked me to marry him, but I think he wanted to. Then I had a dream that he had a girl down there that his mother had picked for him to marry. He was a good boy wanting to do what his family said, but was terribly upset trying to decide what to do. When he came back one Monday, I told him about the dream. He never showed up again and I never heard a word from him. That was the end of that. Soon after that, I went to Washington. That's how a dream saved me.

When I went to Washington, everything changed. I'd landed a tremendous job and a good salary and I had prestige and loved my job. Why get married? That was a different story. Then, of course, I began knowing all those fine women who were working for woman's suffrage and got close to the whole movement. By that time and place, woman's suffrage was a more popular subject. So, although I had been a suffragist, I wasn't a frothing-at-the-mouth one until I arrived in Washington. I still didn't call myself a feminist, though. In those days you were just a suffragette. The word "feminist" was not yet used. They didn't use the term as a title and a label as we do now. We say, "Is she a feminist?" and that's a concrete thing we're asking. At that time, we did not talk about feminists in that hard-boiled way. We just said, "Is she a suffragist? Does she believe in woman's suffrage?" That was the big issue of the day.

So I was getting to be in no hurry to marry. Then I met Hugh. He didn't want to marry either. So I had a boyfriend at last. We went out to dinner every night, Dutch treat. That was a new idea. Women working in offices were new, too. If you were working and he was working, it was natural. I think I was getting a bigger salary than he was, or as big. It was just automatic that I always paid for my own dinner and he paid for his. We just never thought about it. If he weren't there, I'd pay; he's there, I pay. There was no issue. It was utterly natural. After all, we were just pals. We had a marvelous companionship, which I needed. I never had seen any other man in my life that could give the companionship Hugh could. He helped me with speeches, too, though he had never set foot in college. He was just clever.

I think my job had a lot to do with the attitudes I was developing toward marriage. I had an important job. I saw that being like a man had its value, instead of being like a woman. Then also, there was this friend whom I visited repeatedly. She had three children. I thought she was in a horrible position. Her husband had a high position at Yale University and was a wealthy man. But there she was, glued to this home and children and cooking and everything. I thought, Thank God! I'm free.

MARRIAGE AND FAMILY LIFE

I had decided that I was never going to get married, so my life was very simple. I had this gorgeous job lobbying, which I adored. I had never been so completely happy and so completely using every talent I had, and it was heaven. Then I met Hugh, and since he didn't want to get married either, we just had a nice, platonic friendship for four years. We were companions but not future married partners.

Then I reached the age of thirty-three. As I looked around at the women who hadn't married and were forty on, I didn't like the picture very well. They didn't seem very happy. One of the most brilliant women in Washington, who'd had a very high position in the government, was now in a mental home for life. I didn't like the looks of that, either.

Besides, I'd been eating dinner every night with my platonic pal, Hugh. He secured a job at the American embassy in London, so I began to wonder whom I would be eating dinner with. I enjoyed him. He helped me in my work. He loved having me do this kind of work, he was fascinated with it. He gave me titles to my speeches. He was a much more brilliant man, mentally, really, than I was as a woman. He was a Welshman and I was half German, and that's a rather slow-thinking mind. So whenever I landed into a tight place, this alert Welshman always had the answer.

It was one of the most difficult decisions I've ever made in my life: to leave the best Washington job I, or anybody else, ever had, to give it up and get married. There is a long story of the pressure that was on me by his mother not to get married. She came to Washington to help get him away without me. She told me at the first meeting that he was never going to marry. I was not having her plan out my life for me, either. She couldn't tell me what to do with my life! Then I began to want to get married. A little opposition was a good deal. Meanwhile I had grown so used to Hugh that I found, to my horror, that I couldn't get along without him. But the decision to marry was made on a deep spiritual basis. It was the most difficult and important decision in my life and one that changed my life and improved it. I did not realize that my husband would give me a great experience that would broaden my whole life and my career and everything—invaluable. Marriage is that way.

On December 6, 1920, we were married in New York City by the Reverend John Haynes Holmes, the great Unitarian preacher. We were married by him in his office, with his clerk as witness. The opposition of my husband's family to his marriage made him unwilling to have anything but a very simple marriage. Six days later, on December 12, we saw ourselves taking the good ship *Aquitania* for London, terrified at the idea of leaving America. I knew I couldn't carry on my career, but I thought I'd like to see England. I'd heard that the women whose husbands were in the diplomatic service didn't do any cooking. I thought that had its charms. A nice trip to England

and no cooking and a lot of the new world to see. I was a philosopher and full of curiosity.

We arrived in London just a short time before Christmas, and before long we found an apartment in Hampstead Garden. Later on we bought a house there, the only Americans at the embassy to buy a house, and a woman at the American Woman's Club guided me in buying enough antique furniture for the eleven-room house. Soon after our arrival in London I discovered the American Woman's Club in a perfectly beautiful mansion in Grosvenor Square. Almost at once, I was roped in to start a current events circle once a week, and that became one of the most interesting and brilliant activities I had ever been involved in. There were talented women from all over the world; there were reports from Italy about Mussolini's beginning activity, from Ireland. The only trouble was that few of the women had training in public speaking, so they had to read their reports.

Then I found Madame d'Esterre down on the Chelsea Embankment. She had taught public speaking to nine royal princes and many men in the House of Commons and their wives. The British generally took their wives with them to speak on the same platform when they were running for seats in the House of Commons. I thought that was rather neat. That was a period when our political wives were still kept under cover!

Madame d'Esterre was persuaded to come to the American Woman's Club to teach their members how to speak. Oh, was that an experience! That was the first time I'd ever had any formal lessons myself. She was so rough and critical that only about twelve of us survived. I learned later that's the British way of teaching. Madame d'Esterre was from Ireland. She came to England at the same time that Bernard Shaw did. She wore a Romanlike toga, only it was black, and she had short hair. She was, without doubt, one of the plainest women I ever saw. This, too, bothered the American students. But she worshiped the English language and she could certainly teach speech!

I also went to her regular classes in her studio and loved

them. I was a sensation because I was the first American there. They thought I had a terrible American accent, one of the worst. Madame d'Esterre said not to mind, that it would take me two years to get rid of that accent and then I would be unpopular when I returned home.

Meanwhile I had acquired fierce rheumatism in that frightful British climate, though I now think it was arthritis, and something had to be done. Lady Walker Smith advised me to go to Baden-Baden, Germany, to secure treatments from Dr. Eddie Schact. Not only did his program in the hot baths and with the Swedish masseur knock out the rheumatism, but he laid out a plan for my life that was long absent. The question was, How was I to have a baby and still carry on with my interests in public life when we returned to America? By this time it was clear that it was too late for me to turn into a dedicated housewife for the rest of my life.

The doctor advised me to give the intellectual interests a rest for five or six years while starting my family, and to get the British to teach me how to find and keep household help. He said that I must have one day off in seven, though, to continue to pursue my hobbies. "Why, Doctor," I asked, "how can I do that? I thought I could never do that anymore once I had a baby." "That's why you had a college education, to think that one out," was the answer.

It was easy to find a good woman to clean our apartment once a week and to do the washing. There was a cooperative dining room in the building for dinners, so that problem was settled. Then it began to dawn on me that having a baby was not quite the same as being a lobbyist at the Capitol. So I began to visit a huge mothers' clinic in London that was perfectly fascinating. All over England, in the small villages and in London, were these free mothers' clinics. The cheapest medical costs had to do with childbirth. Thanks to Florence Nightingale, most of the nurses in England were also midwives. Most of the babies were born at home, delivered by midwives, for something like one pound. The pregnant women had been so well trained at the clinics, there was seldom a need for a doctor. Pregnant women even from the middle classes went to these clinics to learn how to have their babies.

Then I found Dr. Pink's Nursing Home in Blackheath. The English were making a science of childbirth and child feeding. Dr. Pink had never lost a mother or a baby, and sent every mother away nursing her baby. That did it! Our daughter was born in March 1924, when I was thirty-eight years old. She was breast-fed for nine months. That was the most exciting thing I had ever done, to learn to breast-feed a baby. Our son was born in 1926 and he, too, was breast-fed, though not as long.

Our British home was now established with a governess and a cook. The governess knew all of the tricks of the trade, since she had already brought up three sets of children. Every evening she joined me in the dining room to report every incident of the day and what she had done to meet the situation. She had two days off a week and so did the cook. When I found out how free I was the rest of the time, I was glad to pinch-hit during their absence. So another fear was settled. I was afraid that if I were devoted to child care night and day that I would lose the friendship that had been developed with my husband, a friendship which was very important. I did not want to lose it and neither did he. We were able to explore London together — the political meetings of the House of Commons candidates, the musical concerts, the Shakespearean plays at the Old Vic.

I thought I had to have all holidays with my husband, but the German doctor had pointed out that we needed a rest from each other, too. The doctor was right. Hugh wanted to go to the golf courses in Scotland for his holidays. And I went, for two summers, to the Fabian Summer School where I sat at the same table with George Bernard Shaw. While I was there, I was invited to give a lecture on prohibition, which the British thought was a very undemocratic and strange piece of legislation. While I did not support prohibition, I was able to hold my own during the question period by discussing some American history in the answers to questions. Bernard Shaw supported me with glee, as he was a teetotaler and a vegetarian.

In 1928 I was presented at the Court of St. James'. No one at the American embassy had ever gone to the court except the ambassadors' wives, but I didn't see why we shouldn't go. Hugh said, "Well, okay, but how are we going to afford it?" Then this Englishwoman got hold of me and told me, "Jessie, don't miss it." I told her we weren't rich and I didn't have diamonds to wear. She said, "None of the British have anymore. We're all poor after this World War I. You put yourself in my hands and it won't cost much." So I did. It cost a hundred and fifty dollars for the dress, the footman, the limousine, the driver, pictures, everything. She took me down to an Eva Zorn store where they sold dresses to actresses. All the American women went to Paris for gowns worth two thousand dollars. Mine cost forty dollars and the woman who sold it to me wrote out its description, which I gave to the press when they came around. Guess what! I was the only one who hit *The New York Times*— to the anguish of the ambassador's wife and the other ladies whose husbands had the top jobs.

Well, that's London for you. Hugh's boss, Dr. Klein, came over finally and said to us, "You can't stay here any longer. If you stay here any longer, you'll never want to go home." We told him we didn't want to go home now. Our home was so beautiful, with all those Oriental rugs and antique furniture. My husband had brought his organ over. He's a skilled organist. It took four years to get accustomed to British life and climate, but now we loved it. But Dr. Klein said we had to go home and he made Hugh head of the Department of Commerce in New England. So we packed up all our antique furniture and sold our house, and Uncle Sam brought everything back to America, costing us nothing.

I came back, in 1929, to Needham, Massachusetts, with the cook and a new Swiss governess. We bought a three-story old New England house which we got very reasonably and we put in our antique furniture. Oh, it was just a beautiful home. Nobody at that time wanted big old houses like that. I rented the top floor to three schoolteachers and they almost paid the rent for the house. Why not have a nice home? was my theory.

Beginning in 1930 I started lecturing on "Pomp and Pageantry at the Court of St. James'," and I earned three thousand dollars a year doing that. I taught them a lot more about England than court life, though. All these women's clubs paid from fifty dollars to a hundred and fifty dollars for that lecture. I had to take the court dress and put it on at the end of the lecture and then come in and show them how to make the curtsy. It had cost only a hundred and fifty dollars to go to court, and I made three thousand dollars a year for five years for going!

After the depression came, in 1932, Hugh suddenly lost his job. When Roosevelt came in, he put the father of his secretary, an utterly inexperienced man, into Hugh's position. Everyone told Hugh that it was time he went into private industry, so he secured a job in a big firm in Worcester, Massachusetts. We took all that beautiful furniture and rented another three-story house. My husband had this magnetic personality, but he was not as good an administrator in private business as in government. He was given one of the top jobs over a lot of men who'd been there for years in this big factory which made grinding wheels. But he didn't know anything about the kind of politics that goes on in such a firm. Within six months they saw that he wasn't qualified for that kind of job.

Meanwhile I added to our troubles. I instinctively disliked factory towns like Worcester. One's social status depended on how high the husband's job was in those factories. We did not fit there, socially or culturally. I ignorantly started a PTA to clean up the school situation. There were a lot of Catholics and Catholic schools there, and the top people sent their children to this little private school, so nobody cared whether the public schools had any money or not. That also helped Hugh to lose his job. Women just didn't do things like that in a factory town where the social status was based on where the husband worked. It didn't completely cause his job to go, but it didn't help it any. I was not going to play that kind of game for anybody. Now, do you call that feminism?

The man who employed Hugh said, "We just feel terrible. We've made a terrible mistake." He was getting a big salary, ten thousand or twelve thousand a year. "But we'll pay you a half-year salary when you leave because we made this mistake." By that time, both of us wanted to stay in New England, but we found that few people secure high positions in New England who aren't Harvard graduates—and Hugh had never set foot in a college. He began pacing the streets and I feared he was going to have a breakdown. He had never been without a job in his life before.

One day I said to him, "Come on. We're going into Boston and have a big blow-out," to which he answered, "Are you crazy? I'm out of a job." I told him, "You are getting a big salary for six months. Now we're going into Boston and have some fun." As we were walking up Tremont Street, there on a building was the sign of an astrologer, and I said, "Come on. Let's go up and see her." "I know you're crazy now," he said. "Here I am without a job and I'm going to see an astrologer."

I have something—I know what it is now—a kind of inner wisdom. Anyway, we went up. There at a kitchen table in the middle of the room sat an old woman. She had the most beautiful face and eyes I ever saw. I told her we'd like an interview, and she said it was two dollars. She asked Hugh the date of his birth and all that, and then she started right in, "You are one of the few most gifted men, gifted for public work, that I've ever seen. That's your destiny." She went on about it. We had just walked in there, you see, so she had no way of knowing about us. Finally she said, "Well, I see ships all around you. I see them everywhere. Meanwhile, you go back into public work," and she talked some more.

With that, we left and Hugh said, "Well, that settles it!" We had a big fish dinner at the wharves in Boston and then we went right back to Worcester. Hugh packed his bags and left for Washington the next day. There I was left in that beautiful house with all that beautiful furniture and everything. Within two weeks Hugh landed a job on the ground floor of the Social

Security Administration. Later, he worked with the Maritime Commission. That's where the ships came in that the astrologer talked about.

RETURN TO WASHINGTON, D.C.: THE DEVELOPMENT OF A NEW CAREER

In due course, after Hugh was safely started, I packed myself and belongings and moved to Washington. I stored the furniture and stashed the children away, and Hugh and I went into a boarding house near Dupont Circle for two years. Our son went to Florida for a year with a lovely family that wanted to take him with them and I sent our daughter to a beautiful private school in Colorado, where my family still lived. Hugh and I were then free to struggle with our problems; to help him back into the Civil Service in the U.S. government, where he belonged. I didn't know then what I was going to get into.

At this point I had a bright idea. "Now's my chance to study public speaking officially and to get some college credits." Luckily, there at George Washington University was Professor W. Hayes Yeager, head of the Chauncey DePew Department of Public Speaking. Imagine that! And I'm in a boarding house with no housework to do. So I went there for two years, taking every course in speech. Never in my life was I so happy. You know, after you have been married a long time and had children and had problems and then you get to be forty-five, to go back to school—if ever anything is heaven, that is!

I went every single day except Saturday, and I had nothing to do but prepare those very tough speech lessons. I spent six and eight hours a day on those lessons and came out from Professor Yeager's class with one of the first A's he'd ever given. I was in a class of young people and they were bored with this old woman in the class. The first two or three months they did nothing but giggle at every speech I made. But I eventually discovered the skill of getting the ears of that type of audience, which didn't do me any harm either.

At the end of two years I was within three points of the master's degree, but they had no program there that would give me the M.A. Professor Yeager advised me not to take any more courses, not to go after the doctorate, but to get out into the women's movement where the leadership was developing. That was what gave me my goal. Immediately I found Mrs. McGill Kiefer, who was the most beautiful singing teacher in Washington, and asked her, "Where can I start this speech class?" She told me I could use her studio. That was about 1935 or 1936. I sent out invitations and something like twenty women came. One of them was Mrs. Harvey Wiley, who had been active in the Woman's Party during suffrage and was now the legislative agent for the General Federation of Women's Clubs. She was skilled in legislation, but she couldn't speak without anxiety. As soon as I started this teaching, I seemed to have great success with it and just loved it.

We bought a home in Fox Hall Village and the children returned to Washington. It was a lovely home overlooking a deep park, and it had a top floor that I rented to four medical students. Soon I found Dora Bailey, a Negro housekeeper who ran our home for over six years. She was priceless. So from 1935 to 1950 there were fifteen successful years of teaching, beginning with that small class. From there I went to the Democratic headquarters where they had a large Democratic Woman's Club. Then the Republicans took me up and I taught classes there twice. I also held classes at the Junior League. I finally taught Pearl Mesta, Mrs. William Fulbright, and most of the leading women in Washington before I left in 1950. My classes became a social must. It was Eleanor Roosevelt who eventually put those classes on the map. She came to the opening sessions of the class three years in succession, beginning in January 1939, and urged wives of congressmen and diplomats to learn to speak so that they could share with their constituents what they learned in Washington. Later, testimonies poured back into Washington about the successes of these brilliant students.

Among them were many diplomats that Mrs. John Cabot had gotten to take the eight-week course. It's too bad that Madame d'Esterre of London, whom I had copied in my teaching, was no longer living to hear of this success.

After I started teaching these classes, I realized that there was a drastic need for a textbook for women. At the annual meeting of the Speech Association in about 1944 I encountered William Norwood Brigance, who was the founder of the Speech Association and was then the president of it. I accosted him, saying, "Where could we find a suitable speech book for these women's classes?" Most of the men's books that they used in the colleges were too intellectual and too biased from a man's point of view and they were not good books for women.

"Well, Mrs. Butler," was his answer, "why don't *you* write the book yourself?" I never felt such a cold chill of fear in all my life! The idea of sitting down and writing a book. I asked, "How could I do it?" and he told me, "Write down what you've been teaching, exactly as you are teaching it. Such a book is very much needed for women. You ought to write a book that's slanted towards women's use. They need many things in that book that the men don't need. I'll tell you what, I'll give you a deadline of June first." This was the middle of the winter.

All anyone has to do is to give me a deadline, and I'm sunk. I'll do anything to meet that deadline. Well, we had this hideout in the Shenandoah Mountains that we'd been going to for twelve years. We left Washington Friday nights and didn't come back until Sunday. It was right in the midst of hillbilly farmers and their families, people who had lived for generations in the mountains and who had been moved out of the mountains when Roosevelt built the beautiful Skyline Drive and set it up as a public reservation. They were now living in these modern little houses that the Resettlement Administration had built for them. We bought one of those houses for our hideout. It was relaxing, looking at those mountains. That's the reason my husband is still alive, I believe.*

* Hugh Butler died on November 2, 1975, at the age of eighty-five.

So at the end of May, as soon as school was out, we went to our hideout. I took my typewriter along. I knew I had to get those first three chapters done by June first, but I put it off every day. I kept thinking of everything else that I could do to put off writing. I was really scared. I had never written a textbook before, and didn't know how to start. Every day I'd say, "Tomorrow," and then my husband would come up for the weekend and I had a good excuse for not starting. I remember well the Monday morning when I got up at seven and said, "I am starting that book today." I had a bedroom up in the top of the little barn which I used while Hugh was away. The air was so nice up there and the view was beautiful. I climbed down out of that barn and set up the typewriter in the living room. By the time I had written one sentence, I was off with a bang. I didn't stop until one, and I had the whole first chapter done, "Conquest of Fear." Professor Brigance told me later that no one had ever written a chapter like that in a speech book. I asked, "Don't the men get scared too?" "Oh, yes, but they don't admit it."

I wrote every day that summer, and by September I had the book written. I wrote to a man at Harper's whom I had known in Boston in the Fabian Society. I had the extreme joy of having him write back at once; he wanted to see the book. It was accepted at once, something that happens to very few people who write books. It was heaven! In the end, the book was published in 1946 and Mrs. Roosevelt wrote an expression of gratitude for it and Lady Astor did a testimonial that went on the back cover. It didn't create a howling sensation, though, because everybody said that women didn't want to speak in public; they were too shy, too sweet and not that aggressive. The feeling was that this was a bit premature.

I had also become the speech coach for the General Federation of Women's Clubs, which had five million members. I was on their board, and for eight or ten years I went to their annual meetings all over the United States and put on four speech workshops early every morning during the conventions. I'll never forget the first one, in St. Louis. The president had told me that nobody would come, that they already knew how to speak. There was a workshop on parliamentary procedure and I was going to be in competition with this experienced teacher who'd been doing this for years and years. That morning I kept reminding myself of the few people who came to my first course in Washington, and told myself, "Now just be calm. Maybe there will be just three people, but you just teach them and the next year there'll be more." As I approached the ballroom I heard this enormous buzz. The ballroom was jammed with people. I was so unhorsed, it took a little bit of time for me to gather myself together with my usual poise.

Soon that first class for the General Federation of Women's Clubs was started, and they continued at each annual meeting. Sometimes four hundred delegates came to the speech workshop, and often as many as two hundred endorsed textbooks were sold. The workshops were a great success. They just packed the place. It was delightful because it was needed. I just loved that teaching. It was inspiring, because the minute the women were trained as speakers they seemed to find themselves. Few men can equal such trained speakers, and they know it. That's why they like to discourage women from taking speech lessons.

NEW ROOTS: CALIFORNIA

My career was at its height in 1950, when my husband's job with the Maritime Commission ended. He was showing signs of weariness that I didn't like. I decided that I preferred a husband to a career. Our biochemist lived in Los Angeles, so we beat it there to her office. She caught him just in time. She said that within a week he would have had a severe stroke.

Hugh had the idea, then, that we should go down to Mexico for a while. I didn't want to go to Mexico. I didn't like the sound of it. I couldn't speak Mexican and I'd go crazy. My sister got hold of Hugh and told him, "Look, you go down to Mexico by yourself. You'll never have a minute's peace with Jessie down there. You get down there and relax and rest and get back to your organ." That's what he needed, you see. He went and stayed a year. He was still a colonel in the army, so Uncle Sam paid his hotel bill and this teacher's bill to study the organ. He came back completely healed after watching the Mexicans practice *mañana*.

Evidently we both needed a change. I stayed in California and wrote a book about my life, a complete autobiography. It was sent to two or three publishers, but I've done better writing since. In 1967 I wrote another book, *Adam's Other Wife*, the wife that Adam wants, a companion. The American woman, the minute she gets a baby, never pays any more attention to Adam, see. Then he has to turn to his secretary or somebody for companionship. You can't take care of a baby twenty-four hours a day and continue to be a good companion to your husband, can you?

I thought that when I came to California I'd just carry on with my teaching. But the Federation clubwomen out here killed my book and my career. Californians don't like people with a career to come out here and tell about their careers and how famous they are and what they want to do. They dislike it thoroughly. I didn't realize that you have to start all over again from the bottom in California. I was a babe in arms and just plunged in. I'd never even voted before. You don't vote in Washington, D.C. It wasn't until 1954 that I finally began teaching speech again, at Mount San Antonio College, one night a week. The classes were large; men and women in public life came. I did a good job and a lot of prominent people came. But after seven years, I was ruled out—because of my age.

So after I came to California my life really revolved around writing and two other things. One was that I found Vic Tanney. My sister had bought a ticket and didn't use it, so she turned it over to me. For four years I went to the Vic Tanney gym three times a week and completely strengthened my body. I'd never given any time to my body. It was flabby, my legs were flabby. I thought, Well, to heck with it. If I can't do my teaching and all, I'll just go to Vic Tanney's. You wouldn't believe how I revolutionized my body.

That was smart, at seventy. That's when they all commence to deteriorate, you see. What's seventy? I'm in my eighties now. When I was forty-nine in Washington, I began saying, "Isn't this terrible!" Then a woman who was an editor for McCall's came to speak to the press women in Washington. She was over eighty and she gave this down-to-earth, practical woman's talk. I said, "Well, I didn't know you could talk like that on a public platform, at over eighty." And they never heard another word from me about my age. I thought, I'll fix her. I'll get to be eighty-two and I'm never going to talk about it.

So the dear California Federation of Women's Clubs did me a favor when they kicked me out because the other thing I did was that I found a new religion for the new age. Several years ago I felt I was going to die and knew it. I prayed for a spiritual leader, saying, "I'm not ready to die; there are more things I need to know." I found such a spiritual leader apparently by accident. She had just come to California from Florida. She preaches a religion tied to the Bible and the teachings of Jesus, plus dream interpretation, reincarnation, night flights and healing. All the modern things that can go with a religion, and it's a religion for the new age. My husband and I went over twice a week to Glendale. She saved my life, healed me, and I'm still here. She thinks I'm going to last quite a while yet, and maybe I'll get some of these books printed, or get my speech book into a paperback version.

FULL CIRCLE:
THE WOMEN'S LIBERATION
MOVEMENT

All through those years, although I wasn't teaching or anything, I was reading everything I could get my hands on that had to do with the women's movement. I considered Betty Friedan's book the greatest book I had ever read. When the history of this era is over, that book is the thing that's going to stand out as the leading book of this era, the book that's changed the history of the world for women. A lot of people don't agree with that, but she's got the deadly facts there. The whole women's movement is covered and what needs to be done about it. I don't know how she ever wrote it. I've even heard people pretend that somebody else had written it because they couldn't understand that Betty Friedan, as she is now, was capable of writing such a book. I don't care who wrote it, or where it came from.

I was so excited. Then, immediately after they had that caucus in Washington, D.C., I joined the National Organization for Women (NOW). I never did get back there, but I sent them fifty dollars at once and would have sent more if I'd had it, because I knew they had started something that was perfectly tremendous. The more I know about it, the more I know that's got to be done.

Some time after that some woman came from Pittsburgh to help start the women's movement here. She came out to Claremont and spoke in a hall on the college campus. At that meeting I started talking to some of the women from the Los Angeles NOW and told them, "You must have some classes in public speaking to develop your leaders." One of the women went back and stirred them up and then got in touch with me to give them a class. Of course they didn't have any money, so I said, "I won't give a class unless people pay for it. Otherwise, they'll come and they won't finish it. But I'll give the money back to help start your Speakers Bureau." So they had that class at the home of a woman in Hollywood. There were twenty or twenty-five women there, many of whom later became leaders.

When August 26, 1970, came along and there was going to be that big celebration for the fiftieth anniversary of woman's suffrage, they asked if I had a speech. "Yes, I do, about Tennessee." So I took part in that, and ever since then I've been involved.

I just recently spent two whole days in Los Angeles at the hearings held by the Status of Women Commission. I've never heard such brilliant presentations on the issues that involve women in this state. It was marvelous, beautifully handled, brilliant speakers—and you know I'm very particular—although they didn't all enunciate quite loud enough. These women brought facts and material, well substantiated, and presented their causes and told the Status of Women Commission what they must do. It was a great hearing, those two days. It's a revolution, there's no doubt about it.

Since it took seventy-two years just to get the vote, you can figure out for yourself how long it's going to take to resolve this revolution that involves every part of women's lives. Suffrage just had one thing to do, to get women and men educated to go out and give women the right to vote. But that isn't anything like the depth of all these other issues. They didn't go into these deep issues of their family lives or homes or children and all that. They just said, "We want to vote. We want to get good people in government. We have a right to vote because we're citizens." It was a simple little story and it took them seventy-two years to get that over. What do you think, how are you going to get over these *deep* discussions, *deep* issues that we're in the midst of now? It's a revolution.

We haven't yet found ourselves any plan, any program, any vision, any issue, or any way of working out our lives. I think they're finding their direction today. They're making headway every day. But I don't think the women yet know what their goals are. They're unhappy. They're getting divorces on the slightest excuse, running out of their homes. They'e so unhappy, untrained, unequal to meet the problems they've got. They haven't found their destinies yet. The first thing we've got to do, I think, is to help the girls, help them make a plan for their lives, get a goal for their lives and work it out. They think the way to solve everything is to quick, quick, run away from home and get married. Nothing could be worse. Marriage is a terribly difficult prospect. There's no more difficult job in the world than to make a marriage go—and the most worthwhile job. Nothing else will bring as much comfort and satisfaction as a good marriage, but it's got to be worked at.

We are going into the Aquarian Age, which is the humanitarian age. The women need to be freed to help us in that age. Because they are basically humane, women are, though untrained. I think the men and women are going to join hands and work together to work this thing out. We can't do it without the men to help us. They'll want to help us. There are a lot of fine men, even in the Congress of the United States. Look at the two tough men I had to deal with, Congressman Ben Johnson and Senator Reed Smoot. Yet both of them helped me with that minimum wage bill once they saw the issue. Even to get Woodrow Wilson to understand woman's suffrage took four or five years, but in the end what did he do? When we finally won, he wrote them saying it was the finest thing he'd done. So women can get the men sooner or later. They must make them understand what the issues are.

We're not going to reach all women, though—only the ones who are unhappy. And, there are plenty of them. They're getting more and more unhappy. The Women's Club here in Claremont, where I am a life member, is just so smooth and happy. They don't want to talk about the equal rights amendment. They don't even know what it is. Yet, one by one, every now and then, they're suddenly getting a jolt because the only thing that keeps them from that welfare is that one little man there. When he dies, often suddenly, then where are you going to go, see. Then they find out. Very few of them know how to conserve insurance endowments. Within six years, all but eight percent of the women who get annuities when their husbands die are bankrupt. They don't know how to handle money, they've never been trained.

So, gradually, more and more of them will begin to wake up to what's going on. Then all of a sudden, they'll come to some of our meetings or read a newspaper and hear about the rest of us who've had a lot of trouble. See. I'm personally in a neat position because I have had a fascinating career and a gorgeous education before ever I was married. Then I had a most amazing husband and another amazing career. I went right on developing myself as a writer, a teacher, a speaker, but also as a mother and a housekeeper. That took some doing, also.

I see the work of the National Organization for Women. I want to help them all I can. They're still very amateurish, very ill-advised, and it's going to take a long time to work out these issues. Gradually, issue after issue is going to come up and different women will arise who have leadership abilities and skill in that issue, as they did at that Status of Women Commission hearing.

Several things, I think, have got to be done. One, women have got to learn to work together better. Since the beginning of this eternity, women have been in competition for the same thing, married life and security, and so they have formed an ego of competition. Every woman they meet is an antagonist. It's a terrible situation.

Another thing, women have got to learn how to run better homes. The reasons why men are cashing out on the homes are that they are so chaotic. They're badly organized. There's a wrong theory, a pioneer theory, that the women must do everything: bear all the children, do all the cooking, cleaning and everything. It's a crazy idea and performance. The British have licked that. They're two thousand years old and we're just two hundred years old. I found out from the British the answer to that.

Third, we've got to have mothers' clinics to teach women how to bear children and take care of children. England has made a science of child care. Our girls are marrying in ignorance, absolutely ignorant about having children and bringing them up. This is a terrible country for little children to be born in. They don't have a gambler's chance of growing into normal human beings. Last year ten thousand damaged children were brought into hospitals, and not in the poverty areas either. Another ten thousand died in their cribs in crib death because they're not being breast-fed. Cow's milk is not the milk for little children! We've got to do this.

I have somehow had the vision to do something about this child care program, just as I did in the meat-packers industry. A bill was sent to the President for millions of dollars to start child welfare centers. In the past we didn't start things like that. When our great farms were started, the government didn't buy all the farms and start running them. They let the farmers own the farms and sent out teachers to teach them how to make these farms work. So maybe we have to do the same with children.

The thought came to me that with these tracts and apartment complexes, that's the place to start your child care centers. You're still going to need them in the centers of the cities for the poverty area, financed by city governments, but the middle class, cultured people, need child care centers, too. It occurred to me that we must go to these tracts as they're being built, and put in child care centers at their back doors so that the mothers can take the babies to the centers close to where they live and then get them at night. Forty-six percent of the women in America today are working outside their homes and they're going to go right on doing that. There's no use telling them to stop it. They aren't going to stop it.

How to pay for it? The people who build the tracts must build the child care centers. But first the program had to be endorsed by the Planning Commission. So I started to talk to people about it. I got the endorsement of the Status of Women Commission in Sacramento. I talked to the head of the Planning Commission and to a member of the Pomona City Council and in June 1973, we had the first hearing on this. It was to persuade the builders of the Phillips Ranch to include a child care center in that tract. It was a historical occasion.

The month before the hearing I was appointed chairman of the Task Force for Child Care Centers of Pomona Valley NOW. We received written endorsements from many of our legislators. Eleven junior and senior women's clubs, eleven business and professional women's clubs, the YWCA of Greater Pomona and six other women's groups endorsed the idea of having child care centers in tracts, mobile homes and apartment complexes. To our surprise, there was not a single word of opposition to the idea, though many personal interviews were needed to explain the idea to members of the Planning Commission. A resolution was passed unanimously which recommends that child care centers be part of the development plans. The mayor of Pomona hopes to make the resolution mandatory.

It was gratifying to have the La Verne City Council endorse almost the same resolution passed by Pomona, the first city council to accept this resolution. Other cities in the area here have held hearings, too.

At the moment, because of the present industrial crisis in America, much of the building of tracts has been halted. Within two years, when building will start again, we believe that the groundwork laid in the Planning Commision will begin to have an effect. The builders need it to attract buyers and, at the same time, families need it to achieve more stable family life. By that time we believe that child care centers will have become as vital to families with preschool children as public schools are to school-age children.

I am proud that our National Organization for Women in the Pomona Valley had the vision to see the importance of getting these centers into tracts, mobile homes and apartment complexes for the middle-class family. They have set an example. It took them a long time to accept me, though. At first they thought I was a farce, that I was just putting on a show and had nothing real at all. They're beginning to see that isn't so. Gradually, slowly, I'm digging in. I believe I have something to share with California.

In a strange way, from the time I've been a little girl, I've wanted to help women, and I really have done it. When I worked four years with the Massachusetts Minimum Wage Commission copying payrolls in candy factories and brush factories, that was to help women. To find out what was going on with women that were being exploited like that.

I just love women. I've loved working with them and I've loved teaching them. I know how to teach them and I can forget the fact that I'm critical with women. I see the wealth in those women, the virtue, the character, the goodness. I want to spend the rest of my life helping women to find themselves.

MIRIAM ALLEN deFORD

On the Soapbox

Miriam Allen deFord, despite failing health, was still a disciplined and prolific writer of science fiction and mystery stories at the age of eighty-five. Because she was a prominent longtime resident and observer of San Francisco, articles both by and about her often appeared in local papers. She lived in a suite of rooms in the Ambassador Hotel where my interviews with her were recorded.

The Ambassador had been a respectable hotel when Miriam first moved into it in 1937, after the death of her second husband. During the intervening twenty-eight years it had fallen into both disrepair and disrepute. The neighborhood, the "tenderloin district," is now occupied largely by assorted derelicts, "porno" movie houses and topless bars. Several rooms on Miriam's floor, gutted by fire years earlier, were simply boarded up rather than repaired. The atmosphere of the lobby and the elevators was enough to make even the least timid quite fearful.

Despite all of this, Miriam Allen deFord maintained in her fifth-floor suite a self-defined world which she described as her "oasis in the desert." Her living room was crowded with books of all kinds, including those she had written herself and the reference volumes required for their writing. Some of these references were too heavy and cumbersome for her frail frame to handle any longer. On one desk was her vintage 1935 portable

Royal typewriter at which she worked from six to eighteen hours a day.

Over the two years of our relationship Miriam's physical condition steadily deteriorated. Nevertheless she maintained an active intellectual life and was able to converse knowledgeably on current events and the most recent feminist literature. Even though her life revolved primarily around her writing and her social activities became increasingly circumscribed, she was still able to maneuver with the aid of a cane to a nearby San Francisco restaurant for lunch and an occasional martini.

I spoke to Miriam on the phone one week before her death in March 1975. She was still living in her "oasis," though now with a nurse in attendance. Her fingers were incapacitated, making it impossible for her to type, so she now had to dictate her stories to someone else, but she was still practicing her craft of seventy years.

THE MAKING OF A FEMINIST

I was born in Philadelphia in 1888. My parents were both doctors in a heavily industrial part of northeast Philadelphia. My father's parents were both born in France, and although he was born in Philadelphia, it was in a section of the city that was then entirely French. He and his brother didn't speak English until they went to school. He worked his way through high school and college and medical college. One of the things he did was teach French. That's how my mother met him; she went to his French class.

Although my mother was eight years older than my father, she actually seemed younger, even though she was prematurely gray. She came from a family that had been in Philadelphia for about seven generations, I guess. They were born and brought up in a part of the city that now is slums. Then it was mostly Quaker and all her early friends were Quakers. Even though my mother became a doctor, her mother was not a feminist. In fact, she was proud of the fact that she never in her life had crossed the street alone. When she was a child, her father took her, then her brothers, then her husband and, finally, her sons. When my brother was too young to take her across the street, she had to have her daughters take her.

Nevertheless, my mother had sort of vague interests and yearnings about a medical career for a long time. Then, after she met my father and after they became engaged (they were engaged for four years), he persuaded her that it was possible. I don't think my mother's family was at all pleased, but they had to reconcile themselves to it.

When my father was in his second year of medical school, she started. She was a year behind him. He was at Jefferson Medical College and she went to Women's Medical College of Philadelphia. Her professors were the first generation of women doctors in this country. After all, the Women's Medical College was founded in 1857, when my mother was two years old.

She told us a lot of stories about her years in medical school, and these added to my feminism. First, there were some courses that they had to go to at one of the men's medical colleges. When they demonstrated an operation, they had all the students observe from rows of seats like a theater balcony. The girls had to sit up at the very back. One day, one impatient girl got up and walked right over people's heads down to the front row and sat there. The men made things so unpleasant for her that she never tried it again. The men resented very much having women study medicine with them and they used to yell after them in the streets.

When my mother graduated from medical college in 1887, a year after my father, they started a practice in a neighborhood of shipyards and textile factories. After the workers changed from Englishmen to Poles, I don't think there were many who could read or write in the neighborhood, except for the few doctors and their families. In our house, what was other people's parlor downstairs was the office and waiting room. My mother and father had both their brass signs outside the front windows. They didn't practice together because my mother, I think, did most of her work in gynecology. My father first was a general practitioner and later became a genito-urinary specialist. That would be something my mother wouldn't be likely to do. My father, in later years, had an office downtown, but my mother never did; she always had her patients at the house. She practiced until she was in her sixties, when she had to stop because she became deaf. Until then, she practiced right along.

There were three children and I was the oldest. I had a sister two years younger and a brother five years younger. When my sister was born I was only twenty-two months old, so I don't remember much about it. But when my brother was born, I was five. I can remember that they thought I was too old to leave around the house. I wasn't supposed to know about those things, so I was sent to my grandmother's and I never saw my mother until after my brother was born. I was very jealous of him and hated him. I was never jealous of my sister though we quarreled a good deal. I thought that they were making such a fuss over him because he was a boy.

My mother's family, her brothers and sisters, were pleased because it was a boy. I remember my aunt coming to tell her mother saying, "Finally it's a b-o-y." I was only five, but I could read and spell fairly well. I said, "I know what that is, that's 'boy,' and I've got a brother." And I wasn't at all pleased. I was wishing I had another sister. Now I think they made a great fuss about him because he was always in very poor health. All his life he was a semi-invalid, though he was married and had children.

They talk about penis envy. The first time I saw Allen naked, my mother stood him on the toilet when she was toilet training him, and I saw this thing hanging out from him, and I was terribly embarrassed. I was afraid that I had a deformed brother, and I was so afraid that people would find out that my brother was deformed. It wasn't until a good deal later that I found out every little boy was deformed. I was so accustomed to his being ill most of the time—he always had something wrong with him—so I just took it for granted that this was another thing wrong with him!

As I remember, my mother never nursed any of us. She never could. By that time she did very little home visiting; the patients came to her. It was easy enough to handle a baby and work at the same time. So, my mother, who was a very small and slight woman, practiced medicine and ran a house and even mended clothes. She was a terrible cook, though. Fortunately, she never cooked except when we were out of cooks. As far back as I can remember, we did manage to somehow have what was then called a "girl," a cook and houseworker, and when we were small, we had nurses who were usually Welsh coal miners' daughters from the mines in Pennsylvania.

When I was first sent to kindergarten in this very tough neighborhood that we lived in, there were just a few of us who were not shipyard workers' children. I remember this unfortunate boy who was a doctor's son and his mother dressed him in Little Lord Fauntleroy costumes, and all these tough little kids would go after him. Every day poor Willie would go home in rags and his mother would fix him up with velvet and lace and long blond curls.

My first friend that I ever had was a little girl whom I adored. Her name was Laura. She wore a plush coat and I would go up in kindergarten and just touch it. I remember when I was out one day with my aunt and I found Laura and her mother, and they were carrying a big basket of wash between them. That was the first note of snobbery I remember. My aunt said, "You mean that's Laura?" Because all I talked about at home was Laura.

But the boys were very, very bad, and the worst of the lot was a little boy named Billie. He had his own little group of sycophants that followed after him. The other girls would fight back, but I wouldn't, so he picked on me. The kindergarten had an ordinary rough dirt ground with a fence all around. Billie would come up and bang my head against the fence, just to show off to the boys how easily he could do that, and he'd say, "I won't bang your head anymore if you'll let me show the boys your flannel petticoat." And I'd show the boys my flannel petticoat.

Then one day Billie came up to me and said, "I want to show the boys how to fuck." I had never heard the word before and I hadn't the remotest idea what it meant, but if Billie recommended it, it was something I didn't want, so I said "No." He banged my head hard and said, "Come on," and dragged me to the boys' toilet and all his little group gathered around. He said, "Now take off your drawers." I said, "I can't. My mother does it for me, and I can't do it." So he got one of his little followers to do it, at which point the teacher came out. I don't know what happened to Billie; maybe he was expelled. I was sent home to my mother with a note, and I wasn't sent to kindergarten till the next year, when my little sister, who was a born fighter, would be there to protect me. Then, by the time I was ready to go to primary school, they sent me down to live with my grandmother in a more respectable part of the city where my aunt was a public school teacher.

I think that subconsciously, all through my childhood, that

incident haunted me and I thought it was an awful disgrace. I decided I'd been raped until thirty or forty years later when I had an English friend visiting me. I told her this story and she told me that she was raped by a grown man when she was seven. From that time on, it never bothered me, but all those years I had a subconscious feeling that I'd been raped in childhood. I think that had a lot to do with my attitudes toward men.

The first time I can remember thinking about—well, I didn't even know the word "feminism" then. I think I was about six or seven. We had a Welsh nurse and an Irish cook, and the cook got married. The nurse took my sister and me to this big Roman Catholic wedding. I remember the bride was all in white satin with a veil. The happy couple adjourned to the little row house on a back street that was going to be their home. Gwinnie kept us standing at the door; they were all grown-up people and we were the only children around. I know now that everybody had had plenty to drink at the reception, but, of course, I had no idea of it then.

Some kind of argument came up and the bridegroom had to express his *machismo* somehow. One of his friends said, "Don't let her answer you back, start your marriage right." So he promptly knocked her flat on the floor. Gwinnie hurried us away. I was just wild with indignation and I remember saying, "He knocked her down because she wasn't as strong as he was. If I ever get strong enough, I'll get up and fight back." From that time on, I was very much against most men and very much for most women.

I was terribly indignant. I was used to a household where my mother ran practically everything and my father did as he was told, at least domestically. That was the first time I'd ever seen the old-fashioned male dominance, and it made me very, very angry. I remember telling my mother about it and saying that he'd knocked her down because she was a woman. My mother didn't like to tell a child that age that probably everybody was drunk, so she just said, "Well, that's the way people of that kind act."

Then, a couple of years later, I remember the little old

washerwoman, a tiny German woman with her face covered with smallpox scars. That was very common in those days. When she came Monday, she usually was bruised all over. Her husband got drunk every weekend and beat her up. She took it philosophically; she expected it, that was what married life was like.

All these things, as I found out about them, made me feel more and more the way I'd started to feel. By this time I suppose I was nine or ten. I was back home. I stayed down with my grandmother for just one year, and then when we moved to another part of the city, I was brought home and sent to school near where I lived.

Remember, this is all back in the 1890s, but as far as anybody was, my mother was all in favor of what we would now call women's lib. Of course, as a doctor she got the same pay that a man would get, so we never had that question come up in the house. And it was unusual for a woman to be married and to have a professional career. That was before women were in offices; stenographers were all men. But in the working class, women who were married worked. Our washerwoman was married, and sometimes when a cook got married, she came back.

Ever since I can remember my mother was for "votes for women," which was the thing then. To a certain extent, I suppose my father was feminist. I remember, though, that he refused to march in a parade once. He thought it would be too embarrassing to be one of the few men. But he certainly put nothing in our way and he was for woman's suffrage. If it had been a question of voting, he would have voted for it. But he had no particular connection with it otherwise. My mother had all that she could possibly handle without doing anything active. I don't think she'd have been physically able to march in parades or that kind of thing.

Her feminism didn't come out of any radical tradition. My mother never had any radical connections, and my father was horrified when I became a real radical. He wrote me long, long letters about how superior his mind was and how he's been all through this and how it was just youthful exuberance and I'd get over it. No. I was brought up in what I suppose you'd call a kind of generalized semi-rationalist atmosphere. As far as politics goes, we were Democrats in a Republican city, and a very corrupt Republican city, where kids would jeer "Democrat" at you down the street. Every respectable person in Philadelphia then took *The Public Ledger,* but we also took *The Record,* which was a Democratic paper. I suppose we were the only Democrats I knew. My father considered himself something of a liberal and I think he once voted for Debs. Of course, my mother couldn't vote.

My parents taught us to be independent. I was sent downtown alone by trolley car to run errands for them when I was nine or ten. At thirteen I had my own latchkey. Of course, that didn't keep them from worrying, or punishing us, if we came home late. By the time I was fourteen, I was down at suffrage headquarters stuffing envelopes.

I was at the girls' high school by that time. Usually the principal was a man and all the teachers were women. There were no coeducational high schools then, except for perhaps one in Germantown run by the Quakers. I don't think anybody had ever heard of a coeducational high school in 1902. My grandmother told me that when she was of high school age (I think she was born in 1833), the only way a girl could go to high school was that they had classes on Saturday morning for girls, as a special favor. She went to a private school. I asked her what she learned. She learned some French and to play the piano—after a fashion—and things like dancing and etiquette. Then, by the time my mother went to high school, and she went to the same high school I did, they had it five days a week. But she had to drop out because her father died and she was the oldest girl and had to look after the little ones.

In our high school we were divided into three sections. One was what they called the general course. Most of those girls finished their education in high school or they went on to what was then called normal school, and became elementary school teachers. Then there was the classical course; that was the college preparatory. You had four years of Latin and you took other languages, either Greek, French or German. As evidence of a little snobbery, we considered the Greek classes just a little above the French and German ones.

The third course, the one I was in, was the other college preparatory course; we called that Latin scientific. In those days, science was all German. We had four years of Latin and four years of German. That course was for people who were more scientific-minded. I wasn't particularly interested in science then and I don't know how I got into that thing. It was taken for granted that I was going to study medicine and inherit both my parents' practices. But you know the younger generation. The one thing I would never do would be to study medicine.

I hadn't yet decided *not* to be a doctor. I don't think I so much rejected the idea as just ignored it. I think that what I wanted was lots and lots of English. I got more English in the Latin scientific than I would have got in the classical. By this time I was already writing and had a story published somewhere and got a dollar for it. (Actually, I really began being published a little later, when I was about eighteen.)

When we were growing up, it was taken for granted that we all would earn our living. My sister became a teacher and ended up as a supervisor of industrial arts in the Philadelphia schools. The question of marriage never really came up. As far as that goes, my sister never did marry. I think my family was a bit surprised when I married twice. I never remember any discussion on that point at all. It was just taken for granted that whatever I did I would keep on doing, married or not.

But nobody ever said anything. Remember, this was still in the Victorian age. My mother was extremely Victorian, very prudish, even though she was an M.D. and considered herself very liberal. Nobody ever told me anything. I found out about menstruation and all that kind of thing by reading my parents' medical books. I had read so many of them, especially my mother's gynecological works, that when I was eight years old I gave my sister a long, detailed account of just how one handles pregnancy and childbirth. She said, "Well, what I don't understand is how the baby gets there." I said, "That's the part I haven't found out yet, but it isn't important."

I can remember very well when I was a little older, sitting on the floor in the waiting room in my parents' office when there was nobody else there and reading Krafft-Ebing (*Psychopathia Sexualis*). If I heard a footstep, I'd get up and consult the dictionary quickly. After my father died, my sister sent me the Krafft-Ebing, and I never saw such a boring, dull book in my life. I still have it somewhere.

Even so, I was very prudish. I never in my life talked about anything like that, and my friends, my high school friends, and I never talked about any sexual subject. Most of them weren't interested in anything much except having a good time. And I just didn't know any boys. I remember at my high school senior dance, I simply hadn't any young man to invite, and my father, I think, bribed a young man in a drugstore that he used. I was a terrible dancer, so he should have had a bribe. My brother was five years younger, and, of course, his friends were just children. So I didn't know any boys. When I grew up, I just didn't know any men.

AN EARLY INTRODUCTION TO SUFFRAGE

It was my mother who first sent me down to suffrage headquarters. She had no time to do anything, so I was her surrogate. I don't remember anybody my age. There were young people, but, of course, to me at fourteen they seemed grown up. They made kind of a pet of me because I was so young.

Good Lord, fourteen. It was 1902. I have a very vague memory. I don't even know where the office was anymore. I remember the woman, then young, who was in charge of headquarters. Caroline Katzenstein. I remember vaguely some of the other people; a Frenchwoman who'd lived in England for years and then moved to America, and a few others.

By the time I was eighteen, I was really working for them. I don't think I'd done any writing for them yet, even though I was on the *Philadelphia North American* and was also doing what I suppose we'd now call public relations work. But when we had parades, I always went up. New York would be the national parade. I can remember the parade in 1910, or something like that. I was holding the banner of the Philadelphia contingent. I was in my twenties by then and went there on my own. I was the representative of the family. My mother didn't have time, and my father, though he was all for woman's suffrage, would have been ashamed and embarrassed to have been there. There were usually, out of several hundred women in a parade, a contingent of maybe half a dozen men, and they always looked sort of beaten, as if their wives had said, "You go or else!"

I can't remember which parade it was, exactly, when I was holding that banner. It was an annual thing. I don't know how many states it included, but I know that Connecticut, New Jersey and Pennsylvania were there. Every city would have its own contingent with a banner in front giving our locale. I think there was probably a rally at the end, but I don't remember. For one thing, we weren't at the head of the parade; we were somewhere way in the back. All New York went first, because New York was always the largest contingent.

THE NEW YORK TIMES, SATURDAY, MAY 21, 1910

SUFFRAGE PARADE HAS POLICE GUARD

Strong Force Out to Keep Order in the March and Auto Spin Down Fifth Avenue

WOMEN SEND UP A PROTEST

Will Make Ceaseless War on Legislators Who Have Ignored Their Bill in Albany

The automobile branch of the Women Suffrage procession moved down Fifth Avenue yesterday to the meeting of protest in Union Square, well guarded by the mounted police.

The protest was against the action, or lack of it, taken by the legislators at Albany in regard to the Woman Suffrage bill which they cannot be persuaded to vote out of committee and was read yesterday to an assemblage of people in the square. The women say they have worked quietly and ineffectually for sixty years asking for consideration, and now they believe that the legislators should be made to feel that they are in earnest.

There were 10,000 persons in Union Square who listened to the speeches the women made. It was the biggest suffrage demonstration ever held in the United States.

The women taking part in the demonstration went in procession, some in automobiles and others on foot. Many of them had never taken part in anything of the kind before, and were resolute, but a good deal scared. The automobile branch of the procession started from the Fifth Avenue entrance of Central Park at Fifty-ninth Street. That was where the first auto stood, but the line ran up to Sixty-fifth Street. There were ninety of them all told, and the public ones as far as it was possible were yellow taxicabs, the suffrage color.

THE NEW YORK TIMES, SATURDAY, MAY 6, 1911
EDITORIAL

PARADE OF THE WOMEN

This afternoon the women who believe that their sex will be uplifted if they can obtain the right to vote will try to demonstrate their fitness for the suffrage by parading on Fifth Avenue. The British suffragettes had a monster parade in London which, to be sure, has not yet secured for them the privilege of voting for members of Pariament, but impressed a multitude of onlookers mightily. Women march well, and good marching is always worth looking at. It was proved long ago that if the chief work of soldiers was marching, women would make better soldiers than men. Since the Amazons in "The Black Crook," forty-five years ago, the West Point Cadets and the Seventh Regiment have not been accounted our best marchers. The feminine sense of time is keener than the masculine. The presence of a few men in the ranks, however, may disturb the harmony of the spectacle.

To-day's parade will be a symbol only. Whether 3,000 women are in line, or only 1,500, only a figurative goal will be reached. But it requires enthusiasm and energy to march five miles or so through city streets under the searching eyes of a crowd which will not all be sympathetic. The paraders will be aware that many will watch them with derision, many more with mere curiosity, comparatively few with perfect sympathy, implying belief in the righteousness of their cause. They will hope, however, to make converts by marching, as they doubtless make them by all their other demonstrations.

The idea of the parade is perfectly logical. It will indicate the courage of the paraders, the strength of their conviction, and their determination to win. No cause can be won without efforts of this strenuous and showy sort. If the parade turns out as well as its promoters expect, doubtless many thousands of persons in New York, who have never given much thought to the matter, will feel to-night that woman suffrage is nearer at hand. Perhaps it will not be nearer, but it is worth while for the suffragists to make hesitant and hitherto uninterested people think so. They may get the suffrage some day, but never by reading papers at women's clubs and passing resolutions. We sincerely hope, for their own sakes and the sake of the State, that they will fail. But their parade will give them a valuable advertisement.

THE NEW YORK TIMES, NEW YORK, SUNDAY
MAY 7, 1911

WOMEN PARADE AND REJOICE AT THE END

Bright-Hued Procession for Suffrage, 3,000 Strong, Goes Down Fifth Ave. to Union Square.

CHEERED ALL ALONG THE WAY

Women Farmers, Jewelers, Writers, Athletes, College Students, Shirtwaist Makers and of Society in Line.

The women suffragists in their thousands—the police said 3,000 and some more optimistic estimates gave the number as 5,000 —marched down Fifth Avenue yesterday from Fifty-seventh Street to Union Square as a demonstration against the delay in giving the women votes. Afterward they and many others listened to open-air speeches in the Square. Perhaps 10,000 persons were there. At least as many more, some more eager to see the Marathon runners, who also were out, than the suffragettes, watched the parade.

It was perfect weather for a woman's parade. The procession, however, did not get under way till 4 o'clock. The Marathon races, though they made a small showing beside the woman's procession, were a cause for the late start. The Marathons had an awful fear that they might be taken for suffragettes, though even the suffragettes of Bloomer days would have hesitated at the hygienic Marathon costume, and they tried to sidetrack the women to Madison Avenue. There was a big equal rights cry from the suffragists at that, and they got right of way.

One plan of the suffragists was set aside by Mayor and Mrs. Gaynor. It had been suggested that there might be a large reviewing stand, with the Mayor and Mrs. Gaynor in the high places. But suffragettes have an uncertain political status, and Mayor Gaynor and Mrs. Gaynor were unfortunately called out of town. The Mayor wrote polite regrets and Mrs. Gaynor was equally sorry over the telephone.

The Marchers Elated.

At the close of an exciting if tiresome day the suffragists congratulated themselves and declared that never in the world had a procession like theirs taken place. There were few women in tears, and those who were were women who did not march. One said she did not march because her fiancé objected, another stayed out of line because of her husband's objection, and one stayed away to please her mother's wishes. These were examples of many others who did not march, the suffragists say, and they consider that no objections would keep them away another year.

THE NEW YORK TIMES, TUESDAY, MAY 9, 1911
EDITORIAL

TOPICS OF THE TIMES

A Demonstration That Made an Impression

Just how much Saturday's parade did toward hastening the ultimate extension, now apparently inevitable, of the electoral franchise to women, is, of course, a question to which no definite answer can be given. Judging, however, from the comment one hears on the demonstration, it did do something, if only in the way of giving no small number of their antagonists the first convincing reason for taking the suffrage movement with something of the seriousness which was shown by the women who marched.

Before the parade there was a

good deal of talk to the effect that it was either ridiculous, or shocking, or both, for women to display themselves on the public streets, but those who watched these paraders and noted their quality and demeanor, found little cause for laughter or scorn, and though there was a little badinage from the crowds on the sidewalks, there seem to have been no manifestation at all of anything like hostility. The really trying jokes were directed at the men in the line, and even their experience, while trying, was not a painful one. . . .

We got a lot of jeering from the sidelines, but we didn't retort. There was never any violence. Nobody threw anything or anything like that. They just laughed and made fun of us, just like later when we used to pass around petitions after our soapbox talks. As long as I lived in the East, I went to the parades. I was at that one, whenever it was, when the whole parade was led by Inez Milholland,* who was a beautiful woman, and she was dressed in armor and mounted on a white horse. She died shortly later of pernicious anemia because they didn't have any cure for it then. Now, she'd have recovered.

So, from that initial time when I was a youthful kid around the office who'd fold things and stuff envelopes and run errands, I always had some kind of connection with suffrage. I got to know all those people and they would know other people. After I left Philadelphia in 1912, I became involved in Boston.

"GIRL ON A BIG-CITY NEWSPAPER"

After I graduated high school and until the following year when I went to Wellesley, I worked on the *Philadelphia North American*. It was a daily newspaper owned by John Wana-

* Inez Milholland, an active suffrage worker since her Vassar days in 1908, led the 1912 parade in New York on horseback. After leaving Vassar, she worked closely with the Women's Political Union and the National Woman's Party. It was while on a tour for the National Woman's Party in 1916 that she died.

maker's brother, Thomas, and one of the biggest in the city then. I was in the Sunday Department.

How I happened to get the job is a long story. There was a section called the Women's Section—eight pages on Sunday. It had, among other things, a department run by a then well-known novelist who called herself Marion Harland. She was the mother of the writer, Albert Payson Terhune, and her real name was Virginia Terhune. One of the things she had on her page was a sort of club, by correspondence—girls corresponded with each other on various things.

Somebody in Philadelphia decided to make a real club of it. We had meetings, went to picnics in the summer. For some reason—I suppose just a matter of publicity—the woman who was appointed editor of the section came to one of our meetings. At the time I was just getting through business college. (After I got out of high school, I had a scholarship at Wellesley, but it was just for tuition. My parents couldn't pay the difference, so my father treated me to six weeks in business college during that summer.)

This editor decided that I was just the person she was looking for. It was a combination, I suppose, of typing all the letters and some feature writing. Unfortunately, though, she had already engaged somebody she didn't like and was trying to get rid of. So she'd keep writing me all summer. By then I got a job with the people who published the theater programs. Finally, she got rid of this other woman, and on Thanksgiving Day—I can remember that we were at the table having Thanksgiving dinner—she phoned me and said, "Come right down. You've got the job." I deserted the turkey and went straight down to the *North American* and started working. We didn't have holidays in those days on newspapers.

I hadn't thought about newspaper work until I met her, but it was a chance to write and be published and that's all I was interested in. After I'd been there a few months, I wrote a long series of articles called "A Girl on a Big-City Newspaper" for a Baptist magazine, using up my material as fast as I could. From that time on, I wrote everywhere, especially poetry. In those days I think I must have had hundreds of poems published.

During that first year on the newspaper, I ran a health and beauty column and also did some of "Marion Harland's" work for her, answering letters. A good many of them were commonplace things to which we just sent some kind of printed material. One I'll never forget. A photograph came out of the envelope of a nurse in uniform, a registered nurse, and a letter saying, "Will you please look at this picture before you read any more of my letter. Then, if you've looked at it, will you please tell me whether or not you can tell I'm illegitimate." I wrote her and told her that it was impossible to tell from anybody's appearance. Of course, a letter like that was not printed. We got plenty of others in that line. Some of them my superiors in the office took away from me because they didn't think an eighteen-year-old girl ought to answer them.

I first worked on the paper from November to the next September, when I went to Wellesley. Languages are the thing that interest me, so at Wellesley I took French and Greek and advanced English. I took three English courses. Later, at Temple University, I took Latin all the way through graduate school, but English was my major. Unfortunately, at that time Wellesley made you take freshman math. The part of the brain that thinks mathematically was left out of me. Three days before I was to graduate from Temple with high honors and a graduate scholarship at the University of Pensylvania, I still had to pass off a freshman algebra condition; I'd taken the examination three times and failed. I've never taken math again, of course, and I've completely forgotten all I know.

When I went to college, I don't think I ever thought about how it would aid my writing or career. Everybody got educated; you had to go to school as a matter of course. In the college preparatory courses in high school, most American girls from the classical course went to nearby Bryn Mawr. Most of us in the Latin scientific course wanted to get farther away from home. One of my friends in high school went to Goucher, two to Bucknell, two to Cornell, and so on. One, later an M.D., went to Wellesley with me.

Most of the professors there were women. There were men, but I never happened to have any. (Now, I think, almost half of them are men.) Most of the women were single, I think. I don't remember if any of them were actually married; some were widows. In high school my freshman algebra teacher was an old friend of our family who was a widow, but I don't think there were any women teaching who were still married. They just took it for granted that when you got married you left your job.

Of course, a great many girls take that for granted now. I remember a few years ago a girl I knew who was one of my editors in a publishing house wrote me that she was leaving because she was getting married. I wrote back and said, "What about your fiancé? Is he leaving his job because he's getting married?" She never answered.

I would never have given up my work for the sake of being married—hardly! In my own group, most of my friends didn't marry; most of them became teachers. One of them became an elementary teacher, then left to get married. She had four children. Then times got hard and she went back to teaching while her husband was still alive. That happened sometimes. Most of the girls I knew, didn't work anymore if they got married. Of course, some of them, even the ones who didn't get married, didn't take jobs. They lived at home and took care of aged parents, that kind of thing. I hear occasionally from one of my classmates still who never married; she just took care of her parents till they died.

I went to Wellesley for only one year, my freshman year, and then my scholarship gave out, so I had to do something else. What I did was come back and live at home and enroll in Temple University. I had to get a job right away. I can't remember—I've had so many jobs—just what I did. I think I was then a secretary to a doctor, an eye specialist. After a very short time, though, Ernestine Allen, my former editor on the paper, called on me and asked me to come back. I was too shy and too timid to ask what my salary would be.

I went back and I was with them for three years. At the same time I went to Temple University. Our classes were all in the evenings or on Saturday and the students were mostly teachers. The College of Liberal Arts was very small; it wasn't the enormous place it is now. Temple was coeducational and, as was to be expected, there were more men than women in all my classes. I suppose most of the teachers at Temple in those days were not so distinguished as the ones at Wellesley, but they had very high standards. I got exactly the same kind of teaching as at Wellesley.

I was a year behind because of that year I had off after high school, but I made up my mind that I would graduate the same year as my Wellesley class. So in the summer I made arrangements with the paper and went to summer school at the University of Pennsylvania and then had it credited to Temple. My life was made up of mostly work and study. I was very unhappy about it. I was twenty, and I had just one Saturday evening a month to myself. I'd do most of my homework on the streetcar going to and from work.

When I went back to the newspaper, I did nothing but writing. We then had a stenographer and I was an assistant editor. I recall that I wrote a short story a week for our section besides a long series in verse about an old lady and her canary; she gathered advice from its chirps. I was making fifteen dollars a week then. That first year, I'd been making ten dollars.

I'm pretty sure that the women on the newspaper staff were paid less than the men. Our Sunday editor, who was quite high up in the hierarchy, got fifty a week. I know that. My editor, Myra Wybrant Smith, who also became my very good friend, got twenty-three. Whether people doing the same work got the same pay, I wouldn't know. But I don't think there were any women doing the same sort of thing as any of the men. There were very few regular women reporters; there may have been one or two on the New York papers, but there weren't any on ours. I did have two editors, before Myra, who had been reporters on a Chicago paper. They always wore hats with veils when they were in the office. They said that when they were reporters they had to show they were ready for instant assignments, just like a man. There was a woman photographer, which was very unusual in those days, but she photographed for the society section.

I was on the newspaper four years all together, counting the time before I went to college. Then I left the *North American* in 1912 to go up to Boston to live. Like most young people I wanted to get away from home. In Boston, among the numerous jobs I had, I started doing occasional feature stuff for the *Boston Post*. That was all free lance, though, from that time on.

SOAPBOXING FOR SUFFRAGE IN BOSTON

When I went to Boston, I think I made one or two inquiries at the newspapers there, but there just weren't any jobs and I didn't pursue it. I didn't really see going into newspaper work as an alternative, largely because I was a very shy, timid person. The way I got jobs was having somebody tell me about them and recommend me. I never had the nerve. As a matter of fact, whenever I had to go to an interview, I always got violent diarrhea. I simply couldn't face people and was always glad for a job where I could be alone and do my work and not have people around me.

The main thing was to get any kind of job that would pay my living expenses and then to write in the time I had left. I'd always prefer something where I could do some writing, but if worse came to worse, I'd work for anybody. And I did. I was sort of what they called a stenographer and what they now call a secretary. By this time women worked in all the offices. As a matter of fact, it was getting close to the time when a man stenographer was unusual, unless he was a court reporter. I think that on the many, many jobs I had, I never saw a man in the office except as the boss. Oh, yes, the bookkeepers used to be men usually.

This was actually the second time I lived in Boston. I first went up there in the summer after I had seen my former class graduate at Wellesley. I stayed the rest of the summer and worked in various offices as substitutes for girls on vacation. In one place, I remember, the manager called me aside and told me, "Don't tell any of the other girls what you make because you're a college graduate and you get more than anybody." I was getting seven and a half a week, less than on the newspaper, and they were getting seven.

When I went in 1912, I had various kinds of jobs. For a while I did public relations work for two or three organizations. Later on, I was on the staff of *Associated Advertising*, which was the house organ of the Associated Advertising Clubs of the World.

I lived in what was called a "home for self-supporting women," The Hemenway, in a very bad part of the city, worse even than where I am living now in the San Francisco Tenderloin. The College Settlement was right across the street from us. We had two old four-story houses thrown into one. For a very small fee, we got a room and breakfast and dinner. Usually you had a roommate, but I was nearly always alone.

The head of it was a lady named Bertha Hazard, who was from Alabama. She was a graduate of Vassar and had lived in Boston many years and was a very active suffragist. It was probably through her that I became connected with the Massachusetts Suffrage Society. Every state and large city had a suffrage league. Maude Wood Park, I know, was the head in Boston.

I think I was the only one living in that home who became involved. Oh, there may have been one or two social workers who were more or less interested, but nearly all the girls there were devout Roman Catholics and their whole outside interest was in the church. Boston is a highly Irish city. Most of The Hemenway residents were factory workers. A few were office workers. I was the only one, I'm sure, that took any active part in the suffrage society.

They got out all kinds of literature and had evening street-speaking. In those days every evening in every city the downtown street corners were all occupied by soapboxes, literally sometimes, and sometimes we just called them that when they were little platforms with a flag. There was usually somebody from headquarters who would get up and make an opening talk. Then whoever it was would introduce the speaker.

You would know you were going to speak that night and you'd have some kind of subject to talk about besides the general one. You'd talk for maybe fifteen or twenty minutes and then you'd ask for questions and try to answer them. Mostly we spoke about suffrage, but we also talked about the right of a woman to have control of her own earnings. Those were the days when the married woman who worked could have all her money taken by her husband. Also, he decided where they should live, and if they separated, he got the children. A lot of women stayed in very unhappy marriages because they didn't want to lose their children. I suppose we talked about the peripheral subjects, but we thought primarily that the way to help women was to give them the vote so they could be citizens, too.

The audiences would be people going along the street. I suppose there were people who spent every evening going from one place to another, just like Hyde Park in London. They were just the same kind of people you'd find if you had an auto accident on the corner. People were going by and they stopped to listen. If they were interested they stayed, and if they weren't they left. Some of them went from one to another speaker, just to spend an evening listening to conversations.

In those days there weren't any other women that I recall besides suffragists. Most of the other soapboxers, except for the ones on some special issue that might be coming up about housing or something, were religious. They were missionaries of one kind or another; they were either promoting the Bible or criticizing it. In Spokane and in Los Angeles when I was speaking there for some of the radical martyrs and victims, I can remember there'd be a religious meeting on the other side, and I'd get up and yell, "You people that are listening to fellow-worker Jesus, come over and hear something about the real workers' movement." But that was later on. These religious people didn't pay much attention to us. We all had our own audiences. Of course, we preferred to have a larger audience, but you couldn't hold them if they wanted to go; you had to keep them entertained.

We never had any actual physical violence that I can remember. We got jeers and catcalls. In those days you didn't use four-letter words, but we'd be interrupted, of course, and heckled. That was all part of it. You expected that and learned how to handle it.

Somebody else from headquarters would be passing things around. We always passed out petitions; there was always some bill in the Legislature. When we went over them later, we would find all sorts of facetious phony names like Luke McLuke or Gyp the Blood. But we always got a certain number of actual voters, all men, of course.

As I remember, I'd usually speak once or twice a week. They would say, "What evenings do you have free next week?" or something like that, and we'd make a schedule for the week. A great many people didn't like to speak in public, especially to this shifting audience of strangers on the street. It sounds very radical to get out on a soapbox and stand on a street corner, but everybody did it. I mean, quite conservative political candidates would. That was the day of the soapbox. Every evening when you went downtown, every corner was occupied.

The suffrage movement in Boston was very mild and very conservative. Mrs. Park couldn't have been more respectable and conservative. She was a sweet little woman. She'd been married six months when her husband died, and she wore mourning for him for the rest of her life. So you can see. And Miss Bertha Hazard, who was the head of our "home for self-supporting women," was one of the conservative suffrage people. Though I think she was the one that first suggested that I offer my services to speak in the evenings, she herself would never have dreamed of doing it. I don't think she even marched in a parade. Don't forget this was early—1912 to 1915. She was very much a lady. She did once try to register to vote as a demonstration. That was one of the things they did; different women would go down when it was time to register and try to register, and be turned down and get some publicity for the cause.

No, it was a conservative group. I don't recall talking about feminism with them. I never knew any of them personally. I just went down and offered my services, and since I had some experience in public speaking, they took me on. They never really talked about anything except "What's a good corner?" and "Who will circulate the petitions tonight?"

At that time, too, I wasn't at all involved in radical circles. No, I never was until my first marriage, until I met the man who was my first husband. In a sense, I suppose you'd say I was always open to that kind of thing. I was soapboxing and I also was the official reporter for the Ford Hall Open Forum. We had all kinds of speakers there, and that's the first time I ever did hear any radical speakers. We also had what we called the Town Meeting at which I was the clerk. People would bring up all kinds of "bills" and we would argue and discuss them and that sort of thing. When I finally met the man I married—he was sort of a combination of Southern aristocrat and anarchist— he converted me all the way over very quickly.

SEXUAL EMERGENCE: END OF VICTORIANISM

I guess I was twenty-five before I knew a man well enough outside my family to have him call me by my first name. I'd known some of my classmates in Temple University. Two of them used to call on me; one was a divinity student and I used to entertain him by writing sonnets with him! Then I was in love with one of my married professors, but of course, he never knew it.

I remember saying to my father, when I was down on a holiday in Philadelphia, "Thank goodness, I never see a man in Boston except the janitor." My father was horrified. I suppose he was afraid I was turning into a lesbian! I wasn't. I was simply uninterested. Of course he never mentioned it in those terms. Good Lord, no. He'd have died before he'd have said a word like that.

It was about that time that one of my high school friends married a young doctor and we were at an art gallery or museum, and this young man made some remark which struck me as anti-feminist. So I said, "There's no difference between men and women," and he said, "There's a vas deferens." I was so angry, I walked out on him. He followed me down the path, saying, "It's perfectly natural, it's perfectly natural." So, you see, I was prudish, too.

I wasn't against men, I just didn't know any. From the time I got connected with Ford Hall, though, I did meet a lot of men. In fact, two or three of the men had quite a case on me. I was so unobservant about such things that I didn't even know. One of them asked me to marry him and I just laughed. It was a young man whose name, strange to say, was Jack London. One night he was walking me home from Ford Hall and proposed. I just laughed at him. He said very stiffly, "It isn't funny." I told him that I didn't think he meant it seriously. I hardly knew the man. I hadn't the slightest interest in marrying him.

I remember that one summer we had what they called the Sagamore Sociological Conference on the seashore near Boston. I was there because it was run by Ford Hall. I think it lasted about a week. We'd have talks every day and concerts. That was the first time that Roland Hayes, the famous Negro tenor, ever sang in public.

There was a young Unitarian minister there whose name I've completely forgotten; it was a three-barrel name, George something. He was kind of taken with me. A group of us were at the beach and I can't remember what happened, but there was something we had to get from some house nearby and he went with me to help me carry it. When we got inside the house, he kissed me and I slapped his face. That was my first kiss from any man except my father, and I was twenty-four!

We were pretty near the Victorian Age, and they were still

sending the unmarried daughter out into the snow with the baby in her arms! "Never darken my door again" and that kind of thing. I know I was pretty prudish and easily shocked. I know how horrified I was when some woman on the *North American* told me how some man had misled her. I remember turning cold at the thought that somebody I actually knew had done something irregular like that.

By the time I met Armistead, I knew that a man could be interested in me, but I was just as prudish, and it took him a long, long time, very gradually. But before that, during this period, I went through a sort of semidepressed state. In fact, I was an outpatient in Peter Bent Brigham Psychiatric Hospital for a while. I think probably it was that I did lead such a one-sided life. I was unhappy in general, about anything. I took everything very hard, very emotionally. I remember the doctor said, "You're lucky you didn't get one of the Freudians." That was the first time I ever heard of Freud. But from the time I met Armistead and fell in love with him, why, I never had any more difficulties.

That was in 1914. A friend of mine, Mabel, had talked to me about him. There was a rival to Ford Hall, called something like School of Social Science, where they got all kinds of radical audiences. Mabel used to go to it occasionally and she met him there. I remember the first time she mentioned him she said, "Did you ever meet that anarchist that gets up and talks?" I said, "No, and I don't want to meet him. If you have a normal man for me to meet, I'll be glad to meet him."

At that time I was doing public relations work and I used a big room that she didn't use in her apartment as an office; I rented it. I was working late one evening when Armistead came to have dinner with her. In spite of the fact that I said I didn't want to meet him, I couldn't very well just walk out. As soon as we were introduced, he asked me to join them for dinner. We talked all evening and then he walked me home, and from that time on we were together.

I can remember the first night I met him that he made some remark, and though I was a little old for it, I was like a brash seventeen-year-old and showing off. So I made some remark about how nobody paid any attention to legal marriage these days, or something like that, and he told me later in the evening that I was a revelation. Actually, I was as virginal as you can imagine, and as prudish.

Armistead Collier * was a beautiful combination of a mystic, an anarchist and a Southern aristocrat. He insisted on being respected for all three. He preferred to be known as John Adam, but I would never call him that. I wrote a play about him which was produced here in San Francisco in 1924. The protagonist was called Francis Cain for the same reason; John for the saint in me and Adam for the primal man. He was a very persuasive person with the most beautiful Southern accent you ever heard.

He came from a wealthy family and always had some kind of income. His father owned the biggest newspaper in Memphis, and he had done some work on that. When I met him in Boston, he wasn't doing anything that I can remember. He was writing a great philosophical book that was still being written when he died in 1948. As I know now, he was also carrying on four or five affairs.

This thing was all philosophical with him. He had theories about everything and he believed them. I will say that he was the most honest man that I ever knew in my life. He simply had strange theories and had got himself into trouble on several occasions. Twice he had been sent to a mental hospital by his family. So he really suffered for what he believed, and it wasn't just that he was a philanderer. It was his theory that monogamy was evil and that there should be not only free love, but promiscuity.

The way he proposed marriage was "I'll either marry you and not support you, or support you and not marry you—which would you rather have?" And I said, "I'd always rather support myself, so let's get married." He went on ahead to San Diego, and when he got a house he let me know and I went out from Boston in February 1915. Of course, that meant the end of my

* William Armistead Nelson Collier, Jr.

suffrage activities because California already had woman's suffrage.

We were married in San Diego, on a cliff at La Jolla, by an unfrocked Congregational minister who still had the right to marry people. I didn't let any of my family know. I had stopped by on my way to San Diego to tell them good-bye and told them I had a good job in San Diego. My father had put a detective on us when he had heard rumors. He regaled me with a lot of scandal about Armistead that I already knew. He objected mostly to the fact that he was very obviously a Don Juan and was fifteen years older than I and had been married and divorced twice. He had no particular means of support that anyone could see. In other words, he was a most undesirable son-in-law. So I couldn't tell any of my family. Apparently some stranger sent the newspaper story to Philadelphia papers and I got an immediate telegram from my mother.

I suppose you would call me a demi-virgin when I was married. We didn't live together, but he and some other people rented a place out in the country and I'd go and spend every weekend with him. As I know now, he was an extremely practiced seducer. It was all completely new to me and I was very much in love. And he was with me, except that he got tired of any one woman for too long. We never actually had intercourse before we were married, but just about as near to it as you could get.

There was never any question about children. It was understood that I would have no children. From the very beginning I had been anti-baby. I think it was related to my feminist beliefs. I thought children interfered with your work, for one thing.

THE LADIES' HOME JOURNAL, JANUARY 1907 EDITORIAL

The childless married woman figures a great deal in print of late—a great deal too much, and with a peculiar animadversion which is often undeserved. There is no need to dwell upon the dignity and honor which should be given to the mothers all over our land. These honors are quite obvious, and oft repeated. But there are two classes of mothers, as we all know : those to whom children are a crown of rejoicing, and those to whom children are an unwelcome burden which they would shirk if they could. And just as surely as there are these two classes of mothers, there are two classes of childless women : those whose hearts ache because God has not given this blessing "all of grace," as well as those who are deliberately childless with premeditated selfishness. For the latter there should be naught but condemnation. They are not of the genus woman at all. They are mere parasites in nature : beings who take all that life has to offer and give nothing in return. For these there should be a new reading of the old Mosaic teachings, "a life for a life." They owe the world at least that which they have received of the world. But unto a woman who is a member of the former class let us render—justice. Let us not even offend her with our pity. We must not forget that, childless though she be, she may have uttered Rachel's piteous cry before her God, and she may be, in all her childlessness, more of a mother in her soul than she who has been blest with sons and daughters. For let us not forget that there is maternity and their is motherhood. The one is of the body ; the other is of the soul.

There are women who are mothers, yes, but whose souls have nevertheless remained entirely barren of all the sweetness and beauty which real motherhood endows. On the other hand, there are women who have never had a child, yet whose faces shine with the mystic mother-love of the Madonna, whose arms enfold all little children because they have none of their own to circle. They are world-mothers, and yet sometimes these real mothers are commiserated or condemned by mothers in whom this duty was simply a mere physical function and absolutely nothing else. Is this fair ? Is it just, or tender, or Christian ? Should the woman with children, happy or unhappy, have all the respect due to womanhood, and the other, bravely bearing her burden of denial, also have to bear the disrespect of the world ? Hardly. Let us be honest. In nine cases out of ten it is safe to say the childless married woman longs for children of her own. It is as natural that she should want children as it is that she should want the love of her husband and her own fireside. For the mass of American women are not hybrid, pleasure-seeking creatures who look upon life as a gay playground, and who seek to avoid the responsibility and care of motherhood. They are true-hearted, womanly women, and if childless, then let us believe in them and love them all the more because their burden is heavier than ours, and their happiness is less.

Right before I left for San Diego to be married, I went to a Russian woman doctor I knew in Boston. She was an anarchist, a refugee from Czarist Russia. She instructed me on the use of the "dutch pessary." * Since, as I say, I was rather a demi-virgin at the time, she couldn't demonstrate exactly, but she gave me the information and some kind of suppository to use before I could use that. It was a less reliable form of birth control. I don't know what was in it, but it was supposed to be a germicide or spermicide. I used that until I could use the pessary.

I don't remember how long the pessary lasted or how much it cost, but sooner or later, you had to get a new one. I never had a doctor's prescription for it. You'd go into a drugstore. It was very embarrassing, I remember. You'd get the clerk in the corner—it was always a man—and ask in a whisper if he had any dutch pessaries. I never used anything but the pessary. They told us then what they tell us now, that douching is absolutely useless, but, of course, in those days you always douched afterwards. Even with a pessary. It was safer. As I remember, you put vaseline on the heavy edge. I don't know if its like the modern diaphragm—I've never seen one, and, of course, it's been a long time since I've needed one.

LIFE AS A RADICAL

So, at the end of my four years in Boston, through Armistead I began to meet radicals, mostly anarchists, and this was the beginning of my own radicalism. I suppose I really got acquainted with left politics at Ford Hall because that was the first time I'd ever heard people speak who belonged to those groups. Perhaps if I'd met someone, instead, who'd been far to the right, I'd have been a McCarthyite. I don't know, but I doubt it. I was always very open-minded and never horrified or shocked, as my parents were, by my associations.

* The precursor of the modern diaphragm.

By the time I got to San Diego, of course, I was completely indoctrinated, but my political involvement there was minimal. I was working most of the time as a public stenographer. We lived in Coronado and I went over every day on the ferry to San Diego. It was a funny little office, right downtown, on the mezzanine floor of a funny little office building. That's also when I started writing for *Poetry*. When you're a public stenographer, you've got a lot of time when you have a typewriter and nobody is using it but you.

Working as a public stenographer, I couldn't do much publicly.* The only thing I can remember from San Diego that had any connection with the anarchists was that I once helped to hold a hall for Emma Goldman when she was going to speak. The police had threatened to stop the meeting and some of the people we had met there asked if I would help. I sat at the top of the steps in case a cop came. None did, and the meeting was held. She spoke on birth control that night.

On another occasion, Anton Johanson, one of Emma Goldman's crowd, walked into my office and dictated a long letter to "E.G." I didn't know how he happened to come in—maybe he was just looking for a stenographer—but I asked him over to our house in Coronado. Unfortunately, he didn't make a hit with my husband. Armistead was very puritanical in speech and Johanson was full of four-letter words.

The next day Johanson came in again with somebody else— Tweitmoe, I think—and dictated some more letters. Much to my annoyance they wrote E.G. or somebody else about their visit to our house and made very uncomplimentary remarks about it. I thought that was a very rude thing to do. As a public stenographer, I could hardly refuse to write the letters, but I charged them a lot. As much as the traffic would bear.

It never occurred to either Armistead or me that I wouldn't go to work. I would never be willing to have anybody support me. Also, at the time, he didn't have much money, by any

---

* This was a period when vigilantism was rampant in the San Diego area.

means. I don't suppose we could have lived comfortably if I hadn't been working. As a matter of fact, he had no regular income. He had a very rich cousin who had been brought up as a brother in his house who was then head of all the streetcar and subway advertising in New York, Baron Collier. He used to send money from time to time.

Early in 1916 we left San Diego and went to Los Angeles. We had a chance to rent our house and Armistead had a chance to get in the movies. So we went up to Hollywood in the early days. I was an extra in the movies in both San Diego and Hollywood for a while. Armistead had bit parts and got more money. These were all silent films, of course.

I had various secretarial jobs. For a while I was a secretary to two lawyers. Then I answered an advertisement from this big oil company, Pacific American or something like that. It was Doheny's. The man who was going to be my boss came to see me at the lawyers' office at lunch time. He looked me over. Naturally, we didn't have much money and I didn't have much in the way of a wardrobe. I remember what I had on. It was most unbecoming; a black-and-white striped blouse and beige skirt. He was very much impressed by my qualifications, but he looked at me and said, "Our young ladies only wear black satin." I said, "I'm sorry, but I have no black satin." He asked if I had *any kind* of black dress. I think I had only one. I had to wear that to that office.

It was a funny office, a great big thing. Doheny was a prospector who struck it rich when he discovered oil in quantities. He divorced his old wife who had supported him by taking in washing and married a blond floozy. All the officers of the company were British, and most of them, like the retired Irish Anglican clergyman who was my boss, were very arrogant. That's why I finally left there.

That was a funny thing, though. It was about that time, at my husband's suggestion, really, that I decided that the way to express my opposition to the war would be to join the IWW (Industrial Workers of the World). We went up to the office. The IWW was divided according to industry; you were either some kind of industrial or agricultural worker. Well, what could they do with me? They didn't have white-collar. They finally put me in the oil division, though I knew absolutely nothing about oil outside of writing about the company. (My job was to work on the house organ, and in the end I did most of it.) I'm sure that I was the only woman in the oil workers' division of the IWW. I never took an active part, though; I never did anything except pay my dues. It was mainly a protest against the war, and a year later, in Baltimore, I just dropped my membership.

I think we lived in five different places in Los Angeles in the seven or eight months we were there. At one time we rented a nice little furnished bungalow in Hollywood on Fountain Avenue surrounded by a lemon and grapefruit grove a block square.

I always had a typewriter. I've forgotten whether it was mine or his. I began about then to be writing for magazines like *The Masses*, mostly satires and poems. A. Philip Randolph had a magazine, *The Messenger*, that I also wrote poems for. I remember there was a race riot in Tulsa that I had one poem about.

When I was in Los Angeles I first became acquainted with Schmidt and Kaplan. I can't remember through whom. They were connected with the McNamara case,* the *Los Angeles Times* explosion of 1910, and were in the county jail. Later on, when I was living in San Francisco and visited San Quentin, I came to know them very well, and Schmidt's sister became a very good friend of ours.

Spokane was really the first time that I did soapboxing again since I had left Boston. I went there in 1917 and the Mooney case had already started by then. Actually, the Mooney case† was also the last time I did any soapboxing on the street.

---

* In 1910 two brothers, John and James McNamara, dynamited the Los Angeles Times Building. Although they at first professed innocence and the forces of organized labor rallied to their side, they later confessed.
† On July 17, 1916, a bomb exploded among bystanders watching a Preparedness Day parade in San Francisco, killing ten persons and wound-

I had gone to Spokane primarily to visit some friend who had
been the head of the Associated Charities in San Diego. I was
out of a job at the time and they invited me up, so I went up.
I didn't know it then, but my marriage was breaking up. I had
known it would be non-monogamous and the theory was that it
applied to both of us, but every time a man got interested in
me, or I in him, I was "entirely too fine a person to be having
anything to do with that man." The consequence was that I
remained monogamous and he not only slept with every woman
that I've ever known him to know, but he brought them home.
It got rather on my nerves.

I was just as glad to be going away. I expected to be gone
about a week, but I stayed there for three months. Naturally, I
wasn't going to sponge on my hosts, so I got a job packing eggs
for Armour and Company. I was very bad at it. The idea was
that you took eggs out of enormous crates and put them in
boxes. The only instructions we got was that if an egg was
cracked, we were to put it in the boxes for confectioners. What
they meant by "cracked" was anything that had enough shell
left to put it in the box. Very often the eggs exploded in your
face. I got so that I walked home; I smelled so of sulfur I was
ashamed to get on the streetcar.

I remember this little woman who worked with me. She was
much older than I. She was pasting things under the counter.
I found out her husband was a Wobbly (member of the
IWW). I don't know how she happened to confide in me. I
think I called someone a "scissor bill"* and she said that's what
her husband calls people.

While I was in Spokane I heard from my father. He became

---

ing forty others. Despite massive evidence that they were not guilty, Tom
Mooney and Warren Billings, radical and labor activists, were charged
with the crime. Their case became a major cause célèbre for radicals and
the labor movement, and for the next twenty years it remained in the
forefront. In 1939 Governor Olson pardoned Mooney and commuted
Billings' sentence to the twenty-three years he had already served.

* IWW term for a member of the AFL (American Federation of
Labor), also known as Duke of Labor. Conservative union man.

very much exercised about the general way I was living and somehow he wangled this job for me as the editor of a house organ of an olive oil company in Baltimore. The head of the company was a patient of his. In other words, my father wanted to get me away from Armistead. He wired and offered me the job and my fare East. Things were in an economic state such that I couldn't afford not to take it. I wired back that I'd go if he would let me go by way of Los Angeles so that I could say good-bye to Armistead, which I did.

When I got to Baltimore I didn't know a single person. I rented a huge room on Cathedral Street, which was the very first time that anyone on that fancy street had rented out rooms; it was right across the street from the archbishop's. I was terribly lonely and I used to spend my leisure time reading the telephone book and hoping I'd see a name that I'd recognize.

My uncle was a traveling salesman for a paint company, and Baltimore was in his territory. He came down one evening on business and we had dinner together. We were walking down Howard Street afterwards when my uncle looked up and then said to me, "Why, those people have got even here." I looked up and here was this great big sign, "Socialist Party of Maryland." I didn't say anything to Uncle Clarence, for obvious reasons. I was still spending most of my time in my room alone, not knowing what to do. The next evening after work I went up there, and there was only one man in the office and he told me when their meetings were. I told him that I was a member of the IWW and that I was not a Socialist. My own beliefs were rather generalized. I knew I didn't believe in the political orientation of the Socialist party, and I always considered the Socialist Labor party too hidebound.

But I was interested in anything. When the man found out I was from California, he asked if I knew Maynard Shipley, the editor of their paper, *Progressive World* or something like that, who was also from California. Well, as it happened at that time, Maynard had never been south of Menlo Park and I'd never been north of L.A. except to pass through on the way to

Spokane. I don't know why, I suppose I didn't want to seem ignorant, but when this man asked if I knew Maynard Shipley, I said I'd heard of him. But I'd never heard his name in my life. I did go to the meeting Friday evening, and that's when I first met Maynard.

My marriage wasn't over. The idea was that Armistead was to come East. We had every expectation of rejoining, but, unfortunately, I met Maynard and that was the end of that. It was a very complicated thing. It wasn't like an ordinary marriage in a great many ways. (As a matter of fact, several years later when Maynard and I were living in Mill Valley, Armistead came up and spent six weeks with us. He made it very embarrassing by taking walks and telling everybody he met that he was staying with his wife and her lover. We were posing as brother and sister, so it made it a little uncomfortable.)

Maynard had gone to Seattle as a boy of fifteen and spent most of his youth between Seattle and San Francisco. At this time he still had two brothers left in Baltimore, and when he went back to visit he was asked to edit the Socialist paper there. He was an organizer for the Socialist party and, in fact, from 1906 to 1922 he was very prominent. He had, before I met him, worked as Eugene Debs's campaign manager in 1912 or 1916, and Debs was a friend of ours.

We got an apartment together in Baltimore, but before that we used to go to a little third-class hotel up near the railroad station. The first time we went there I remember how shocked I was that Maynard signed the registry Miriam Collier and husband. I was still very shy and timid and frightened, and I remember that we'd have dinner downstairs in the restaurant— it was an old wooden place—and then I'd run up the stairs to our room. Maynard said, "Why do you do that? It's so conspicuous. People will look at you when you run. Why don't you just walk quietly!"

The company that I was working for, that I edited the house organ for, sold olive oil and products made with olive oil. All the oil came from Spain, and with the war, there were no more ships. So the company folded and I was out of a job in a strange city.

Frank Lang, a member of the Socialist Labor Party whom I had met through a mutual acquaintance from L.A., told me that because men were being drafted, the Maryland Casualty Company was thinking of training women as claims adjusters. There had never been any. I think there were a half dozen of us who applied but I was the only one who stuck. I was four or five months in the home office in Baltimore, then they sent all their adjusters to Chicago, which was the training center, for three months. When I joined the company, it was on the condition that I be transferred to San Francisco.

When I left for my training in Chicago, Maynard gave up his job and started on a lecture and organizing tour across the country. It was then a very hazardous, risky thing to do—talking against the war for the Socialist party. It was months before I saw him again; he'd been all over little towns you'd never heard of in Montana and Wyoming and Idaho. The plan was that the two of us would join each other in San Francisco. By that time we'd lived together for several months. We couldn't marry for another three years because he was married, too. We both had to wait till we got our divorces. The day I got my final decree (his was not due for several months, but then his wife died) we were married in Santa Rosa.

At this time my political activity was general. The primary thing was the war, which we were all fighting, and then later the Palmer raids. People were being arrested, headquarters were being broken up, they were deporting people. The consequence was that even all the different kinds of radicals who ordinarily would be at swords' points with each other were cooperating against the common enemy, so I can't say there was any doctrinaire atmosphere. The whole thing was fighting the capitalists, all of us, so we helped each other out. Nobody was allowed to speak. People were sent to prison for twenty years for just saying they were against the war. People we knew, people with names, were being arrested, and some of them got long prison sentences. When I was in Chicago, the IWW trials were starting.*

In fact, my company wanted to take me to the Cook County jail to see what the inside of a jail was like. I knew what would happen. I knew half of those people there, and I didn't dare go. I'd have been greeted immediately with "Why, hello, fellow worker, what are you doing here?" and that would have been the end of my career as an insurance adjuster. I told them the truth, that I had been inside a jail in Maryland and that it had made me sick to see those men in cages and that I didn't know if I could go through it again. Of course, as an adjuster, I was in county jails much of the time, interviewing burglars to find out what they had done with the loot, that sort of thing.

I remember what a terrible shock it was to see those IWW's get twenty years apiece. That was when Bill Haywood had escaped.† But the others got twenty years, I'm sure of it. Yes, I remember that day because I felt so terrible that I went out to the cemetery to see the graves of the Haymarket victims. It was about all I could think of doing.

It was in Chicago that I had a post office box and found, among my mail, a letter addressed to the district attorney—which showed that my mail had all been on his desk. The day after I left Chicago, someone blew up the post office with a bomb. I'm sure that I was expected to have been involved in that.

There was a radical club called the something or other Pud-

* On April 1, 1918, 101 members of the IWW were charged with sabotage and conspiracy to obstruct the war. It was clearly the IWW philosophy which was on trial.
† "Big Bill" Haywood was one of the more prominent members of the IWW who stood trial, being among the founding members of the organization. He and fourteen others of the leading defendants were sentenced to twenty years' imprisonment and $30,000 fines. They were released on bail while their case was on appeal, and when their conviction and sentences were upheld, Haywood and nine others refused to surrender. Haywood went to the Soviet Union, where he spent the last years of his life.

ding Club. Some people I knew introduced me to it and occasionally I'd go there. I met a man that, I know now, must have been some kind of provocateur; he kept on advocating violence. He insisted he wanted to see me at such and such a meeting. I finally got very suspicious and told him I couldn't go. I stayed away, and that was the day they raided the place and arrested everybody there. I wasn't known, but that I would be in such a place would have been enough. I called on Mrs. Parsons, who was the last surviving widow of the Haymarket. I had all kinds of radical connections, thanks to my first marriage and all the anarchists. I presume my name had somehow gotten into the files. I must have a thick dossier at the FBI.

After my training in Chicago I went on to San Francisco and joined Maynard. I stayed with Maryland Casualty from 1918 to 1923. At that time, I was the only woman claims adjuster, as far as I know, in the world. The only difficulty I had was that the manager was a Marylander from the eastern shore, very conservative and not at all pleased that they sent him a woman. He tried to do everything he could to discourage me. First, I did mostly workmen's compensation cases. He sent me up to Fort Bragg to see a man who'd been cut in pieces by a circular saw. I took that without a flinch. Incidentally, by that time I was writing detective stories for the pulps. Then he sent me down to Lindsay to see a farm hand who had been crushed by a tractor. When he found out that I wasn't going to be put off by any of these gruesome things, he took another tack.

This was before prohibition, of course. One of our policy holders was a saloon keeper named Cassidy on lower Market Street. Mr. Morris sent me to interview Mr. Cassidy, who had a claim, to see whether he was back at work. In those days, women didn't go into saloons. I still remember how I had braced myself to open the door. All these male heads turned around and glared at me, and I said very quickly, "Is Mr. Cassidy here?" and he was and was working. So that ended that.

Maynard and I lived in Mill Valley for almost two years, and then the woman from whom we rented the house wanted to sell it, so we moved back to San Francisco for a year. By that time I had softened my antipolitical views. In other words, Maynard persuaded me. His arguments had finally won me over. It was up to me if I wanted to join the Socialist Party or not. It was the only thing we ever disagreed on. Once he got so angry with me that he went over to Oakland and stayed for two days. I had to go over to get him back.

I felt that as long as we were here in the city (San Francisco) we ought to do something active, especially as Maynard had been one of their prominent people and organizers for so many years. So, in 1919, when Maynard stopped editing the *World* in Oakland (he had edited it before, from 1909 to 1913), we both joined the San Francisco chapter of the Socialist Party and did go to the meetings.

We both left the Socialist Party in 1922 because they were going too far to the right—they were practically a branch of the Democratic party. Maynard had been in the left wing of the Socialist Party. I suppose we would have said that though neither of us ever was a Communist, and were not entirely in sympathy after the promising early days of the Revolution, we were certainly not liberals or reformers. I've always been for complete revolution, not reform. I suppose you'd say we were good Marxists. We were probably among the very few Socialists who ever read more than the first volume of *Das Kapital*.

In 1919, though, the local in San Francisco was still pretty left-wing. Then, by the end of that year, the Communists had started. They would raid the place and invade and made things actually not safe to go to a meeting. You never knew when they were going to bust the door open and begin throwing things around. They even stole the lists of subscribers to the *Oakland World*. They played very rough, so that I can't say we were on amicable terms. I see one of the men from that group of young Communists. He is now aged with gray hair and missing teeth. I see him over at Oakland at the Humanist House there. We don't refer to those days.

I was doing every kind of writing during this time. I had been writing for all those magazines like *Scribner's, Nation, Masses,* and then when the Federated Press was founded in 1920, I wrote and asked them if they could use me. They were a labor wire service. By this time, I had a reputation in those circles. I wrote a weekly column at first. I can't even remember what it was about. After a few months they made me the Bay Area correspondent. I was the whole reportorial staff there. I was with them for thirty-five years until they expired in 1956. I probably became one of their best-known and regular people. When they expired, they sent me a hundred dollars.

When you're doing work like being a claims adjuster, you're out on the street all the time, and nobody knows how much of your time you're spending seeing people you have to see and how much you're calling for news. So, beginning in 1920 or 1921, while I was still with Maryland Casualty, I was also covering labor stories for the Federated Press. I had my regular rounds. I covered not only all labor conventions but meetings of every kind, including those of the Labor Council. Every kind of labor news was in my province, for the whole Bay area. I covered all the various Mooney hearings and trials and retrials, the Bridges* hearings when they tried to deport him, and so on.

One of the places I had to visit was the IWW headquarters, which was just around the corner from the Maryland Casualty office in the financial district. It was the old Russ Building, one of those old-fashioned buildings with galleries. This was 1923, just before I went on vacation that summer. And I walked into a raid. As soon as I realized what was happening, I just made some noncommittal remark and got out.

I got away as fast as I could, but was not fast enough, because what they called the Red Squad, Mulberg and O'Brien—much to my pleasure, Mulberg later shot himself to death—followed me and went around to my office and informed Mr. Morris that I had been at IWW headquarters. He didn't say anything then. The next day he called me in and said this report had been made. He also then told me what he hadn't told me for five

* Harry Bridges is an Australian-born longshoreman who rose from the ranks during the 1934 maritime strikes to become president of the West Coast Longshoremen's Union. Because of his ties to the Communist party, efforts were made to deport him.

years. When I first came to San Francisco in 1918, Mulberg and O'Brien had called on him and told him that I was out here organizing for the IWW. He told them then that he would keep an eye on me and that if I didn't try to convert any of the staff, he wouldn't do anything. The idea of converting those dumb little Irish Catholic stenographers and file clerks was pretty funny.

Now he told me, and said, "Well, your vacation is due, and when you come back we'd better be separated." So I was out of a job in 1923, and had a pretty strenuous time for a while. I was only making twenty dollars a month from the Federated Press and so I could hardly live on that. Fortunately, by this time I had pieces in several places. I was moving up in the world. But I wasn't able to live purely by writing (until about thirty years ago), so I took various substitute jobs. Maynard lectured all the time and made most of his income from lectures.

Then we discovered Haldeman and Julius' Little Blue Books in Gerard, Kansas. For about five years we both wrote prolifically for them. You got fifty dollars for fifteen thousand words. Maynard wrote something like thirty-five Little Blue Books for them, mostly science, and I wrote at least fifteen, mostly biographies and translations from the Latin authors. I also wrote one on Mussolini and the Fascist movement, one on how to teach yourself how to play the piano and another on how to teach yourself to type. In other words, the fifty dollars came in regularly. That was our main source of income during that period. We both earned all we could and pooled it, never thinking whether it was his or mine.

By this time we were living in Sausalito. After we got burglarized in San Francisco, we decided we were better off in a suburb. Sausalito was a funny kind of place; it was part fishing village, part artists and writers, part suburban, and also a pretty tough gambling and criminal joint. It's always been a hangout for criminals. Baby Face Nelson hid out there. I accidentally bought his Tommy-gun case when I was buying containers to move over to San Francisco. We lived in Sausalito for fourteen years, until Maynard died in 1934. First we rented a flat, almost on the waterfront, until we found the house that we lived in for almost thirteen years.

All during those years, I covered every labor story; every kind of labor convention, including the founding of the CIO, every kind of strike, and labor cases of any sort that involved arrests or imprisonment. Of course, I was involved in the Mooney case. You couldn't very well be working for a labor wire service and not be involved. It was the biggest case we had in the whole country. I did a lot of reporting also on the Schmidt and Caplan case.* I remember during the founding convention of the CIO coming back early from lunch. It was at the Civic Auditorium, and there was no one in the whole building except John L. Lewis.† He was striding up and down talking to himself and I discreetly hid in the shadows and heard him saying, "We disaffiliate, we disaffiliate."

I was purely a labor reporter and I certainly couldn't be affiliated with any party. The Federated Press had no politics. It was always accused of being a Communist outfit, and there were quite a number of Communists connected with it. But there were also quite a number of non-Communists. What it was was pro-labor. At one time we even had ordinary newspapers, even the *New York Herald*. At the peak of our prosperity I think we had something like three hundred papers all over the country.

Neither Maynard nor I were active after we left the Socialist Party in 1922. Most of my political activity was through writing. Not only with the Federated Press but also, through covering all these things, I got material that I began writing articles about for *The Nation* and *The New Republic*. I wrote for them frequently and for a long time—on criminal syndicalism cases and things like that.

* Matthew Schmidt and David Caplan were arrested many years later and accused of participating in the dynamiting of the Los Angeles Times Building in 1910.
† President of the United Mine Workers and one of the founders of the CIO (Congress of Industrial Organizations).

After 1922, when Maynard had his first heart attack, he was not well enough to do very much. It was enough to be going around doing all the lecturing and all the writing. And then, from 1924 until 1932 we were absorbed in the anti-evolution fight. That took up all the energy either of us had.

Maynard founded the Evolution or Science League because one state after another began having these anti-evolution bills. He had written to every scientific and scholarly organ you can think of and they all answered that "yes, somebody should do it, but it wasn't their line." Finally, in despair, when he was doing a long lecture series, at the end of one of them he outlined the situation and we started right there. That night we collected eleven dollars and nineteen members, and that was the beginning. This was before the Scopes trial. In fact, most of the witnesses for Scopes were our members. We were very, very select. We had practically every well-known scientist in the country, but we didn't have an awful lot of them.

We had a secretary who was supposed to do the office work, but his salary got so far in arrears that he had to get a job somewhere and I did most of it from that time on. We organized branches in Los Angeles and San Diego and Sacramento and we'd take organizing tours. Sometimes I went along, sometimes I didn't.

At one time we had something like a thousand members, not all scientists, of course. Anybody who wanted to could join. I remember there was an old man in Nevada who hadn't any money and he used to send rabbits he'd kill. Once a rabbit arrived on Saturday, when we weren't there, and when we opened the door Monday morning, it was horrible. It was like a grave. There was another old man, in Georgia, an old Spanish War veteran who would sometimes be paid five dollars for someone to sleep in his bed while he slept on the floor. He'd send us the five dollars, which was very touching.

The League lasted until 1932, when Maynard's health got so bad that he couldn't go on with it. We just had to let it go, and by that time it was long after the Scopes trial. About this time, too, I was having my first book published.* And, of course, I was still working for the Federated Press.

The 1934 general strike is one that I shall never forget because it was when Maynard had his stroke and I was going in to San Francisco every day and covering the strike. I'll never forget that. There were four months when I was doing all that and was also the nurse and the cook and the housekeeper. For some unknown reason, after he began to get a little better after his first stroke, our doctor thought it would do him good to have all his teeth pulled. So I'd bring him over on the ferry and go on the Market Street car. He would always walk, but he couldn't talk. We'd see long lines of strikers coming out. He died in June, right in the middle of the strike, just before the general strike. He was only sixty-one. The day he died I sent in my story, as usual.

During the general strike I tried to get in as close as I could to cover it. I remember very well when the strike lasted three days there were funny signs in people's store windows saying "Going fishing" or something like that. The small shops closed. There were no street cars. The department stores closed. Everything was absolutely dead for about three days. I was at "Bloody Thursday." † There was a kind of bridge over the Embarcadero, and I stood on that and could see the corner of Stewart and Mission. I was standing as near as they let any civilian stand so I could report just what happened. The police shot these two men down. I didn't see it, but I saw the police mob up and when they threw the tear gas it came up to where I was standing on the bridge.

After Maynard's death, I went to Honolulu for a long time with close friends of mine who are now dead, and then I went back East. That was the last time I went back home, for my mother's eightieth birthday. I was to come back the next year

---

* *Love Children* (biography), published 1931.

† On July 5, 1934, two striking members of the longshoremen's union were killed and one hundred others injured during a battle with police. In retaliation, a general strike was called which paralyzed San Francisco for four days.

for their golden wedding, but she was dead before then. I returned to San Francisco in 1935 and that's when I became involved in writing a complete history of Tom Mooney from birth until 1935.

What happened was that Mooney heard the Communists were going to get out a book on the case. Sometimes he was chummy with them, sometimes he wasn't. At that time he wasn't. So he wanted his own biography, and I was paid twenty-five dollars by the Defense Committee to go up to San Quentin. By that time I had begun to write a little on criminology and I knew Warden Duffy. His sister, Duffy-Turner, was a very well-known novelist and I knew her well.

For several months I went up to San Quentin every week. Mooney told me what he wanted said, and I had my questions prepared. I wasn't allowed to take notes, though, so when they took him away I'd go down to the ladies' room and write down everything I could remember. About a hundred copies were made of the book and they were sent all over the country.

I hated Mooney. Everybody did who knew him. I got to know Frank Walsh, the distinguished New York attorney who came out here free of charge to help defend Mooney. He had two ambitions. One was to get Mooney free because he was obviously framed, and the second was to push the son of a bitch in the bay. That was about the way we all felt. Of course, there were people like poor Rena and his sister Anna, who got to be a good friend of mine, and his old mother. I knew the whole family and everybody connected with it. Our lives were all interlocked over the years. Sometimes in strange ways. I remember covering the tenth-year memorial of the U.N. in 1955 and running into Tom Mooney's sister, Emma, who was acting as a waitress in the canteen.

After the Mooney project, I became one of the few non-relief workers on the Writers Project for the WPA, from 1936 to 1939. That's how I happened to be on the editorial board of the California guide. I wrote up all the big cities. In fact, my book *They Were San Franciscans* was originally a WPA project, and then after the Writers Project died, I got possession of it myself and had it published in the regular way.

By 1939 they were trying to weed the Communists out of the WPA, so there was more or less a battle on, especially since the old-line Communists were willing to perjure themselves and deny they had ever been members of the party. I found out that it was one of these crypto-Communists who reported to the supervisor that I was spending all day at the Bridges Deportation hearings, which, of course, I was covering for the Federated Press.

Paul Johnson, who was the last supervisor before the WPA died, called me into his office. He was a very strait-laced arbitrary kind of man and he informed me that I had committed a felony and I could be sent to the penitentiary. I told him that if that was the way he felt, I didn't belong in the project. We used to say you "were separated." You weren't fired, you were separated. So I separated, that's all. That was the last steady job I had except that during the war I spent two years doing public relations, working with a man I'd known from the Newspaper Guild.

By then, though, I was actually earning a sufficient living as a free-lance writer. I wrote stories, I wrote articles, and as I developed new interests I got better acquainted with the periodicals that dealt with them. Whatever I was doing, I wrote about. I can't remember exactly how I got involved in crime writing, unless it goes back. I was always interested in crime, and then Maynard did a great deal of important pioneer work on the history of the death penalty. Largely through him, I wrote a number of articles. A convict at San Quentin wrote me that he read my article "What Do Detectives Detect?" making fun of the stupid things they do. He was heartily in favor of the article and told me that one time when he was on the lam and his picture was in every post office, he attended a detectives' convention in New Jersey and drank in the bars with them and nobody ever paid any attention. Well, I got to know him very well, Ernest Booth, one of [H. L.] Mencken's discoveries. I got to know several others through Ernest and by going up every week to see Mooney. I just got to be fascinated by crime, and back in the 1920s I was writing a whole series of detective stories for the pulp magazines. I guess I've always been interested in crime. Maybe I'm a born criminal myself, I don't know, getting my catharsis that way.

I didn't start the science fiction work until much later, about 1938 or 1940. I think that was largely because of Maynard's work in science. I'd type his things and read his books and just got interested in it. I still do more mystery than I do science fiction. I sort of alternate. I'd rather write true crime more than anything else, but there's nowhere to sell it now, so I have to let it go. I'm interested in the psychology of the criminal, and if he's a real person, naturally it's more interesting.

Over the years I've written just about everything. When people ask me what kind of writing I do, I say, "I do hash." I've written everything except Westerns and love pulps. I even wrote confessions for a while. My nonfiction was largely biographies and literary history. And, of course, I did all kinds of articles and was a labor journalist for thirty-five years.

Actually I was in one of the few professions where there is no sexual discrimination. I have never heard an editor say, for instance, that he didn't want a story because it was by a woman. There are people who write what they call ladies' novels, especially those mawkish Gothic things that other writers make fun of. But the women are just as mocking as the men. No, I should say there's less prejudice. For instance, it's almost impossible for a woman to get a good job as the conductor of an orchestra, but there's no trouble at all about becoming a successful writer if you can produce.

REFLECTIONS ON FEMINISM, WOMAN'S SUFFRAGE AND WOMEN'S LIBERATION

The whole suffrage movement, after its earliest days, was divided into two camps, a conservative camp and a liberal camp.

As far as I know, the conservative suffragists were interested in nothing else. They weren't feminists, really. I mean, they didn't care much about working conditions or birth control or anything of that sort. They were just after the vote.

The liberal camp was more or less favorable to other causes, like the birth control movement, but nobody active or prominent in the women's suffrage movement ever endorsed abortion or anything of that sort. That would have been fatal. Even if they believed in it personally, they wouldn't do a thing with it. It would have ruined the whole movement, besides themselves. Remember, they were not a radical group, they were liberal. They were only left as compared with the extreme right. Most of the feminist leaders, anyway, were interested in nothing but feminism. They might be interested in related things. Many, like Lucretia Mott, were Quakers, and the Quakers— the Eastern Quakers, not the Nixon Western Quakers—were always socially minded. They were generally fairly open and tolerant and had views on other economic matters, but it took so much of their strength and energy and interest just to speak up for women that they just didn't have time to think of anything else.

The old-time feminists go way back, keep on going back to the 1840s. And usually they believed in a lot of other things that the more respectable didn't, like free love. And a good many of them were actually anarchists. Of course, Emma Goldman lectured regularly on birth control and Margaret Sanger was an anarchist in her early days.

My own feminism just came from my own emotional stand. I became a feminist at the age of six, and ever since then, I was always on the side of the girl against the boy. Since that was the period when you read all the classics, and I was too busy getting acquainted with every well-known author, it wasn't until after I graduated from college that I started reading feminist literature and writers like Charlotte Perkins Gilman. One thing leads to another, a great many books have bibliographies and look interesting, and so you go from one to the other.

Until the modern women's lib movement, though, you rarely

heard the word "feminism." I don't think most people would have understood what it was. I think in the minds of a great many people who would have called themselves liberal, feminism was a fighting word. It belonged too far to the left. They weren't radicals, politically. And it was the political radicals who were also feminists. I think that's probably the fundamental reason that the movement died after 1920. A great many people who wanted the vote didn't want anything else, so when they got the vote they were satisfied.

I also think that women expected too much from the vote. You know, politics was going to be purified and everything was going to be lovely as soon as women got the vote—which was pure nonsense! My argument always was that we're human beings and citizens and we have a right to vote. I never thought that women legislators would be any less corruptible than men, because we're all human together and we have all kinds.

I think that is one of the chief reasons that a good many people who had worked hard for suffrage gave up in disgust and despair. They found that they weren't entering into an Elysium. Then, of course, we've had two world wars since then and two private wars. World War II was the time that "Rosie the Riveter" appeared.* I imagine that a great many of those people who had never been interested in anything except their own private lives were turned out summarily at the end of the war and men got their jobs; I imagine a good many of them began to think of women as women. But I don't have any definite answer at all as to what happened, except that you know how people are—they get tired, they get bored, and then they get out.

But I have known women all my life who were lifelong feminists. For instance, Congressman William Kent's widow, an active suffragist who gave Muir Woods to the country, was an old-time feminist from way back. I remember going up to her

* Women who went to work in defense industries during the war were dubbed "Rosie the Riveter" by the popular press, where they were regularly pictured in coveralls, carrying their tools and lunch pails. The term came to mean women war workers.

house and making a speech once to a little group of old-time feminists. At one time I did a great deal of public speaking and was actually a professional lecturer. It was mostly women, to women's clubs, and you were supposed to talk about anything that they were interested in. I would usually give them a not too strong dose of the kind of thing that they wouldn't hear from anybody else. My subjects, otherwise, would be according to under what auspices I was speaking.

But this particular group were feminists and still identified themselves as such. I think this was about 1929 or 1930; it was the day our house caught on fire. An old lady of ninety-three drove me back and told me about her fight for feminism seventy years before. These women were all very old people and they weren't doing much of anything. I don't think there were more than a half dozen at that meeting.

I can remember, though, occasionally at Maynard's lectures there used to be an old lady who came up from Palo Alto who had been a lifetime feminist. In the question period she always managed, no matter what the scientific subject, astronomy or anything, to get it around somehow to women.

There were plenty of feminists and you knew who they were and they wrote individually, or spoke individually, but there was no organized movement outside of birth control. There was nothing for them, they had no organ, no avenue, to speak through. All they could do would be on their own and it was only writers you'd know about, because they could write.

But most of the women, especially the more conventional ones, joined or organized the League of Women Voters. They were the kind of people who thought that once we got suffrage, politics was going to be purified because women were so holy and saintly and all that. They found out very soon that women were just as corrupt. I think a lot of them were made quiescent after that. Of course, there were always some who kept it up. Then when the bohemian crowd began to make Greenwich Village famous, most of those people, like Edna St. Vincent Millay, were also militant feminists.

I didn't change any of my own feelings but there wasn't anything, no movement, nothing to join. The only thing was that if, individually, anybody had anything to say, I told them what I thought. I wrote dozens of letters that were published in newspapers. Whenever anybody would make an anti-feminist remark, I'd call them on it. I had an article or two or three, mostly in Midwest farm women's magazines, bearing more or less on the subject. I remember one, "Do Women Really Want Children?" It was surprising the sort of responses I got. These were all farm women from Iowa and Kansas. I got a lot of anonymous letters that were scurrilous. I remember one that started "You creature in the form of a woman." But the ones that were signed were from the farm wives and they were almost entirely commendatory. One woman wrote that she had eight children, that she never wanted any of them, that she never liked any of them. I knew the so-called maternal instinct was nonsense. I probably wrote half a dozen articles on more or less that line and always from a feminist slant, even if it wasn't the exact subject. Some of my science fiction is more oriented towards feminism; for instance, my collection *Xenogenesis* is all about matrimony, reproduction and sex on other planets and in the future.

I did at one time ask one publisher's representative whom I knew about doing a book on feminism. It was about the time that women's lib began. I think it was at the time that Betty Friedan's book came out. I had an idea for a book and he was very much interested in it, but New York finally said, "No." They didn't think there was enough interest. Afterwards, there was a terrible flood of such books, but I was busy doing other things by then, so I just dropped it.

I was closely connected to Planned Parenthood, to what we first called birth control, and in the 1920s I used to write for Margaret Sanger's later magazine, *Birth Control Review*. I've kept my interest up, and when Patricia McGinnis * started her work here for free abortion, I helped with writing their publicity.

But except for Planned Parenthood, I don't remember any-

---

* One of the leaders of the San Francisco Planned Parenthood movement.

thing. Until women's lib started, there wasn't anything in the way of an organization. I still don't know why there was this sudden recrudescence in recent years. I mean, there was not one event, unless it was the fact of the two big wars and that women for the first time did things they had never done before and didn't want to give them up.

I certainly don't like some of the extreme manifestations of today's movement. I mean, they seem foolish. The ostentatious anti-man business and some of the demonstrations seem to me to be a trifle exaggerated. But I'm all for women's lib, naturally. In fact, I'm a member of NOW (National Organization for Women) and have been from the beginning.

I remember I went out to a NOW affair in the courtyard of the First Unitarian Church about three years ago. There were all kinds of stands, you know, with literature and things. There was one girl who had made elaborate printed poems on big plaques, printed by hand. I'd never seen anything quite so vicious as one of them she had posted, very anti-man. I went up to her and said, "Look, we don't hate *all* men. We hate male chauvinist pigs." She said, "They're all male chauvinist pigs."

I think there were many respectable middle-aged women who had always thought of themselves as feminists who were scared off by that kind of thing. As the more permissive era arrived, too, many of the older women began worrying that there were only lesbians. They scuttled out in a hurry for fear that they might be considered lesbians. This was just before the most recent movement, the women's lib movement, started.

All kinds of women are feminists. Some of them are lesbians, some of them are bitter, soured spinsters who have been rejected all their lives and are taking it out and hating men, and some of them are people who are intellectually convinced. A good many of them, I hope, are people like myself who think of human beings as human beings, not distinguished by color or sex or age or anything else. In other words, the kind of psychology that is against minority status of any kind, just the same whether it is against blacks or against women or against Jews or against Catholics.

I think the so-called women's lib movement is very different from the earlier movement. To begin with, it has a much better background atmosphere. People are much more receptive than they used to be. It used to be just a grinding fight, and male chauvinism was practically universal. In fact, there was even a lot of female chauvinism: "I'm perfectly happy, and Nora * didn't bang the door" and all that. It was only the political radicals who weren't like that. As far as I know, every political radical I've ever heard of—no matter what he was, Socialist, Anarchist or Communist—has always taken feminism for granted. It wasn't the most important thing to them, but if you asked them, they would have always said, "Yes, we agree." But very few of them would do anything in that particular line because they had plenty of other things that they were fighting about. I suppose there's always a tendency, in any group, that if there's domestic work to be done, the women do it. If you'd call it to their attention, they'd be embarrassed and they'd wash the dishes.

I suppose that I feel we have been let down since those early days, but I always realize that there's a great deal still to be done and that we have to keep on doing it. I'm always afraid that with every movement you get that first enthusiasm and then you accomplish a few things and then you get tired. Though I think the women's lib movement has a lunatic fringe, as every movement has, I think it is a good, solid useful movement and I certainly hope that it's not going to attenuate or die out.

* Reference is to Nora in Ibsen's *A Doll's House*.

LAURA ELLSWORTH SEILER

In the Streets

Laura Ellsworth Seiler, at the age of eighty-two, though not an active participant in the current women's movement, closely follows its literature. She is particularly interested in vocational guidance for women as a result of her own long professional career. She has written a manual, as yet unpublished, on career management for women.

Laura is an attractive, perfectly coiffed, gray-haired woman who appears twenty years younger than her actual age. Her manner is very proper and businesslike, and her speech seems to bear the mark of lessons in elocution. Despite this outward formality and a clear reluctance to discuss her private life in any detail, Laura was quite cordial and eager to share her suffrage experiences.

When we recorded the first of two interviews in October 1973, Laura had just moved into a retirement facility in Claremont, California. Her apartment was tastefully and simply decorated with the artifacts obtained uring her extensive travels. Among her books were several on the suffrage movement, a few on today's women's movement and a scrapbook covering her career in advertising. Though she is on congenial terms with the other inhabitants of the retirement facility, it is obvious that her life has been very different from the lives of most of the others and that her support of feminist goals is not shared by them.

Laura Seiler is an accomplished public speaker and a gifted storyteller; it is difficult to capture in print the marvelous vitality and perfect timing of her accounts. Nevertheless, it is hard to imagine that this well-groomed, dignified woman participated in that part of the suffrage struggle that today might well be called "guerrilla theater."

A PROPER BACKGROUND

All of my ancestors, on both sides, so far as I know, were in America before 1700. So it's a straight New England background until the generation in which I was born. My grandfather had a period of retirement because of a breakdown in health. When he decided to practice law again, he settled in Ithaca. It was a family joke that he moved to Ithaca because he had four daughters and a new college had just opened, that he moved to Ithaca to marry them off. Two of them did marry Cornell men. So even though they were in New York, I always thought of my family as New Englanders in exile. It seemed to me that they bore down more heavily on New England traditions than if they'd still been living there.

I was born in Buffalo in 1890, but when I was only six months old my mother and father separated and we moved to my maternal grandfather's household in Ithaca. My grandfather had been a judge, and though I don't think he was anything very important in the way of a judge, he was always called Judge Ellsworth. The household consisted of my grandmother and grandfather, a maiden aunt, my mother and the three of us children. I was the youngest. My sister was seven years older than I, and my brother five.

The house was very large. That was the day, of course, when you still had sleep-in servants. Down in the rather large, halfway basement was the dining room, a large pantry, a huge kitchen and what was called the maids' sitting room. It was called that because it was furnished so that they could have fun there. Beyond that, there was an enormous cellar. There was an outside entrance to the maids' sitting room so that their guests could come and go, and that's where the deliveries were made, too.

The first floor had a big central hall, a music room, a library, front and back parlors, and a very large bed/sitting room and bath for my grandfather and grandmother. On the other side was another bedroom with a room off it which was used for storage.

Up on the second floor there were one, two, three bedrooms and a bath in the front of the house, and what was then called the sewing room. Then you went down a flight of steps to a door, and there were one or two rooms for servants, and a big storage room, out of which came the most peculiar things when we had to break up the house (among others, a straw frame for hoopskirts). I don't think anything had been taken out of the room for twenty-five or thirty years.

When we first came home to my grandfather's, my mother was very ill, and for a while they weren't quite sure she was going to recover. But then she grew stronger. Of course, in those days it was unusual for a woman to be divorced, and I think that my mother, when she returned to the bosom of an orthodox Episcopalian family, was definitely made to feel it was improper; this living away from the husband was not the thing to do.

I definitely suffered very much when I was a small child because my sister told me, very early, that I must not ask my mother any questions about it. So I really hadn't the remotest idea where my father was or what was the matter with him. It bothered me a great deal. Some of the children might have had fathers who worked in Buffalo or someplace like that but they came home on weekends. I was the only one who had no father.

Of course, I have since thought that, in spite of the enormous disadvantages of not having a father, it was probably also partly responsible for my somewhat more friendly and less critical attitude toward men. I really never, in my family, encountered the thing known as a dominating male. My grandfather then was too old and too mellow, and, of course, charming with us children. He never was the tyrannical sort. I just grew up liking men and never have seen any cause to change my mind.

Grandfather was really the most important person in my group. When we moved into his house he was seventy-four and still practicing law. Later, after he retired, I used to spend a great many hours with him. He mostly sat about in a chair on the porch or in the house. My grandfather was what used to be called a "freethinker." He got his Phi Beta Kappa key back in 1835, when he was in Union Law School. In those days Phi Beta Kappa was an organization of freethinkers; that's what it means, its philosophy, the key of life. I can't remember any big lectures on ethical subjects, but I do think his attitude must have somehow been bred into me. It seems to me that very early in my life I realized that you didn't judge people by what they had, but by what they were. I have an idea that these things were offshoots of my grandfather's conversation and of other things that went on in the house.

My grandfather was a Democrat, and a Democrat in upstate New York was an oddity. He didn't think much of the local papers, so he always had the *Rochester Democrat* and *Chronicle* sent to him. It was a family custom to gather around the table in Grandfather's bedroom while Grandfather read the things he considered important that day. My older sister and brother sat in on these. I was too little—I knew that and never participated.

All the rest of the family were very orthodox Episcopalians, I should say. I can still remember my grandmother asking him to go to church and he, retorting with a grin, "No. I'm glad to pay for the pew, but you go and sit in it."

My grandmother was a rather protected Victorian woman. She was quite an attractive woman, rather small, and led a quite normal social life. My grandfather didn't like very well having people asked to meals. I remember that it had to be arranged with him beforehand, and there were not very many people he liked to have invited. Usually, when people came to the house they were calling on my grandmother, aunt and mother, and we entertained them at the front of the house. Only occasionally were they taken back to my grandfather's room.

I don't remember my grandmother going out to anything like club meetings. They went out to receptions, as they were called in those days. And I also remember that in the winter they had perpetually going what was called duplicate whist.

There were boards just big enough to hold four hands of

cards under elastics. They had a series of them, I would guess probably twenty. As I recall, they had two tables always in the front parlor. And they played the boards all the way through, and kept track of their scores. The boards were shifted one to the right, so they went through again playing the hands their opponents had played, and then compared the scores at the end. That was called duplicate whist, and they did it all winter long.

One of my earliest and most charming recollections of my grandmother and grandfather was when I was quite small. Theoretically the door to my grandfather's bed/sitting room was always closed, and you knocked before you went in. But being small, I disregarded that and swung the door open and discovered my grandmother sitting on my grandfather's lap. I was so surprised. I'd never seen anything like that before in my life.

My mother's life was mostly concerned, of course, with us children. She wasn't too active outside the household, though since she had grown up in Ithaca she had plenty of friends. She didn't do anything special that I can recall in the way of church work, though we all went to church very regularly. One of my happiest recollections is that during Lent I always went with my mother, across the park where our church was, for the five o'clock Lenten services, which I enjoyed very much.

I didn't have any contact with my father or his family until I was eight when, for the first time, we were invited by my grandmother to spend the Christmas in Buffalo. That was the first time I ever saw my father. Then we also went back the year they had the Pan-American Exposition in Buffalo, in 1901. We spent almost the whole summer in Buffalo going to the fair every other day and staying with my grandmother and my father. That was about all, just very minimal contact.

My mother and father were originally just separated. My mother didn't get the divorce until 1900. My grandfather insisted she get it because he felt he wasn't going to live much longer, and wanted that all settled—for matters of the estate, I suspect.

My grandmother died of pneumonia very soon after she and my grandfather celebrated their golden wedding anniversary in 1899. That was a very exciting affair. My eldest aunt came back from St. Louis, where she lived. My grandfather retired about that time, when he was eighty-one or eighty-two. He died two years later, when he was eighty-four, in 1901. The last year or so, we had an old Civil War veteran who acted as companion to him, helping him around.

When we were growing up, it was always taken for granted that we would all go to college. My sister and I were really the first generation of women in my family to go to college. Mother had wanted to be a doctor, but they told her that she didn't have the physique for it. I think many girls were discouraged in that age by telling them that it was too strenuous and they could never do it. So she didn't go to college. She was always quite resentful, I think, that she hadn't. I don't think there was a finishing school in Ithaca in her days. I don't recall that she did anything in the way of a special school after she finished high school.

But we were all infected with the Cornell idea. My father had been a Cornell man, and also students frequently came to call on my sister. It was just taken for granted that we would all go to Cornell. We were always invited to parties at Sigma Phi fraternity, my grandfather's fraternity at Union. I think it was assumed that my sister, at least, would pursue a career. At that time she was utterly devoted to my grandfather, and she herself wanted to be a lawyer. I think she must have discussed it quite often with Grandfather. She abandoned the idea only after she took a year off between her junior and senior years in college and came down and worked for a year in New York. Then it was that she fell in love with Wall Street and decided that she preferred to go into the bond and stock business rather than be a lawyer.

While she was in school, she was determined to do well. She got the Phi Beta Kappa, too, and has always had my grandfather's key. I was so cross that there was only one large key, so that when I got mine, I bought the smallest one there was—it's about an inch long. I was furious that I couldn't have my grandfather's.

When my sister was a student at Cornell, Nora Stanton Blatch, Harriet Stanton Blatch's daughter and the granddaughter of Elizabeth Cady Stanton, was also a student there. They were great friends. I can remember Nora coming to dinner and much discussion of suffrage and so forth. Nora was in and out of our house in 1903 or 1904 when I was still in high school. So it was no surprise when my sister graduated that she should take a very active part in working for suffrage in New York.

I don't think my mother and aunt were much involved in these discussions, though my mother, being very maternal, was sympathetic about suffrage. I would never say that she was a confirmed suffragist; I don't think it would ever have occurred to her if her daughters hadn't been so much interested.

I remember something I thought was quite funny that happened when I was in high school. The speech teacher thought it would be highly instructive to have a debate on woman's suffrage. She picked out two girls, of which I was one, to do the affirmative, and two boys to uphold the negative. And we had a spirited debate before the school assembly. The really funny thing was that in the heat of rebuttal, I announced in firm tones, "The more responsibility you give women, the more they'll have," and there was a burst of howls from the audience, and I couldn't imagine for the moment what I'd said that was so funny. I heard about that for years afterwards.

Well, we won the debate, but then I was not especially interested in suffrage. I don't remember being interested in it again until I was in college. One day the boy that I was engaged to—somebody had said something about the law about suffrage —I heard him saying, rather smugly, "Laura doesn't believe in suffrage or any of that nonsense," and all of a sudden, I knew I did! That must have been around my junior year, and I forthwith started the Suffrage Club at Cornell among the coeds.

I didn't go to Cornell until 1908, though I graduated from high school in 1907; Cornell didn't take girls until they were seventeen, so I had to wait a year. I spent the winter of that year down in Panama, from about October till February. My father was an architect and he was the official estimator on buildings for the Canal Zone when they were building the canal. My grandmother had been down there with him, and he thought it would be very nice if I came down and spent the winter with my grandmother and him. So I did that, not doing anything special, just having a lot of fun.

I got back just in time to take the last semester in high school again and then I took some postgraduate work. The following autumn I went to the University. I took an arts course, as my sister had done. My brother was both an engineer and a naval architect. I took the number of courses in modern languages to get by for my major. I just took the courses that interested me: evolution, comparative religions, lots of philosophy, some psychology. Every year, when I took my list of courses to be okayed by my faculty adviser, he would heave a large sigh and say, "I suppose if you don't intend to teach, it doesn't matter, because this is a salad course."

I got Phi Beta Kappa, for reasons that were a great surprise to me, since I had not especially concentrated on high marks. Meeting one of my professors coming up the hill one day, I expressed my surprise. He said, "Well, it was kind of a relief to be able to vote for somebody who hadn't always had her nose in a book."

I expected to do something after I graduated. My sister would never have let me get to that point without a definite idea that I was going to have a career. I wouldn't say that I had any clear idea, though, because years afterwards, when I was invited back to Cornell to make a vocational speech to girls, the dean of women said to me laughing, "Laura, do you know what you put on your application when you came in? As a freshman, you were asked what you intended to do. You put down that you intended to be a teacher, and the next question was why, and you said, 'Because they have such long summer vacations.'"

I definitely was engaged when I left Cornell, and I also was definitely planning to do something. You see, when my grandfather's estate was settled, it was divided evenly among his four daughters—except that he subtracted from my mother's part the very considerable sums of money that he had advanced to her during her most unsatisfactory marriage. So my mother with three children got very much less than the other three who had no children, which made it quite tough.

By the time we were ready to come down to New York, I don't think there was very much capital left. I always expected that I would be doing something in the way of earning a living, but I had no very definite ideas about it.

BECOMING AN ORGANIZER
FOR SUFFRAGE

It was while I was at Cornell that I became involved in the suffrage movement. It was a very natural thing for me to be interested in suffrage because of my sister's association with Nora Blatch. My sister graduated in 1908 and went to New York and was the vice president of the Women's Political Union, which was, I think, the most militant of the national organizations. So by the time I went to Cornell, my sister was already working furiously for suffrage in New York.

I wasn't doing anything about it except reading some of the books. Of course, I took time off and went down and marched in the suffrage parade at my sister's behest. I think I probably marched with the Women's Political Union. That was, I think, the 1912 parade which Inez Milholland led, looking very beautiful, mounted on a white horse. There were also about a hundred men in the parade. Believe me, they had courage! Whoo! It took so much more courage for a man to come out for woman's suffrage than it did for a woman. They were quite remarkable.

EDITORIAL

THE HEROIC MEN

The facts are all in print now about the masculine adherents of the woman suffragists who will march in the parade to-morrow. There will be 8oo of them surely. They will represent every trade and profession except the clergy. This is clearly an oversight which should be rectified. There is no lack of clergymen ready to support the cause of votes for women. For the rest the list includes bankers, manufacturers, students, librarians, dentists, musicians, booksellers, journalists, as well as dancing teachers, egg inspectors, capitalists, watchmen, ladies' waistmakers — and authors. A lawyer will carry the banner, and a drum and fife corps will head the division.

This is important news and not to be trifled with. The men who have professed to believe in woman suffrage have always been numerous. But these men are going to do more than profess, they are going to march before the eyes of the more or less unsympathetic multitude. It is one thing to sit on the platform and smile at a woman's meeting, quite another to march behind a gaudy banner to the inspiration of the squeaking fife, in order to indicate one's belief in the right of women to the ballot. The men will be closely scanned, but they will not mind that. They will be called endearing names by small boys on the sidewalk. But doubtless they will study to preserve their gravity. They will not march as well as the women. Only trained soldiers can compete with the amazons in keeping step. There must be strong inducement to make men march in a woman's parade. Some may be looking for customers. We suspect both the waistmakers and the dentists, for instance. But the majority must firmly believe in the righteousness of the cause, and also in the value to it of their public appearance in line. They are courageous fellows. The march of the 8oo may be renowned. We hope they will all hold out from Thirteenth Street to Carnegie Hall, and we extend to all the 8oo our sympathy and admiration.

THE NEW YORK TIMES   SUNDAY, MAY 5, 1912

SUFFRAGE ARMY OUT ON PARADE

Perhaps 10,000 Women and Men Sympathizers March for the Cause.

STREETS PACKED FOR THEM

Cheers for the Women and Some Good-Natured Jesting at the Men.

AGED LEADERS APPLAUDED

They Rode in Flower-Bedecked Carriages— Women on Horseback and "Joan of Arc" Win Plaudits.

Part IX. of this morning's Times consists of four pages of pictures of yesterday's suffrage parade.

Ten thousand strong, the army of those who believe in the cause of woman's suffrage marched up Fifth Avenue at sundown yesterday in a parade the like of which New York never knew before. Dusty and weary, the marchers went to their homes last night satisfied that their year of hard work in preparing for the demonstration had borne good fruit.

It was an immense crowd that came out to stand upon the sidewalks to cheer or jeer. It was a crowd far larger than that which greeted the homecoming of Theodore Roosevelt and the homecoming of Cardinal Farley. It was a crowd that stood through the two hours of the parade without a thought of weariness. Women, young and old, rich and poor, were all banded into a great sisterhood by the cause they hold dear.

THE NEW YORK TIMES   SUNDAY, MAY 5, 1912

EDITORIAL

THE UPRISING OF THE WOMEN.

The parade on Fifth Avenue last evening of possibly 10,000 women of various ages, many of them young and personable, all surely representative of good types of womanhood, for they were obviously healthy and presumably intelligent, will be discussed from various points of view. Most of the comment it provokes will be humorous but amiable. Men generally view the woman suffrage movement calmly, seeming not to care much whether or not the women get the right to vote, and heeding little the consequences of the social revolution which would result from the triumph of the present agitation. A few men believe that the right of suffrage should be extended forthwith to the women. Our observation does not justify the inference that they are wise and thoughtful men, but they are certainly more admirable and entitled to more respect than the men who, believing the contrary, possessed of the knowledge that the vote will secure to woman no new privilege that she either deserves or requires, that the enfranchisement of women must inevitably result in the weakening of family ties, yet look upon the woman suffrage movement complacently and dismiss it with idle, trivial comment.

The situation is dangerous. We often hear the remark nowadays that women will get the vote if they try hard enough and persistently, and it is true that they will get, and play havoc with it for themselves and society, if the men are not firm and wise enough and, it may as well be said, masculine enough to prevent them. The agitation has been on foot for many years. One does not need to be a profound student of biology to know that some women, a very small minority, have a natural inclination to

usurp the social and civic functions of men. But that is not true of a majority of the women in yesterday's parade, or of their thousands of sympathetic sisters who lacked the physical vigor, the courage, or the opportunity to join in the march. Their adherence to the cause is largely factitious, born of much agitation and much false theorizing. There are, however, unhappy creatures to whom the state of being a woman is naturally burdensome. Their influence would not count for so much if their less unhappy sisters, who have no real grievance against Mother Nature or society, would not give them countenance. There are numberless explanations of the conduct of otherwise nice and womanly women in this matter. There are few that can fairly be called "reasons."

We are told by some sages that education has made women discontented. It has made men discontented, too, for that matter. The equality of opportunity all men possess in this country has not allayed the discontent. There is no reason to suppose that the right to vote would allay feminine discontent. Granted the suffrage, they would demand all that the right implies. It is not possible to think of women as soldiers and sailors, police patrolmen, or firemen, although voters ought to fight if need be, but they would serve on juries and elect themselves if they could to executive offices and Judgeships. Many of them are looking forward to an apportionment of high offices between the sexes. This may seem preposterous to some of the men who chose to smile complacently at the aggressiveness of the women's rights adherents, but it is true. It is a state of things these men will have to cope with before they die if they do not arouse themselves and do their duty now.

We have said that the ballot will secure to woman no right that she needs and does not now possess. That is a true statement, and we hold that it is not debatable. Woman is thoroughly protected by the existing laws. Her rights as a taxpayer, a holder of property, are not in danger. Her dower rights are scrupulously upheld in the probate courts. In her pursuit of all the privileges and duties of men, however, she is deliberately endangering many rights she now enjoys without legal sanction. . . . It will be a sad day for society when woman loses the respect she now receives from all but the basest of men. Yet yesterday's parade demonstrates that she holds male courtesy in slight regard, or would, if we were willing to regard the parade as a demonstration of the feelings and opinions of all our women.

Millions of men labor all their years to keep up a home, of which a woman is mistress. Poor enough the home may be, and the measure of toil its upkeep demands of the man may age him

prematurely and deprive him of all the freedom which he instinctively desires. But most men throughout the civilized world have been doing their duty as husbands and fathers, as citizens, according to their lights. That the triumph of woman suffrage would tend quickly to change the point of view of these millions of plodding men is not to be doubted. If woman declares her independence, and forces the State to recognize it, the cry of the men will be "Let her uphold it and enjoy it as best she may." From the beginning "man that is born of woman" has been "of few days and full of trouble." Presumably he will continue to be born. Presumably he will continue to respect his mother, as ISHMAEL did. But with the opportunity afforded to him by the refusal of woman to recognize his manhood as a title of supremacy in the world's affairs, he will be at pains to avoid some of the troubles which he has hitherto regarded as part of his heritage.

This we hold to be inevitable. Let the women who are not yet avowed suffragists consider it. Above all, let the complacent multitudes of men who have accepted the full responsibility of citizenship consider it. There were, at most, 10,000 women in yesterday's parade. If their cause triumphs there will be 700,000 women voters in this municipality. Have the 10,000 thought much about the measure of influence they would exert if the

whole number voted under the
control of their associations and

environment and as their intelligence impelled them to?

There were not very many people interested in suffrage at
that time. But, I started the Suffrage Club in 1912. I don't
know whether it was my idea or whether my sister asked me
to do it. I just called, or put up a notice, or something. I didn't
live at the dormitory; I lived at home. I called a meeting in our
general auditorium and explained to them about the suffrage
movement.

Cornell at that time had only about three hundred women
and some four thousand men. I'd say we probably had a
pretty big club before we got through. And, of course, it went
on after I left. I should guess that we must have had at least
seventy-five, something like that. It was fairly popular with the
women.

Of course, we were not very aggressive suffragists. We met in
the women's dormitory and mainly just had meetings by ourselves. But after the group had been going for a while, we staged
a debate. One of the men students came over to see me one
day to say that his mother, who was a prominent anti-suffragist,
was coming to visit him. He asked if I would like to arrange a
debate while she was there. I was entitled to ask that one of the
big auditoriums be set aside, and so I said, "Yes, I would."

I didn't think it was suitable for a person my age to debate
his mother. This was fairly early in the suffrage movement and
there was no suffrage group in Ithaca. If there was, I would have
asked the head of that. But the Women's Club was vaguely
interested in suffrage, so I consulted the president, the wife of
an instructor and she agreed to debate. She was a very earnest
young woman but not a skilled debater.

The woman who came from New York was a true *grande
dame* indeed, with all the polished manner to go with debating.
Sitting up on the platform, as chairman, I became congealed
with horror because what was developing was a hair-pulling
performance, sending the audience into fits of laughter. The
woman from New York would say, "Now my esteemed op-

ponent has said so-and-so," and the other woman, who was by then furious at the customary misleading statements that anti-suffragists specialized in, would say, "What she says is not so!" or, "That's a lie!"

I, of course, grew frantic realizing that the people in the audience, many of whom were townspeople as well as students, were going out to laugh their heads off. Certainly, it was going to do suffrage no good. I also knew chairmen were supposed to keep their mouths shut, but I was a suffragist and I wasn't going to let this thing go down the river!

So I rose at the end and thanked both of them and then proceeded, rather crisply, I think, in about five minutes, to point out to them the difference between personality and causes. They could leave either confirmed in reaction with the anti-suffragists or planning to go ahead with the suffragists. And, as sometimes happens in those circumstances, I was so convinced that I was right that I felt about eight feet tall and I've never spoken better—with the result that I got an ovation at the end.

It did result in more women students joining our suffrage organization. All together it turned out well in the end, except that I received a letter of reprimand from my sister, who said, "Well, I hope you realize now all you did was to furnish an audience and a platform for an anti-suffragist." But I continued to believe that people should hear both sides of the story. It may not have been good maneuvering, but I thought it was the honest way to do it.

Then, in 1913, when I graduated, the Women's Political Union decided that it would be a very good thing for me to go and "organize," as they then called it, the two counties of Chautauqua and Cattaraugus in New York State. My mother, who was not a confirmed suffragist, but a very charming Victorian, went along to chaperone me.

Nobody had been in those western counties before. More work had probably been done up in Westchester and places like that, but I think perhaps mine was the first attempt to organize those western counties. They were basically manufacturing towns like Jamestown and Silver Creek and places like that. Of course, there was lots of farming in between. In those days, the population was much, much less than now, and they were small towns with one factory, let's say, or some kind of business in which people worked.

I had a little list given me of people thought to be sympathizers, and I was supposed to go in and organize them and leave a chapter of the Women's Political Union behind to go on working. Ahead of time, I had to send the newspapers a little publicity, telling them what it was going to be about. When I got there, I had to contact these women. In most of the small towns I had the names of three or four women who were thought to be sympathetic. Usually they were definitely upper-class or upper-middle-class, married and in their later thirties or middle forties. They were people who had traveled and for some reason or another had expressed some interest in suffrage. I don't recall any laboring-class women who were ever on that list.

That was very fortunate for us. We were trying to reach the local leaders in small towns and let them conduct the local organization work. It was called an organization trip, and that's just what it was. These contact women would arrange a house meeting for the purpose of forming a local group, and I would talk to the women there and provide them with the materials and tell them how to organize. Then it was up to them to do the local work on all classes.

Then, I had to make a street speech. That was in the days when you could still rent cars where the back went down. So we would rent a car and put an enormous white, green and purple banner across the back. The white was for purity, of course; the green was for courage; and the purple was for justice. That's supposed to be the explanation that we gave. The banner was a big one, and it covered practically the entire back. It made a very effective device for public speaking. I would stand up on the back seat to make the speech. Of course the most difficult moment for a street speaker is getting a crowd. As in all small towns, the most popular corner of the street was the one that held the bar. I always directed the chauffeur to stop just outside the bar.

My mother, who was small and charming and utterly Victorian and convinced that all good things started with the favor of the male, would go through the swinging doors, and say, "Gentlemen, my daughter is going to talk about suffrage outside, and I think you would be interested. I hope you'll come out." And just like the Pied Piper, they would all dump their drinks on the bar and come out and make the nucleus of the crowd.

I was always embarrassed to have to take up a collection. I was convinced they thought we put it in our own pockets. But Mother had no such qualms. She would circulate about giving out the pamphlets and holding out a basket and saying, "I'm sure you want to help the cause," and the folding money would come in. She was invaluable!

My speeches varied according to the type of town. In general, it was on the injustice against women and the fact, also, that the injustice affected men indirectly; it held down the wages of all of them if women were underpaid.

Once, in a small town, I had a very amusing experience. We'd been the guests in the house of a man who owned a factory, a very charming young man and his wife. I made a speech and, in the course of it, I reminded the crowd that the only way men had been able really to affect their wages and conditions was getting together into unions and bringing pressure to bear. A ripple of laughter swept the crowd and I couldn't imagine why until I got back to my host's home. He told me that he had spent all the last year fighting their efforts to form a union. So here I was, under his auspices, advising them to do it.

Well, thinks like that happened. And we also, of course, were aware that there were still dreadful conditions in factories in those days. We bore down on things of that sort. Child labor was by no means unheard of—any more than it is today. We focused on the importance of the vote to change these kinds of social conditions.

I did these street speeches in the evening, after dinner, in order to catch the men off work. The crowd would be mostly working-class men, the people you're likely to pick up in a street crowd, except for a few others that might just happen to be roaming around. In general—how much was due to my good mother, I don't know—I remember considerable enthusiasm for the speech and, also, a great deal of good-natured tolerance on the part of the men. And, as I say, rather good collections. I'm quite sure that that kind of campaigning did a lot of good because we reached people, I'm sure, who were not in the least interested in suffrage up to that moment.

On the whole, I think it was a successful tour. It bore fruit, definitely. We left behind a good nucleus of women who would then start in to plan and to work actively and to do things themselves. And, of course, it gave the central organization a chapter with which to work directly; the chapter could ask questions and get material to us, just the way a political organization would work.

Some of these women that I organized went on into quite extensive suffragist experiences. One of them, I remember, somewhat to my dismay, later joined Alice Paul's group and was hunger-striking in Washington.

I think we spent about six weeks in each of the counties, which made it about the first of September when we got back to New York. There was no question of where we were going. My sister was there, working on Wall Street. My brother was there, too, but I don't remember what he was doing. He had degrees in marine architecture and mechanical engineering. Though he wanted very much to do marine architecture, there was absolutely nothing like that going on when he left college.

I had been engaged and in October we married. At first we lived in the same apartment as my mother and sister. I was already working for the Women's Political Union and continued with that. My husband was not against my doing it. He was a

charming man, a very gentle one, and a very open-minded one
—a very good-natured person. I don't think, left to himself,
that it would ever have occurred to him to advocate suffrage.

SUFFRAGE TACTICS IN NEW YORK CITY

After we settled in New York, I went to work full time for the
Women's Political Union. The president of the organization
was Mrs. Blatch and my sister was the vice president. Mrs.
Blatch, of course, was always in the office, which was just off
Fifth Avenue on Forty-second Street, almost opposite the
library. I think she was the only one of the officers who was at
headquarters all the time. The others all had jobs of their own,
of one kind or another, and were just serving on the board.

It was a fairly good-sized organization and, of course, we had
many, many volunteers. As you know, most of the suffrage work
was done by volunteers. Most were probably in their late thirties
or early forties, though some were older. We had a large roster
of very famous older women who came in and stuffed envelopes
and did things like that.

My job was being head of the Speakers Bureau. I had had
training in Cornell in public speaking. I was training speakers,
giving them their assignments, as well as doing a lot of speaking myself. They were on a voluntary basis and some did much
more speaking than others. We did have, especially at campaign times, a certain number of women who were just taken
on and paid small sums, probably just enough to cover their
expenses. You were supposed to be giving your time and yourself as much as you could afford. The secretaries, of course,
were paid, and I might have been paid a small sum, too, but
I don't remember.

THE NEW YORK TIMES   NOVEMBER 5, 1911

CIRCULAR INCENSES WOMEN AT A RALLY

Handed Out at the Doors, It Calls Suffragists Destroyers of Homes.

NO NAME IS SIGNED TO IT

But Women's Political Union Speakers Charge it to Cuvillier, on Whom the Suffragists Are Making War.

There was an unexpected development at the women's big political rally in Alys Dancing Hall last evening, which marked the close of a campaign the Women's Political Union made to defeat Louis A. Cuvillier, candidate for Assemblyman in the Thirtieth Assembly District.

The development came through an anonymous leaflet handed to the people going into the rally. In large letters it announced that the women suffragists were "Destroyers of Home and Country," and "The Greatest Peril to Civilization and this Government."

The Women's Political Union was the most militant of the suffrage groups. Mrs. Blatch had been married to an Englishman and had lived in England for a time. We, as a society, were much closer to the English groups than were the other American suffrage organizations like Mrs. O. H. P. Belmont's Woman's Suffrage Organization or something like that, or Mrs. Catt's National American Woman Suffrage Association. These groups felt that what the women were doing in England was rather outrageous and they wanted no part of it. Mrs. Blatch, on the other hand, felt that the only way they were ever really going to get anywhere was to exert political pressure.

Consequently, the name of the organization was patterned after the English, which was called the Women's Social and Political Union, and there were friendly relations with the Pankhursts and with many other English people. Mrs. Pankhurst came over and addressed a large dinner meeting. Sylvia Pankhurst and Beatrice Forbes-Robertson also spoke and, I think, we raised money for them at one time or another.

The Englishwomen were very fond of talking about free unions and how their children were going to have hyphenated names. Like Havelock Ellis and his wife, they were going to have houses on opposite sides of the park. They felt that conventional marriage was not right, wasn't fair to women.

I was a little more conservative about things at the time and I felt the family had a place in society and I didn't go along with that. I thought it was kind of funny. But they took it all very, very seriously, you know. There was a whole cult of that sort of thing, especially in England. I think not to any great extent here.

I did meet a few women living in Greenwich Village at the time whom my sister knew, who were living with men without being married to them. You know, there was a certain amount of talk about it but they were still very valuable suffragists. They weren't making as much propaganda about it as the Englishwomen were. The attitudes of the Englishwomen reflected, of course, the much more difficult position of women in England than in America; American women have always had more freedom.

You may or may not recall that famous little curtain raiser of Ethel Barrymore's called *The Twelve-Pound Look*. That was marvelous. It played in England. The twelve-pound look was the cost of the typewriter with which the woman made herself economically independent from her husband—left him as soon as she learned to type. The twelve-pound look.

The Englishwomen generally were much more radically oriented than the Americans ever were. We did no chaining of ourselves to lamp posts, though the nearest approach came later with Alice Paul and her hunger strikers, in 1917. Mrs. Blatch was working on these things long before Alice Paul came into the picture at all. I think Alice Paul carried them to the extreme, and my impression is that she went far beyond anything Mrs. Blatch would have suggested herself.

What I have in mind when I speak of the Women's Political

Union as being the most militant is that earlier, before Alice Paul's activities in Washington, we believed much more in demonstrations, in street speaking and in things of that kind, which I don't remember as being characteristic of the other organizations. For instance, we spoke on street corners every night of the week, using soapboxes with handles on them which every suffragette carried and plunked down on the curbstone. We had to have permits for speaking, but we got them from the police department. Now the other groups may have done street speaking, but if so, I wasn't conscious of it. They mostly spoke in halls. But we believed that you had to get to the people who weren't in the least interested in suffrage. That was the whole theory.

I would say that we had at least ten or twelve women out of our office speaking on street corners every night. As I recall it, there were always two women; one would be the speaker and the other would give out pamphlets and things of that kind. You carried the soapbox until you got to the corner. Of course, it was considered outrageous by many people for women to be speaking out on the street corners. Sometimes, depending on the neighborhood, those soapboxes on which we stood were rather dangerous little things. Things would be thrown down from the roofs. Sometimes stones would be thrown into the crowd. I don't remember anybody actually being seriously injured, but they weren't fun!

But there were lots of funny little things that went on, too. It wasn't all difficult. Once, a tiny little man in very shabby clothes, a clergyman from a parish somewhere out in the wilds of Long Island, came in and asked for a speaker for an evening meeting. Mrs. Blatch brought him out to me.

I had already assigned all my speakers for that evening, so I said I'd have to do it myself. My family was not exactly charmed by my taking these evening meetings, but I did when I had to. He said he would prefer a little older and more experienced woman. Mrs. Blatch came down hard on him and said, "Laura is one of our most experienced speakers," and went back into her office. He was a little crushed, but he began to explain to me how I had to get there. I had to change buses twice and so forth, and also that his wife was in a wheelchair; she'd been in an accident. She was very anxious to have me come out for supper.

After dinner we went over to the church and there was a small group of women. His wife was a very ardent suffragist and she had started this little group. The first thing he did was to ask me to play the Doxology [on the organ]. I had never opened a suffrage meeting with a Doxology before, but I was lucky enough to be able to play it and so I did. The women clustered around afterward and told me all about this wife and I said, "How come the Doxology?" They said, "Well, Mrs. whatever-her-name-was puts more faith in God than in politicians."

The organization was, of course, always trying to think of ideas which would get us publicity. Mrs. Blatch's whole idea was that you must keep suffrage every minute before the public so that it gets used to the idea and talk about it, whether they agree or disagree. It must be something that everybody was conscious of. I think she was quite right.

There were some women reporters who were very helpful to us, and they tried to get us all the publicity they legitimately could. But, of course, they didn't mind how ridiculous the thing was. One of the stunts was to make speeches from horseback.

One morning I was sitting in my office and they came bursting in from Mrs. Blatch's office and said to me, "You ride, don't you?" I said, "I haven't ridden since I left school." "But you do ride and you have a riding outfit? Well, so-and-so is ill. The horses are already ordered and we're going to ride down to City Hall park and make a speech, and you'll have to take her place."

You didn't argue in suffrage. You took orders! I went home and put on my riding habit and came back. By the time I got back, the horses were dancing out on Forty-second Street, very annoyed. I climbed on and they put big boards on the side of each horse announcing a meeting. Of course, the boards didn't please the horses; it hit them every time they moved.

All the sidewalks were lined with people and the buses were

going by. There was much shouting at us. The policemen were furious with us for gumming up traffic. We got down to City Hall park just at noontime; it had been calculated that way.

Everybody came out from their offices, and Nora made a pretty powerful speech from her horse. Mine was behaving very badly by then. I began to say, "Ladies and gentlemen," bouncing up and down. (They were English saddles and I'd never ridden in anything but an army or a Mexican saddle before.) Then, just as I was launching into my speech, I glanced across the square and there stood my astonished and astounded new husband.

At that very moment, a horrible little office boy jabbed a pin into my horse and she *reared*! I hung onto the front of this terrible English saddle and sawed on the curb bit and finally got the mare calmed down. But that was the end of my speech. We then took off back toward the office.

Between all the excitement and the saddle sores from not having ridden in a long time, I was in bed for a day. It was a little difficult to explain to my husband why suffragists had to make fools of themselves. That was the only time I remember specifically upsetting him.

Then we presently did another thing. They decided it would be nice to hire a motorboat and run up and down the shoreline yelling through a megaphone, "Suffrage votes for women," at all the men who were loading cargoes. I was assigned along with Nora for this job. We always took reporters with us when we did things. This time, women reporters evidently had rebelled and we got two men, both of whom were definitely anti-suffrage and *furious* at the assignment.

The man who was hired with the motorboat, which, by the way, was only ten or fifteen feet long, evidently had not been told what we were going to do. When we explained, he said, "Oh, what the men are going to say to you!" Of course, that was perfectly true. As soon as the men began understanding that we were yelling about votes for women, they made replies that you might expect. I acquired a good many four-letter words on that boat trip.

Meantime, as ferry boats went by everybody rushed to the side of the boat and the waves bounced us up and down. Then, a group of men going on a fishing trip thought that it was funny to annoy us. They went around us in circles, leaving each time, tremendous waves behind them until they almost swamped us. Both reporters, I remember, had to bail us out with their hats—just furious every minute. The whole excursion lasted about two or three hours. We were all exhausted and thought we were going to be submerged.

When we finally got back, Nora said, "Now see that you give us a good write-up." I looked all through the papers the next day. There was a *tiny* little paragraph in a column. A few days later I met one of the reporters who said he'd always hated suffragists. I said to him, "You certainly didn't do very well by us in the way of publicity." And he said, "Well, next time just get yourself drowned and I promise you the first page." So there were lots of funny things as well.

I don't remember the Women's Political Union actually endorsing anything outside its own interests. I don't think they could have; the women in it were much too diverse. There were all kinds of women who believed in all kinds of things. The only thing, you might say, that they all believed in was that women ought to have the vote. So, for example, though many of them were very interested and admired Mrs. Sanger very much, that would be an entirely individual affair. She was quite a good friend of my sister's.

But there were many issues we *did* talk about. They were all interested in child labor—which still existed. You may recall, that was the period of the horrible Triangle Shirtwaist Fire * and all that sort of thing. We had a very marvelous woman, Florence Kelley, who was on our board, who was especially interested in the trade union movement for women.

* In 1911, 146 young women perished in the Triangle Shirtwaist Fire. Locked in the shop, on the eighth floor of the building, and unable to escape the fire, they either leaped to their death or were consumed in the flames. This tragic episode did help to publicize the miserable working conditions in the sweatshops.

There were plenty of other abuses of women, too. I remember when I visited my sister for a summer vacation before I was through college. She got me a press card to the old *Morning Telegraph*. The editor sent me on assignments, one of which was the Hobo Convention at which [Eugene] Debs was supposed to appear; he didn't, because I think at that time he was in jail. Bill Haywood came to the convention and spoke in place of Debs. There were lots of reporters there.

We all held a little spoofy meeting when we discovered we were not going to have Mr. Debs. Reporters made speeches and they asked "Sis Hopkins"—which was me—to make one; we all wrote that up for the papers. I remember that the *Morning Telegraph* published two versions of this, one by the man and one by the woman—me—side by side.

What really reminded me of that was that, among other things, the editor told me, for my own education, to visit the women's night court, which I did. I was quite horrified at what seemed to me the disregard of women's feelings and rights. I remember one case, especially. It was the trial of a prostitute, and, no doubt, she was a prostitute. Her lawyer said something about it was her word against the word of the policeman. There were no witnesses. The judge said pontifically, "The word of an officer needs no corroboration." I was enraged! That's the one thing I remember clearly out of that assignment.

That attitude was, of course, general: women were viewed as second-class citizens. There's no two ways about it. Their advice was not taken seriously and their opinions were not given the same weight as those of men. I don't think anybody argues about that anymore. It's still true, of course.

I don't know what all the individual women did in their street speeches. I don't remember the moral superiority of women being borne down on much. I do remember a great argument, following that same workers' meeting I was supposed to write up. I went home with a woman who had been a friend of my sister's, who was much more radical than I, and we fell into a discussion of the single standard. I remember it very well because I was a little shocked at the time. She said, "If we ever do get to have a single standard, it'll be the men's standard and not ours." She spoke from experience, and she was a newspaper-woman.

I don't remember women's moral superiority being especially emphasized. In the first place, we had this little ultra-radical group within the movement. I think it would have been a rather difficult argument to sustain. I certainly never used it in my speeches.

I used often to bear down on what I still believe: that there were certain things affected by politics about which men were relatively unfit to judge, such as things that concerned children, schools, similar things. I felt women should have a much larger voice in controlling these things, and that there were just naturally a whole lot of facets to be considered.

I remember once going to make a speech somewhere, and on the way up there on the train an idea occurred to me and I used it. I picked up a copy of the evening paper and held it up in front of them and took one headline after another and showed how the things talked about in that headline applied to women. I went all the way across the front page and there wasn't a single thing in the news in which women didn't have a stake. That was the thing we tried to get over.

I doubt very much that there was anything you could call a uniform position in our speeches. There was too much diversity among the women involved. I don't think you could have a uniform policy. We had all faiths and all types of people work-ing for suffrage—most diverse. In fact, for me it was a liberal education, meeting the kind of people I'd never come into con-tact with before. Some of them were most admirable. Every once in a while, they'd provoke some funny things.

The daughter of Robert Ingersoll had a house in Gramercy Park and they used to have little committee meetings there. Among others, one of the best workers in certain districts was a young Jewish girl from Russia, as I recall it. She attended a meeting one evening and took off her coat and gave it to the butler. Then she said, "Where is my check?" The butler said haughtily, "It won't be necessary, madam." Of course, that little story went all around with great entertainment.

But it's a very good example of the complete cross-section that we had in the suffrage movement, and I must truthfully say that I never saw any hint of snobbishness. There may have been some here and there, but it seemed to me that we all worked together for this one thing, without regard for anything else.

I was, for instance, assigned to make campaign speeches in the section that was run by this same girl. I went and I did exactly what she asked me, and she said very approvingly, "Well, it's nice to know you really take orders!" I said, "Of course. I came over, as my assignment, to do what you wanted done in this area." Evidently she had encountered others who hadn't been quite so cooperative.

But I do think that all kinds of women were working together for suffrage, with great unanimity on the whole. There was a great feeling of cooperation and admiration among the women who worked together.

I think many of the suffrage leaders, though, were very difficult to work with. It's quite understandable; you certainly have met plenty of what are colloquially called bossy women. They are apt to be women with a great deal of drive, women who get things done. They are very apt to be so sure that they're right that they don't want to waste time hearing arguments against their point of view.

Certainly Mrs. O. H. P. Belmont had a reputation of being difficult. I never worked for her. Certainly I think Mrs. Blatch was. From my point of view, she was very autocratic both in how she made decisions and the way she related to the workers. I violently disapproved of some of her policies. Considering that we were a women's organization, I felt that we should be especially fair in our treatment of employees.

I don't think that Mrs. Carrie Chapman Catt ever had that kind of reputation. I never heard that she did. I think she had very firm opinions, but I always gathered she was a person rather easy to get on with. And Anna Howard Shaw, of course, was a wonderful person. She spoke for us very, very often. I think of her as a national suffragist figure. She stands in my mind with a little group of very fine and prominent women who lent their support to suffrage, but I don't associate her with any special group.

Florence Kelley, too, was quite a marvelous person. I remember doing a brochure in which I had carefully dug out of the library all of the instances where women were discriminated against. When the pamphlet came out, Florence Kelley sent for me and she said, "I wonder if you have any idea how really unfair this pamphlet is?" "It's all there in black and white," I responded. "Yes," she said, "but so often there are the balancing laws against these." I remember her saying to me, "In addition to the dower rights,* there are the things called curtesy rights† which help to offset these. And that's true of all statements. It's true of all the statements you've made." I was crushed. What I had said was true, but it was not true in the sense of the whole truth. I think she impressed that on me forever more.

Actually, I left my job with the Women's Political Union because of my feelings towards Mrs. Blatch. I felt her very arbitrary and I didn't like her too well. So I didn't do the Speakers Bureau job for more than six months. But even after I left the organization, I spoke for them every so often—rather often, as a matter of fact.

FAMILY, WOMAN'S SUFFRAGE, AND A CAREER IN ADVERTISING

I left the Women's Political Union in 1914. Then I had to figure out what I could do. A friend of my sister's came over and they were consulting about what kind of business I could

* Dower rights refer to the legal right to a life estate in a husband's real property which a wife acquires by marriage for her use and the use of her children after his death.

† Curtesy rights refer to the husband's life estate in his deceased wife's property.

enter. Among other things my sister long before had told me, "Don't ever, ever, ever study stenography. What man studied stenography to get started in his job? You'll just get sidetracked, so be sure to say you just don't know it." So I didn't have that to offer to anybody.

I remember very well, this friend of my sister's said, "But you've been doing an awful lot of writing this summer." You see, I had sent advance releases, and then when I got through in the town, I gave them another big interview and a release. So I had been doing a whole lot of publicity writing. The friend said, "Why don't you try the advertising business? You can write copy quite well."

I didn't even know what advertising copy was; they had to explain to me that it was the text of the ad. She gave me a list of agencies and I called on some of them. I presume I looked exactly like Sis Hopkins, fresh down from the country. None of them was at all impressed. The agencies said they preferred people who had retail experience—women, that is.

Then I tried some of the department stores; no, they didn't have any time to try to train anybody like that. By then I got quite annoyed. The only store I hadn't called on was Macy's. I went in and demanded to see the advertising manager and told him about my experience trying to get a job in agencies and stores. And I said, "Now, I will come to work for you for ten dollars a week for two weeks. At the end of that time, both you and I ought to know whether I can write advertising copy." He was so flabbergasted that he hired me. At the end of two weeks, they were running the copy the way it was written. So then it became a real job.

I was there about six months and then I got pregnant. I hadn't really thought about a family, one way or the other; I certainly hadn't planned to have one at that time. My daughter was born in January of 1915, so I must have gotten pregnant quite soon, though I didn't quit work right away.

I was out of business until my daughter was about two and a half. I didn't do much outside the home; I was involved basically with the baby. We had moved out of my mother and sister's apartment, and we went to East Orange. Things were very tight. I've forgotten what my husband's salary was, but it was tiny. Of course, everything cost less in those days. My house allowance was five dollars, I remember, for food, and I wasn't a very good provider—knowing nothing whatever about it. When it got to be Friday, I remember nearly always we had to have cabbage because it was only five cents a head.

We had always had servants of some kind or another and I just never did have anything to do with running a house. I was very lucky because I had a marvelous black woman from Virginia, Emma, who came to work for me. Mother, as I recall it, paid for me to have Emma once a week. Emma told me later that I was the only woman for whom she ever washed in the morning and cleaned all the afternoon. I knew nothing whatsoever about domestic things.

I remember very well the day my sister said to me, fixing upon me a beady eye, "When are you getting back to business?" I, of course, felt mildly surprised, to say the least, and said, "How can I?" She said, "You *should* manage."

Presently, an apartment became vacant right across the hall in the place she was living with my mother. She immediately said, "This is the opportunity to move back here; then Mother can help and it will be much easier for you to get a maid." So that's what we did—moved across the hall from my mother and sister, and Emma came and stayed with us the whole time my baby was growing up. She was marvelous.

So, you see, my sister really shamed me into going back to work. I didn't think it was possible to both work and have a young child, but I discovered, of course, that it was. It was difficult, I have to say. Our apartment had these deep window seats, and I had to walk every morning past that front window on my way to the subway to work. My small daughter used to stand up in the window with the tears running down her cheeks. I used to feel like a dirty dog. It was very difficult. And, yet, I did think it was the right thing to do. My husband didn't make any fuss about my going back to work. I think he was probably rather pleased. He wasn't getting a very big salary in those days, and it was quite helpful to have a second salary.

I had decided I didn't want to go back to the department store field. I did try Macy's first, and I told them I wouldn't work after three o'clock in the afternoon (because that's when the baby came home from the park). Well, they wouldn't hear of that. "You can have hours off in the middle of the day," said one of them, who would like to have had me, "but you've got to be here to sign out with the rest of the employees, and sign in." I said, "Well, I'm going."

Then I began on the agencies again. Now, of course, I had a lot of good copy samples and I didn't any longer look like Sis Hopkins. But most of them would hear nothing about leaving at three o'clock in the afternoon—that was out. I got to one agency called the Federal Advertising Agency. It had nothing to do with the federal government; it had been named that because of the building they happened to be in. They had started out basically as a trade agency and were developing in the consumer field and they'd never had women except as file clerks or typists.

When I said this about three o'clock in the afternoon, the head of the copy department considered it awhile and then said, "Well, we've never had a woman on the staff. Might as well try it. I like your copy." So I was taken on to work with the arrangement that I would go home at three o'clock every day.

After a relatively short time at copy writing, I was made what they called an account executive and did some copy still, but mainly edited other people's copy. I continued my suffrage activities, too, actually until we finally got the amendment through. I spoke occasionally, when they needed a speaker, especially in the evening. Also, when we were trying to get the state measure passed in New York, I took time off and had my daughter looked after and spoke continuously for the last two weeks.

I well remember the attitude of men—both in my office, the

subway and on the street—the morning after that state measure was defeated. They openly jeered! There had never been any discussion about it before, in the office, but there were two or three men who took the occasion to make disparaging remarks the morning afterwards. "Well, I guess we know what we did to you yesterday!" and that kind of thing. But it was a passing phase.

Of course, many women I knew didn't believe in suffrage, either. An awful lot violently disapproved. They thought it a lot of nonsense. I didn't happen to number among my friends any ardent anti-suffragists who did anything about it. Most of them were just plain indifferent and thought it was a great waste of time, that it would just all be the same. And, you know, oddly enough, they anticipated what really happened. Most of my friends said, "This isn't going to make any difference; they're all going to vote the way their fathers and their husbands do anyway." You see, that was the burden of their song. As it happened, that's just about the way it turned out, unhappily.

But I remained interested and involved to the end. I remember when Alice Paul and her group started their demonstrations in 1917. I understood quite well the reasons she did it, and I wasn't ever disapproving. I remember being very horrified at what was done to the women, especially to this very delightful woman from Chautauqua County whom I had enlisted in suffrage and who was one of the hunger strikers. I think everybody was just sort of nauseated over the whole thing; it was so horrible, such a dreadful thing for the women to go through. But I also felt that it was a very admirable and probably a very valuable demonstration. There's no doubt about it, her effort is what precipitated the President's decision to bring the matter before Congress. I think we should give her due credit. I'm very sure that if Alice Paul hadn't carried on those demonstrations, it would have gone on years more before it ever got to the Congress.

I worked again during that final drive, and I do remember that there was a vast celebration when we finally had the fed-

eral amendment approved. Tennessee, I think, was the last one.
But that spread over a long period of time. My daughter would
have been five when that happened.

I don't have any recollection if the Women's Political Union
survived after that. After I fussed with Mrs. Blatch and departed from them and when I went into business, I no longer
was as close to them, organizationally speaking. I can't imagine, though, why they would have stayed on as an organization
because there wouldn't have been anything for them to do, if
you want to put it that way.

At that time, I think it hadn't occurred to a great many
women that once they got the vote, the rest wouldn't be easy.
I think most men felt that. I remember once, when watching
at the polls, I was talking to a Tammany boss who was also
watching. He said, "Of course I'm opposed to woman's suffrage. Once women get the vote, they can get practically everything they want."

That was more or less the attitude. It didn't occur to them
that women's groups were going to break up as soon as the vote
was won. They let their organizations go and most of them
paid no further attention. A very few of them, of course, began
to work in politics, but I think they were few and far between.
From what I know, at least.

I didn't stay involved at all after we got the amendment,
though I did belong to a couple of clubs and a certain number
of business organizations, like the American Marketing Association. I joined the Women's Fashion Group fairly early; that
was necessary. The clubs I belonged to were the Women's City
Club and the Town Hall Club. They were made up of women
who definitely were the suffrage type.

There used to be a very interesting club of unusual women
to which my sister belonged. One of these women had a big
fuss with the head of that club—you can imagine they were all
women with minds of their own—and she broke off and formed
another organization. Later on, after it had been going for
some years, my friend, Blair Niles, insisted on my joining that.
It was called the Query Club, and was extremely interesting

because of the women who belonged to it. Most of them were writers, and one woman was an explorer. They were all quite well-known women, as a matter of fact.

For a while I belonged to the Phi Beta Kappa Chapter in New York, but I got bored with that very quickly. I didn't do that very long. I never have been much of a joiner.

I did continue to do quite a lot of speaking during those years, too. I had to talk very often to boards of directors and things of that kind which you may or may not consider public speaking, but it falls into the same category. Once I went up to Cornell to speak to the coeds. And once I remember going to Philadelphia to address an advertising group. Things like that, but nothing else special.

Eventually I was made a vice president of the Federal Advertising Agency and the head of a department, mostly handling women's things, but not entirely. By then, we had plenty of other women, too. Many were in the copy department. I had several executive assistants. Also, women in other departments, like research, were assigned to me from time to time.

You know, up until World War II, I never did work past three o'clock in the afternoon! I enjoyed it. I could, by condensing my lunch hour, always go to matinées and do all kinds of things. It was very pleasant. Then, when personnel problems grew so difficult in the war, of course I was working till all hours myself.

After I'd been there some thirty years and they were giving me a testimonial dinner, one of the vice presidents stood up and said, "Well, I discovered in the records of the accounting department the other day that you were hired on a temporary basis. I would like to suggest that you be put on the permanent payroll."

I was extraordinarily fortunate. I sometimes think I worked for the only advertising agency I ever could have worked for. I had complete authority. The president discovered, after about five years, that if he'd just let me alone, I would make money for him. So he did exactly that. I was responsible to no one but my clients, really. I sent him memos about what we had decided to do but rarely consulted him in advance.

As I discovered in the course of my life, there were practically no other women in the advertising business who had any such degree of authority. In the big agencies, for instance, one or two of which flirted with me later on, I discovered that everything was *à la* committee; the plan went up here and had to be approved, and went up again and had to be approved. Of course, I couldn't possibly have worked that way. I discussed things with my clients, and came back and dictated the work reports, and got their okays on the estimates, and that was it! I wasn't discussing it with anybody, except occasionally with the research department.

This was very unusual, I must say. I began to appreciate how unusual it was, because sometimes my clients were the bosses of the women who were supposed to have authority. I knew, of course, from my work with their bosses that they didn't. That was particularly true of the women in the fashion group who were always supposed to be sort of heads in their own particular departments. But I discovered in working with them that all the things they did had to be okayed, and I grew gradually to realize how unusual my opportunity was. I became a stockholder, eventually, and I was never really tempted to go to another agency.

I retired in June of 1948. I was worn out with the whole advertising business and I just stayed home for six years. I might have done a little writing here and there, but I didn't do much. I was utterly worn out. I had no idea of going back when I retired.

One day, one of my old clients, one of my smaller clients, as a matter of fact, called me up and was bitterly unhappy with his agencies, and had been ever since I retired. He asked if I would meet him at the Union League Club; he wanted to talk to me about something. I went, and he had his general manager there. He said, "I'm about to go to Europe on a buying trip and you can think about it while I'm gone, but I wish you'd go to some small agency, any one you pick, and make an arrangement with them to work only when you want to and as much as you want to, and take my account to them."

I thought about it. I had been fairly bored in the meantime, I may say. And so I did just that. I didn't go in at all in the months of July and August—we had a place in the country. I worked about three days a week the other months, perhaps four or five hours a day, whatever was necessary to handle his accounts, basically. I did some other things for them, too. That was for four years.

Then my husband was ready to retire. So I went too. We began to travel a great deal, mostly in Europe. My husband is a European and we had most of our friends over there. (I had, by the way, been divorced in 1928 and married my second husband in 1929.) We'd always been going back and forth. Right after he retired we spent the winter studying at the Instituto de Allende in Mexico, and then the summer at our place in Bucks County. The next year we went to California to try to make up our minds whether we wanted to live out here, and we drove all over. We ordered a cottage at Mount San Antonio Garden, and in 1960 we went abroad for a year until it was ready. We've lived in California since, though traveling a lot, until recently.

FEMINISM, SUFFRAGE
AND WOMEN'S LIBERATION

Looking back, I realize how great an influence my sister had on me. For instance, I don't think I ever would have taken public speaking in college if it hadn't been for my sister. She won the prize for the Woodford Oration for an original speech she titled "Men, Women and Human Beings." I came along and survived the competition and was, what they called, "on the stage"; I was one of the eight speakers on both the Eighty-sixth Memorial and the Woodford Oration. I didn't win either one of them, much to my sister's chagrin. The title for my original oration was "Crimes against Criminals."

Then, too, I think the emphasis on a career must have probably come from my sister. After all, she had gone ahead and done it and was getting to be quite well known. I certainly don't think I would have gotten those ideas growing up in Grandfather's house. In fact, I would think that the whole attitude of the family at that point would have been that you married and stayed home and had children. And if you were a maiden aunt, you would stay always in the home. I think it was assumed that my Aunt Lil would always live in my grandfather's house. I would say that that was the pattern of a perfectly orthodox Episcopal family.

Economics might have been a part of it, but unquestionably my sister would never have allowed me to think of living without doing some work. My daughter thinks that I would have climbed the walls if I had tried to stay home, but I think it would have been very easy for me to give up after I had the baby. I remember how taken aback I was when my sister suggested that I return to work. To her, of course, the arguments were absolutely unanswerable. She just is, and always was, a feminist. She did all kinds of things, including starting the Women's Bond Club on Wall Street.

I don't think it ever occurred to me to call *myself* a feminist. I was a suffragist. "Suffragist" is how we spoke of ourselves. It was mostly the newspapers, I think, that called us suffragette and that was an attempt to put us down. When you said "feminist," I thought of people like Olive Schreiner, Mrs. Pankhurst, Charlotte Perkins Gilman. They were so interested in the one thing that they hardly had time for other things. I think that always, all my life, I have always wanted to be interested in a great many things—just like my courses in college. Of course, that's the reason those women got things done, because they did channel all of their interests in one direction.

No, I never thought of myself as a feminist. In fact, all my life, until I was retired, I had more men friends than women. This was partly because of my choice of business. And I always got on extremely well with men. I have ascribed that, truly or not, to the fact that I grew up with absolutely no feelings of having been put down, as it were, by a male and I never have felt that way. Consequently, I don't have any of the bitterness that many women, I'm sorry to say, in women's lib have.

In spite of the fact that my sister was also very popular with boys, I think that, in some way, I associated "feminist" with a bitter anti-male position. I never thought of it, really, in college. I discovered very early that if you danced well and skated well—and I was a fancy skater—and did such things, that boys were also very pleased to discover that you could *think*. I was never brought up to feel that you had to pretend to be an imbecile to be attractive. I always got the kind of response I expected. The same thing was true in business. I can only remember twice when there was an attempt made to what you would call "put me down."

One of them, oddly enough, came about in a very curious way. I had become a little distressed at how rapidly the things we learned in college became obsolete. I wrote up to the president of Cornell and suggested that perhaps when twenty-five-year reunions came around it might be a very good idea to set aside at least one day and arrange workshops with the heads of departments, particularly the scientific departments, in which the changes had been the greatest, so that the alumni could be brought up to date. And they could say, "This is what you were taught in physics when you were in college; this is what we think now."

He thought it was a good idea, and he wrote down to the man who was the chairman of the twenty-five-year reunion of men that year. He came to call on me. He listened in a rather supercilious way to this idea, and when I was all through he said, "Where did you get the idea?" I said, "The same place where most of my ideas come from—out of my own head! Good evening." I was enraged. That is one of the few times I can remember. Otherwise, I have always found men very open and willing to meet you on your own grounds.

It's very hard to compare the modern women's movement to the original suffrage movement because today's movement is so much wider and deeper than suffrage. That was really a political job, and it was handled like a political job, more or less. This movement now, I think, springs from much, much deeper grounds. It involves really women's estimate of themselves and what they feel they could contribute to the world.

I think that whereas women felt it definitely unfair that they couldn't vote, I think women now conceive of the inequality as something a great deal more serious than a personal affront. They realize that it has a lot to do with the kind of world we have and the mess we're in, and that the only valid hope for the future lies in *true* equality.

I think women have a lot of changing to do, too. I listen with *horror* at the chitchat that goes on in a normal group of women, and I'm not surprised that men make snide remarks about "girl talk." But that isn't true of the present movement. I'm talking mostly about women in my own age group. They're not going to change, and most of them are quite horrified, I think, at the changes the younger women want. Of course, it just so happens that I go along with the younger women, so I mostly have to keep my mouth shut.

Yes, I think this movement that's going on now goes back to the roots, to those early feminists. And they wrote well. Charlotte Perkins Gilman, for example. Olive Schreiner, of course, I always think of with special feeling because I felt that she, of perhaps all of them, had the least bitterness; she thought of it in terms of what it could become. I also felt that she was very much fairer to men.

I can't help reminding women that up to the time the suffrage amendment was ratified, *every single thing* that American women legally had, in terms of consideration, was *given* them by men. They had no way to get it. I think they were very unappreciative of how much they had actually been given because of men's own sense of justice.

That's one reason I get very impatient with women when they are too bitter. Perhaps if I'd had a different kind of life and different association with men, I too, would feel bitter. But I don't, and I think it's a great drawback because, as I have written my daughter, I look on bitterness as a kind of cancer of the heart. I think you get nowhere with it, and it's one of the most deadly things that one can give way to.

I think this is a major failing today. I'm astonished by some of the things I read. Now, how much they've been blown up by the media, of course, one doesn't know. And I'm far from saying that I'm silly enough not to know that a great many women have ample reason for the bitterness they feel. But I think it's a defect when you're working for equality. Many women felt very bitter in suffrage days, too—many of them, and with good reason. But it's never a help, that's my feeling.

I'm not particularly eager to make unkind comments about the women's movement today. I have every sympathy with their goals. It's just that when I hear them speak, I find so many of them strident and disagreeable. It's the old, old story; people don't really get outside themselves enough. I get very impatient with their bringing up individual grievances about things. I don't understand why they don't work more through groups of women.

I have very definite ideas about what they could be doing with groups of women that, as I see it, they are not doing. Women's groups seem to feel that they have to operate in a vacuum. If they belong to one little group that's dedicated to doing this particular thing, they're not at all concerned with what's going on out there and around. I think that's all wrong for this movement of women. I think that *every* woman's group has a stake in this movement, even though they are not organized to fight for *it*.

I don't care what the individual's special interest is in that group—she should have an overall interest in women. And every organization speaks with a louder voice than its individual members. If a group especially interested in a movement could only learn how important it is to approach other groups. If you say to them, "Look, we know that you give ninety-nine percent of your time to your project, but how about, just this once, writing a letter as an organization regarding this women's movement." I think they'd be rather surprised at the network of influence they could bring up.

That is what happened in suffrage, basically. We had a great deal of that. I'm amazed that modern women don't do more of it. They don't, from my point of view, make very good use of women as a whole. I mean, just think what a small number of women are ever going to get involved with NOW, for instance, compared to the number that sympathize with the overall aims and would be glad to lend their hands, perhaps to advocate the passage of a specific bill or something of that kind. Not to expect that they're going to spend much time with it, but that they are a group of women. They can take a vote and will probably be sympathetic to doing this little bit for equality. It would add up to a great deal.

It was quite interesting when we were doing the organizing, of course, to see which women in these very small towns could be interested. In general, it was the women with better educations. Once in a while, you got a woman from the blue-collar group, but not very often. And in some cases, you got women whose husbands definitely were not crazy about suffrage at all; they just said, "Well, if you want to, go ahead," even though they didn't really go along with it. In other words, they were mostly very substantial women—those who were willing to come right out for suffrage and form a suffrage group.

I think this movement today, though, involves all women, and I think that in a curious way women recognize that—even though they get awfully mad about the thing. Even the older ones who want to hang on to everything they have and not let anything go, even they, I think, have a certain sympathy with it. I have always felt that's why they are so nit-picking about the smaller things. In a way, I nit-pick myself, but I just feel that sometimes the women in today's movement are antagonizing a lot of people by some of the things they do. They shouldn't—just out of pure wisdom.

It's perfectly true that marriage has been one of our most stable institutions, but that's no reason that it can't be reexamined in the light of our present-day situation, and especially now that there is so much clamor for a decrease in population. I think it's awfully silly the way many women talk about these things.

However, to the young people belongs the future, and whether the older generation likes it or not, these things are all going to be reexamined and rearranged. At the moment, of course, I don't see very much possibility of creating a permissive institution which can offer the stability that marriage has offered us. I think it's going to be a very unhappy environment for children if we marry and divorce at such a rate as we're doing now. It *is* tough for children. They have enough things to learn about the world without having to adapt themselves overnight to a completely changed environment.

I would hope that a good many people would try it out; they have a nice name for the marriage that isn't legal, a colloquial name for it, which I've forgotten. At any rate, the Swedes have done this for years, tried out the thing first. Fine. But after they've tried it out, I would hope that people who had lived together for three or four years and found it companionable would go and get married before they have children. It seems awfully tough on the children to have their homes changed by divorce. These are things the younger generation are going to work out for themselves.

I heartily endorse the efforts of the modern women's movement. I think it's ridiculous that women shouldn't participate in government, and I'm very happy that we succeeded in electing that nice Mrs. Cohen to our City Council here in Claremont. We are now getting more women in such positions, all around. Of course, just getting them in where their faces show isn't the answer until they get some real authority and knowledge.

There is something to be said for the statements made by

big organizations about minorities—that one of their troubles is not so much unwillingness to hire as the difficulty in finding qualified applicants. The same is true of women. That's changing, of course. I just hope that there is going to be a considerable change in the vocational advice that's handed out—beginning much earlier than college, way back in junior high. There isn't any reason on earth why girls shouldn't plan all kinds of careers. For example, if they find they're especially good at mathematics, for goodness sake, then let them do it! Let them take part in the new technology.

ERNESTINE HARA KETTLER

In Prison

Ernestine Hara Kettler, at the age of seventy-nine, is a woman who seems to bridge the generation gap between the suffragists and today's feminists. Her ideas on the family, on sex roles and on patriarchy, ideas which have been part of her thinking for almost sixty years, coincide with much of the ideology of the contemporary women's movement. She, like Jessie Haver Butler, joined NOW (National Organization for Women) in the late 1960s; she is one of the few older women in the Los Angeles chapter.

When I first met her in 1973, Ernestine, a petite woman with gray hair and thick glasses, was rather young-looking for her seventy-seven years. She was living on her union pension and Social Security in a hotel in the MacArthur Park area of Los Angeles, a somewhat run-down neighborhood inhabited largely by pensioners. Her room, where we recorded five interviews over a period of two months, had a disquieting air of impermanence about it. Though she had lived there for many years, there were no signs of her own decoration and, except for the books scattered about, no imprint of her own personality.

This seemed to be a transitional period in her life, a time of passage from health and activity to illness and inactivity. This change was painful to observe. Shortly after we completed the interviews, Ernestine was preparing to make a long-deferred move to San Francisco when she suffered a series of "minor strokes" and was hospitalized.

For the past year and a half, Ernestine has been living in a convalescent home in Los Angeles. I visit her periodically and we talk about the women's movement and other current developments. Up until a few months ago, when she lost her eyesight, she would often send me newspaper clippings pertaining to feminism, underlined and with marginal comments. Though now cut off from the world of print, she still manages to keep abreast of current affairs and still argues about "capitalist" politics and feminism with a great deal of perception and conviction.

THE MAKING OF A RADICAL

I was born on January 25, 1896. It seems awful to know that I'm of that age because of the way I think and the way I feel. I cannot understand old age. I feel today the way I used to feel years ago—extremely interested in ideas, aroused by all kinds of unhappy things going on in the world. The only thing is that I realize that I'm physically not as capable of navigating as I was before, that I'm reaching the end of my life. I'm talking about the end of my life without having told you anything about the beginning.

I came out of an anarchist family. My mother followed my father's ideology, as happens quite often in this world—aside from the feminist liberation movement. I was young at the time and their anarchism didn't make any impression on my mind. Anarchism was part of my own experience only later after I came to this country.

I was not born in this country. I was born in Rumania, in like a suburb of Craiova. Just before we left Rumania, we lived in Bucharest, but I don't remember too much about that because we were poor and didn't get around too much. We were Jews, but my family were not Orthodox. They were agnostics, so we had no religious training of any kind. My mother used to tell us stories of heroes and heroines out of the Old Testament. Just to amuse us. They were better than some of the children's books.

What I do remember about Rumania are my reactions and attitudes toward superstitions. The children used to follow funerals. I was one of the children and I used to go along with them from one funeral to another. Sometimes we used to get good things to eat. At the last one I attended, we went up to the corpse and stood there looking at her—an old woman with her arms crossed over her chest. The vision was so strong that it shocked me—the realization that I was doing such a morbid thing. I thought, What am I doing here?! Why do I follow funerals? Why do I come to look at dead people? Since that time I have never, ever, looked at a dead person again.

Because I was Jewish, some of my friends said, "Now, Ernestine, be careful when you see a priest coming down the street. Take three steps back and three steps forward, and the devil won't get you." I used to do that. I did that one day when I was quite alone and a priest saw me. He asked why did I do that. Do you know, I had no answer. It suddenly seemed very irrational to me. That's the last time I was ever afraid of a priest. Those were some of the childish things.

My father died when he was only about forty, and after that we had no money. Like a lot of immigrants, we had relatives in New York who helped us to come over. That was 1907. So my mother came with the four children, my two brothers, my sister and me. I was eleven.

My mother got a job, a sweatshop job. She had to bring the work home in order to take care of us. My sister and I were going to school, but my youngest brother, through the persuasion of the relatives, was put in an orphan asylum. That was the saddest thing that happened. It used to break my heart whenever we'd go to visit him. The tears in his eyes when we left. I've never been able to forget that. But she couldn't afford to feed him. She couldn't feed five mouths. I can remember a distant cousin who fell in love with my mother. He used to come and visit us and bring us a whole big package of food. We just loved him because of the food. After all, we were hungry. But my mother was very much attached to the memory of my father and couldn't see anyone else.

We lived in two rooms, one was the kitchen and the other was the bedroom. It was quite crowded, especially when all four of us were home. My older brother didn't stay around too long, though. He went back to Rumania, served in the army there, and then after his service, returned to the United States. He was an adult by that time.

We lived in a poor neighborhood. There were Spanish-speaking people there, Italian-speaking people. It wasn't really a Jewish ghetto; there were all kinds of Gentiles and Jews in the same district. We were Spanish Jews. Whatever Yiddish my mother knew she learned in this country. I never learned it because I didn't like the language. We were accused of being anti-Semitic. "What do you mean, we're anti-Semitic. We were Spanish Jews. We simply don't know the language and we can refuse to learn certain languages if we don't like the sound of them."

My mother was always an anarchist, but she wasn't active. The only activity I had was through my friends. I became involved with a group on the streets where we lived—two or three girls—and we were all political. When I was about thirteen we began going to the Socialist Party office around the corner. We didn't join YPSL (Young People's Socialist League), but we were nevertheless curious about the place and became friendly with them. If there was a strike on, we'd join the strike. When there were meetings on Union Square, we'd go to the meetings. I don't know how much of it I understood then, but it sort of strengthened my political ideas and fulfilled a more immediate need than the anarchism in which I was raised. It was at a later age, at sixteen or seventeen, that I became more aware. Though really, my political education didn't begin until about thirty years ago.

When I was fourteen I started writing. I had never thought much about it, but we decided to get out a bulletin of some kind, a monthly magazine, on the block where I lived. We were going to publish our stuff—type so many copies and give them around. I wrote a couple of poems and a long Edgar Allan Poe type story, of all things. How I wrote it, I don't know, but it just seemed to come without any effort; I was just on another planet. When it turned out that there were only two things to publish and that my story was too long, we gave up the idea.

All the girls and boys who wanted club experience or different kinds of craft work would go to the Labor Temple in New York. They tried to make Christians out of us. A Greek woman there, Alexandrochas or something, became extremely interested in me. I was the talented one in the family. She got hold of this millionaire who lived in a single-tax colony in Massachusetts with his wife, Fisk Warren. They sponsored me at a private academy in Massachusetts. This was after I'd gone a year to high school. It was a school where foreigners, mostly, were sent to be given a Christian education—in the hopes of making missionaries out of them. They tried to make a Christian out of me, but they couldn't make me a Christian, or even religious, in any sense of the word. I was raised without religion and it had become merely a philosophical question for me. I wondered why people felt the need of a religious crutch. It seemed to me that if they had a political conviction of some kind, that would be just as good, just as effective, as a religious one. Anyway, while I was at the school I did have to go to church every Sunday. It was more like a Unitarian church, and I used to read throughout the service.

During the summers I went back to New York and stayed with my mother. When I was about sixteen, during summer vacation, I worked in the same shop with my mother. I think we were working on hats. That was my first, my only organizing campaign. The girls were complaining there, so I told them, "Well, why don't you join the union? If you'd join the union you'd get certain conditions." I must have said that at least once too often because either the owner or the forewoman talked to me and said, "You know, we can't have that sort of talk around here. I'm sorry, but I don't think we can keep you." That was the end of my factory work. In fact, that was the only factory work I ever did in my life.

I came back from that academy in Massachusetts after about one and a half years and tried to finish my high school in New York. But, you know, I couldn't stand the kids. They were not merely too young, but they were too immature for me. I had been studying with adults, you might say; I was perhaps the youngest in the class, but still they were adults, and had a different way of thinking and I was starting to learn to think in that manner, too.

So I went to Oberlin, Ohio, where they had both an academy and a college. This millionaire paid for my year there, too. For my books and tuition. I had to work four hours a day for my room and board, but I couldn't do that too long. I was much too little and not a muscular person. After attending classes all day long, it's pretty rough to go home and have to do housework. I would stand on a chair to dust the shelves, but most of the time I still couldn't see the top of the shelf. I couldn't do it. So after a couple of months they started to give me money for my expenses, too.

New York kept drawing me. I had my friends there. You know, when you're young, you're looking for thrills of all kinds, and I was in a kind of situation where there were quite a few. I met a number of IWWs (Industrial Workers of the World, known as Wobblies) and a number of socialists and general radicals who were not committed to any particular ideology or to any particular party. So I was running around with a radical group, getting all kinds of ideas on how to destroy capitalism. But we didn't do anything illegal, really. It was just a lot of talk, mostly.

My own position was actually the current anarchist ideology, but rather on the ephemeral side. I guess the only anarchists I knew were the big ones. I met both Emma Goldman and Alexander Berkman, and later when I was in jail in Virginia I received a letter from Berkman. I didn't know them well; I used to go to their affairs and to their forums, and met a number of people there. I became acquainted with Hippolyte Havel through them.* He was about fifty at the time, between forty and fifty.

I was just like a daughter, like a little puppy. In fact, he called me "Keo"—which I think was the name of a puppy he once had. I think he was still putting out a magazine then. It seemed to me he was always running around looking for paper and string to tie the papers, and perhaps for money for

* A rather eccentric veteran anarchist of Czech extraction whom Emma Goldman met in Europe in the late 1910s; he became her lover for a brief period of time and returned with her to the United States.

postage to mail them. I saw him quite a bit. He used to invite me to dinner, and would take me to the Brevoort Hotel. Sometimes he had money, and sometimes he didn't. When he didn't, he'd send me around to the tables to get some money. I don't know what they'd have done to him if he hadn't been able to get any money. But nobody would allow the proprietors to kick him out or send him to the kitchen to wash the dishes. They all knew him, and so they always gave money.

I saw him quite a bit in Provincetown, too. I went to Provincetown in 1916 with the Zorach family. He was a sculptor and was with the New York School of Social Research. She was a painter. They wanted somebody to go along and look after their young boy. He was a year and a half old. I stayed with them for about a month and then I left them and got a room.

I met all the people who were there in Provincetown: Eugene O'Neill, Louise Bryant, Jack Reed, Max Eastman, Mary Heaton Vorse. There must have been about a dozen people I met who were all either writers or artists. I even met one actress. I think it was Crystal Eastman, Max Eastman's sister. I was offered a part in one of Louise Bryant's one-act plays, but I turned it down because I wanted one in Eugene O'Neill's. I couldn't act worth a darn, but do you know, I chose the biggest role there was and the most difficult.

I wrote my first long story and took it to Hippolyte to read. He said it was very beautiful, but unpublishable. Eugene O'Neill read it, too. They both thought I had talent. As a matter of fact, I was told I had talent before then—by a dramatic critic in Boston who had read a play I had written. As I recall, it was a pretty bloody play, but he said that it had the markings of a near genius. I had a thought all my life about becoming a writer. I should have gone to school and learned the craft of writing. That would have changed my whole life.

Instead I went to a commercial school and learned some bookkeeping and stenography and typing. I went to work with *Smart Set* magazine, run by Frank Harris. Then I got other jobs, office jobs. The European war brought on a great deal

of employment and affluence in this country. You could just
get a job anyplace. I was offered a job in the office of a defense industry in Brunswick, New Jersey. There were many
girls from New York there and we all boarded somewhere together. I don't know how long I was there. The work was
awfully heavy for me. I had to use one of those wide type-
writers and I didn't have the muscular strength to shift, to
work on such a huge typewriter. So I went back to New York.

About that time I met Katherine Hodges. She was from
Everett, Washington, and had come to New York as a delegate to a Socialist convention. Evidently I was doing some
work for the Socialist party and met her. We started talking
and she told me about the National Woman's Party in Washington, D.C., whose members were picketing the President.
She asked if I cared to go. Of course, anything as exciting as
that would have appealed to me.

I might have been taken as an adventurer because during
that time I was having a good time. I had walked in the suffrage parade of 1915, or whenever it was, but I wasn't fighting
for feminism. I was interested in the theater, in writing, in art.
I was a bohemian in the real sense of the word. My associates
in Greenwich Village were mostly dilletantes and they were
mostly nonpolitical. The politics were sort of brought into it
because you live in a political society. Certain ideas would be
expressed about which I felt offended, and if I corrected them,
I would try to correct them politically as well as philosophically. But politics, like feminism, was part of the general life
I lived. All these issues were outstanding. I can't pick on any
one subject and say it had a certain influence on me. They
all had an influence on me. For instance, I've always had an
attitude toward sexual freedom, in favor of free love. For the
very reason that engaging in it was "immoral." That was so
puritanical, so false. Unless you were legally married, you were
not a moral woman. Naturally, in those days we talked about
the legal prostitute; a woman would marry a man for money,
therefore, she was a legal prostitute. I've always had these
ideas. It was part of my radical background.

Much of my radicalism I learned outside because my mother had mixed ideas. She had a Victorian attitude about sex. She hadn't overcome her own mother's training about sex and she turned it on me. She started telling me lies when I was four, five, six. You see things, hear things. Children are very curious, rabidly curious. I asked all the questions and was told all the lies. I would say, "How is it possible that men always have love nests if sex is abnormal?" The papers were rampant with stories about love nests, especially in those early years of the century. "Is it possible that men are abnormal?" I began thinking in that fashion and straightening out my own ideas on it. I couldn't quite accept the fact that if sex was dirty my father and mother engaged in it. I couldn't accept that.

I was already rebelling against much of the stuff that I didn't know and some of the stuff that I had already figured out for myself. I couldn't coordinate them. I couldn't coordinate them until I found out that sex was not only normal, but that without sex, there would be no human life. This I was able to grasp very quickly and I was already fifteen at the time. I went home and gave my mother quite a lecture. She was in tears. She said, "I thought you would find it out in the street." I said, "I did, I just did, and I'm bawling you out for telling me lies all my life." So there was never any period in my life when I had these ideas and another when I didn't.

Of course, I also believed that women should work after their marriage. That would give them more independence. If they wanted a trial marriage, they could try it—provided they had sufficient knowledge about contraceptives. Two issues that bothered me very much in this free-love business were getting pregnant and getting a disease. People—girls, especially—have no right to engage in sexual activity if they are not properly trained and educated in how to prevent these two situations.

All these issues were part of the whole philosophy that we carried, and I can't separate one from the other or distinctly remember any special struggle that we fought. The ideas were all meshed together.

THE SUFFRAGE STRUGGLE:
DIRECT ACTION IN WASHINGTON

I don't know how this conversation with Katherine Hodges started, but she told me what the suffrage party was doing in Washington—the picket lines and so on—and she said that I might be sent to jail. Well, I'd never been to jail. It was kind of romantic in my mind. I thought it would be a thrilling experience. I was both serious and light-headed about it. Not light-hearted, but just a little light-headed.

THE NEW YORK TIMES, WEDNESDAY, JANUARY 10, 1917

SUFFRAGISTS WILL PICKET
WHITE HOUSE

Plan to Post "Silent Sentinels" Bearing Emblems, Whom President Must Pass

WILL GUARD ALL EXITS

New Campaign of Militancy Arranged When President Says His Views Are Unchanged

Special to The New York Times
WASHINGTON, Jan. 9.— Women suffragists, representing all parts of the country, disappointed over the result of an appeal which they made this afternoon to President Wilson in the East Room of the White House, held an indignation meeting and decided to adopt a new plan of campaign. They intend to post women pickets hereafter about the White House grounds. Their purpose is to make it impossible for the President to enter or leave the White House without encountering a picket bearing some device pleading the suffrage cause. The pickets will be known as "silent sentinels."

THE NEW YORK TIMES, THURSDAY, JANUARY 11, 1917

PRESIDENT IGNORES SUFFRAGE PICKETS

Six Silent Sentinels Posted at Each of the Main Gates of the White House.

BUT HE GOES BY OBLIVIOUS

While Police on Duty Only Smile—Women to Post Guards with Military Regularity

Special to The New York Times

WASHINGTON, Jan. 10.—The White House has been picketed before, but never until today by hostile suffragists. It was placed in the beleaguered state this morning under the new "silent sentinel" campaign begun by the Congressional Union for Woman Suffrage as an outgrowth of the failure of President Wilson to declare in favor of the proposed Federal suffrage amendment when he received a delegation of 300 suffragist leaders at the White House yesterday.

The first guard mount of the suffrage sentinels marched across historic Lafayette Square a few minutes before 9 o'clock this morning, under command of Miss Mabel Vernon. The detail consisted of six young women. The Sergeant of the guard for its first day of picketing was Miss Mary Gertrude Fendall of Baltimore.

THE NEW YORK TIMES, THURSDAY, JANUARY 11, 1917
EDITORIAL

SILENT, SILLY, AND OFFENSIVE

Suppose this impossible piece of news should be printed tomorrow morning:

WASHINGTON, Jan. 11.—Socialist leaders visited the White House to ask the President to support Socialism. He replied that his views on that subject were unchanged. Upon leaving the White House they held an indignation meeting, at which it was resolved to post Socialist pickets hereafter about the White House grounds and to make it impossible for the President to enter or leave the building without encountering a picket bearing some device pleading the Socialist cause. The pickets will be known as "silent sentinels." At the indignation meeting a fund was started to finance the movement. EUGENE V. DEBS started the fund with $1,000, BOUCK

WHITE contributed $100, and a prominent member of the I.W.W. pledged $100 a month.

The popular feeling at this organized harassment of the President can be imagined. It would not have much chance to gather headway, of course, because at the first manifestation of so impudent an attempt to annoy the head of the nation the police would unceremoniously assemble the offenders in a patrol wagon and deposit them in a body in the District jail. However, no one can imagine the Socialists, the Prohibitionists, or any other party conceiving of a performance at once so petty and so monstrous; one could not imagine even the I.W.W. attempting it. Why? Because they are men, and men's minds may be wicked, virtuous, wise or foolish, but are not made so that they would work in just this way. There is something in the masculine mind that would shrink from a thing so compounded of pettiness and monstrosity, if for no other reason than that he would dimly feel the absurdity and futility of it.

Yet nobody is astonished that woman suffragists should propose such a thing, and therein lies a matter of deep concern in dealing with the whole woman suffrage question. The granting of suffrage would intrude into govermental affairs a great body of voters comprehending many whose minds do work in just that way, a great many to whom that compound of pettiness and monstrosity seems natural and proper. It would introduce into the management of the Government many persons so constituted that they can see nothing wrong in trying to influence the President himself by duress when they cannot convince him by argument. That the female mind is inferior to the male mind need not be assumed: that there is something about it essentially different, and that this difference is of a kind and degree that with votes for women would constitute a political danger is or ought to be plain to everybody.

But it wasn't just an adventure. As a radical, I believed in justice. It was very just for women to vote and it was highly undemocratic and an outrage that so much opposition had been placed against their getting the ballot. There were, after all, as many women in the country as men. What is this business? Is a woman so far below a man intellectually that she's not fit to vote? When I think of it, it's just incredible! I can't believe it! I condemned it. I was actually outraged that women didn't have the vote! That's why I went down to Washington, D.C.

I don't know how I got there. I didn't have money, so someone must have paid my fare down there, perhaps this Katherine Hodges or the suffrage party. All I remember is that I
found myself in Washington, and that I was met at the station and taken to the headquarters of the National Woman's
Party. The headquarters was the Little White House; that's
where President McKinley died. I was given his room and his
bed. I wanted to get out of that room, fast. I didn't want to
sleep in anybody's deathbed. Of course, he was only killed,
you know, he didn't die of a disease.

What they were doing was picketing in groups of four. Each
group had a shift. As soon as one group was arrested, then they
sent out another group of four. There was a continuous picket
line. That's what drove the policemen crazy—they saw no end
to the number of women who were picketing!

I met the other three women in my group at the headquarters. One of them was Peggy Johns from New York. Another, whose name I do not remember, was an organizer in
the needle trades in New York. The fourth was a lawyer from
one of the Western states, either Wyoming or Arizona. They
were all between twenty-five and thirty-five. I was the youngest in the group, twenty-one.

We started picketing the second or third day I was there.
We walked back and forth, right in front of the White House
gates. We had a banner, but I don't remember whether we
each carried one banner or whether the four of us carried one
long one with four posts on it. There must have been a saying
on it. You can't just have a plain banner without something
on it to draw the attention of the people passing by.

A pretty big crowd would gather every day—at least it
seemed pretty big to me. There were always men and women
standing there harassing us and throwing some pretty bad insults—and pretty obscene ones. The women weren't obscene,
but the men were. Our instructions were to pay absolutely no
attention to them. I ignored them. I was brave. My goodness,
I was fighting for a cause.

We had some support, but they took their lives in their

hands. If any of the bystanders supported us, they could be beaten by the rest of the crowd. Towards the end, they started throwing stuff at the women. In fact, during this period somebody fired a shot through the windows of the Little White House, the headquarters. Any woman that happened to be in the right position for it could have been killed. And we couldn't get police protection. We just couldn't get it. The only protection we had was when we were arrested. Then we were protected!

THE NEW YORK TIMES, WEDNESDAY, JUNE 27, 1917

Nine More Pickets Seized at White House

Court Hearing Today—Rumors of Hunger Strike Plans Are Revived.

Special to The New York Times
WASHINGTON, June 26.— The coveted goal of the American militant suffragists—a hunger strike in jail—appeared in sight today when nine White House pickets who were arrested this morning were released on $25 cash bail each for their appearance for trial before Justice Mullowny, of the Police Court,

tomorrow morning at 9 o'clock. After their trial date had been fixed the suffrage leaders let it be known that they would go to jail before they would pay a fine. This is taken as substantiation of oft-repeated talk in Washington that the militant suffragists are manoeuvring for a jail term so that they can start a hunger strike.

On one of the picketing days, the police hauled us in and took us to jail. All four of us. Immediately the lawyer or somebody was sent to the city jail to bail us out, so we were in jail only about an hour or so. We didn't have to wait too many days for our trial. After all, the National Woman's Party had to board us, and that costs money.

At the trial we all made statements that we were not obstructing traffic, but that the traffic was obstructing us—which was true. Obstructing traffic and loitering were the charges. We weren't doing either one of them. We were marching. "There were only four of us," we told them, "so we couldn't possibly obstruct traffic. We were on the sidewalk, there was only one row of us, only four of us. There was plenty of room. But unfortunately, a lot of people stopped and they obstructed traffic. None of them were arrested, except us." We were very bold.

The judge asked how old I was, and when I said twenty-one, he was so mad. He scowled. He couldn't believe it. But he had to believe it because he knew that the suffrage party was insistent about that; we had to be twenty-one or over, otherwise we couldn't march.

So we were given thirty days. Before then, only the hard-core criminals like Alice Paul had been given thirty days. After we were sentenced, we were taken to the city jail. That's where we cooked up our political prisoner demands: We were political prisoners. We were not guilty of obstructing traffic. We were not guilty of the sentence as charged. Therefore, we did not owe any kind of work in the workhouse. That workhouse in Occoquan, Virginia, was a real workhouse—you worked or else.

We made all these decisions in the city jail where we were taken and kept overnight. That really gave quite a different tinge to the whole struggle. Peggy Johns was the one who suggested it. She was the truly political person in that group. We all agreed with her. I'm surprised that the trade unionist didn't mention it first, but a trade unionist doesn't necessarily find her experience in political prisoner activities. I didn't even think of it.

The next morning we were taken in a bus to the Occoquan Workhouse. When we got there, we had an immediate discussion with the other women and told them our decision. There was already a group of either eight or twelve of our women there. They were very enthusiastic about the idea and accepted it, without question. The next day we appeared in the workroom and we just sat there with our hands in our laps.

All the women in that sewing room took an example from us. I think there were probably about a dozen other women in that room. When they saw that we weren't working, they took heart. They could be real courageous. They wouldn't work either. There was nothing that could be done about the whole room. I think that's what bothered the superintendent. He wouldn't have cared so much if the others had continued to work.

It wasn't long before he asked if we would at least, please, hold the work in our laps. We were demoralizing the other prisoners in that workroom. I suppose we were to be making sack dresses; that's all we wore, just sack dresses. We said, "No. We decided that since we were unjustly arrested and that we were political prisoners, it would be just as wrong for us to hold the work in our hands as it would be to sew it. We were going to abide by our decision—that we had to be respected as political prisoners."

We'd go to the workroom and we'd just sit there all day long. We talked, you know. All we could do was talk. Since we were all sitting at one table, we did a great deal of talking as to how to comport ourselves. We lived in dormitories; we slept in one long dormitory with beds on both sides, about three feet apart from each other. It was just like the ones you see in motion pictures of prison wards or hospitals. There were about thirty in the dormitory—not just suffragists, but other prisoners, too. We took turns washing ourselves every morning. There were several sinks and we took turns. Then we went into the dining room.

I think twice a day we went out for our "constitutional." We had certain prescribed prison walks through the gardens there; it was a lovely fall time of the year, you know. The leaves were turning red and they were falling, the air was fresh.

We were allowed some correspondence, but that was limited to receiving books, letters and newspapers from our relatives and friends. To my knowledge, I was the only one who was permitted a visit; my mother was permitted to come and see me. The people in the office were mad as hell because we spoke in Rumanian and nobody understood.

The food was the greatest problem we had there. It was just unbelievable—the worms that were found in the oatmeal we ate, in the soup we ate. I don't remember anything else. The coffee was God knows what—it wasn't coffee. It might have been chicory. To me, that was the most terrible part of the whole prison experience, the food.

We all suffered. This was before the hunger strike, but some of the women were acutally on a hunger strike already! They just couldn't eat. The only thing they could eat was bread, if it wasn't totally moldy and if it didn't show rat tracks. That prison was paid hundreds of thousands of dollars to feed us, and it raised beautiful vegetables, but we had none of them. Instead, they bought this old stuff that was rancid and sitting in warehouses heaven knows how many years, and fed us that.

In those days a lot of food had worms in it; you had to be careful. When you bought it, you had to eat it right away. The prison didn't buy the food right away or didn't cook it right away, and it bought the worst of all possible foods, anyway. It was all loaded with worms. I just didn't know what to do; I used to pick out the worms. If I found some clean oatmeal or clean soup, I'd eat it. But most of us lost a lot of pounds during the thirty days in that workhouse. I just couldn't go through the job of picking out the worms, weevils, or whatever they were. It was really miserable in that fashion. Otherwise, we weren't punished. There was nothing the superintendent could do if you refused to work. There was only one occasion when we actually suffered brutality. You see, my friend Peggy Johns became ill and was taken to the hospital. I used to visit her in the hospital every day. One day I went to see her and she wasn't there. I asked the nurse what happened and she said she didn't know. I asked all the other nurses, whoever was there, and they all said, "We don't know. Just go and ask the superintendent."

I rushed into the other building. There was a long hall with a dining room at one end and the superintendent's office at the other. As I walked along the hallway, there was Peggy—all dressed up in her civilian clothes. "Peggy," I said, "where are you going?" "They're taking me to the psychopathic ward in

Washington, D.C. Go tell the other girls, and all of you rush back here." So I did.

We all rushed back to the superintendent's office. He was absolutely dumbfounded when he saw us. He thought he'd be able to steal her away without us knowing. If I hadn't been such a loyal visitor, we wouldn't have found out. When we got into that office, we told him that he couldn't do that, that she would have to be picked up by our lawyer in Washington and taken to the hospital, that she couldn't be sent just by the prison alone, that we had no assurance what would happen to her, and that, above all things, we wanted security for our women.

He wouldn't abide by it. One of the women rushed to the telephone to phone our headquarters in Washington, and he rushed over, too, and just tore the phone right off the wall. Then he called in deputies. Of all the dirty tricks, he called in Negro girls to come in there, and I'm telling you, they beat the hell out of us. I was so little that I was scared to death to get in the crowd and I was on the outside.

I saw some women on the floor, being trampled. The Negro girls—considering how badly they were treated—got the most intense joy out of beating the hell out of the white women. The superintendent was frightened when he saw the zeal with which these women were beating us. He didn't want us killed or hurt in any way because he would be held entirely responsible, so he had to call in the men deputies to haul the Negro girls off us and get them outside. He then allowed us to call Washington, and we told them at headquarters what was going on. So Peggy was sent to Washington, and the lawyer met her and took her to the hospital, or wherever it was. Anyway, it wasn't the psychopathic ward.

'PICKETS' MUTINY IN WORKHOUSE

Eighteen Suffragist Prisoners Attack the Superintendent of Washington Institution.

SUPPRESSED BY NEGRESSES

Fierce Rough-and-Tumble Fight Attends Removal of Mrs. Johns to Asylum Hospital.

WASHINGTON, Oct. 4—Militants of the Woman's Party serving time in the District of Columbia Workhouse for demonstrations before the White House were charged today with mutiny as a result of their rough-and-tumble fight yesterday with guards and negro women prisoners. The development furnishes a new phase for the investigation of conditions at the workhouse, undertaken by the Board of Charities on complaints of the militants.

The charge of mutinous conduct is made in a report by Alonzo Tweedale, auditor, in charge of the workhouse while the Superintendent is suspended pending outcome of the inquiry. A long story is told by the report of how the eighteen suffragists attacked the Acting Superintendent, the prison matron, and three male guards who had been called to the rescue when the officers sought to remove one of their number, Mrs. Margaret Johns, for medical treatment at the Washington Asylum Hospital.

It tells of negro women of the prison kitchen force rallying to the aid of their boss, the matron, when she was threatened with a blow on the head with a club, of a general wild scramble about the workhouse corridors and yard, and eventually of Mrs. Johns's departure for the hospital in a doctor's automobile after she and her guards had been much mauled and hauled about. The Acting Superintendent emphasizes the statement that extreme forbearance was shown the prisoners, the male guards obeying orders to handle them with every possible consideration in spite of all that happened.

Miss Alice Paul, head of the women's party, made a statement denying many of Mr. Tweedale's statements and declaring that the women interfered because they were not told where Mrs. Johns was to be taken, and feared that she was to be placed in confinement on bread and water. She also said Mrs. Johns was not removed for proper medical treatment when she really was ill, and that she had recovered when the authorities decided to take her to the hospital.

The workhouse is a big, unbarred structure on a farm near Washington. Its open doors made it easy for the suffragists, when they started on the warpath, to give their custodians a lively time.

The next day, after this fracas, they sent us back to the city jail. The superintendent didn't want us there any longer at the workhouse and he maneuvered to send us to the city jail to finish out our sentence. We had about three days left to serve. We had lost our automatic five days off for good behavior after the first day we were in the city jail. Or perhaps we had lost it at the workhouse because we initiated that work strike.

In the city jail we raised Cain! I remember that after we ate, we'd take the tin plates and throw them through the bars of the gate, of the doors, right at the windows. I think we broke some windows. We raised so much hell. We had all kinds of notoriety. The newspapermen came to interview us. They'd even bring us food from the outside. The food in the city jail was much better than at the workhouse. But we were mad; we were so darned mad. They put us in solitary confinement, two in each cell. We were held there in the city jail three days and then released.

The next group that came in was the one that went on a hunger strike, and they were brutally treated. They received very severe treatment. They were beaten and dragged across the patio from the superintendent's office to their cells. (These later women were segregated; they were put in cells.) Some women had broken ribs and were bleeding profusely and they weren't treated. Others had all kinds of lacerations.

After we were released from jail we went back to headquarters. I don't know how long I stayed there, perhaps another week or two. I was even tempted to go back again on the picket line, but I just couldn't stand the thought of going back to that workhouse again. After thirty days of that dreadful food and the fear of what might happen to the next contingent that was arrested, I just wasn't courageous enough to go back again. I felt horrified by the different things that could happen to you in prison. It wasn't as exciting as I had thought it would be; it was exciting in a frightening way, but not exciting in a joyous way. That was one reason why I decided not to go back again on the picket line and then be tried again and sentenced again.

THE NEW YORK TIMES, THURSDAY, JANUARY 2, 1919

MEN IN UNIFORM ROUT SUFFRAGISTS

Demonstration in Front of the White House Arouses Wrath of Soldiers and Sailors

RESENT ATTACK ON WILSON

Women Carrying Banners Are Knocked Down by Charging Crowd—5 Women Arrested.

I don't think any of the women in my contingent signed for another commitment. The only one I kept in touch with was Peggy Johns. She wasn't much taller than I am. Maybe we just stood together and supported one another; it gave us this additional muscle that we needed. There didn't seem to be any bond with the others and I never saw any of them again except for Peggy. She was in New York, too, and until I went West I saw quite a bit of her.

Then, after forty-four years, I saw her again—about twelve years ago. There was a man writing a biography of Eugene O'Neill who had written to newspapers throughout the country asking for everyone who knew Gene. I wrote him and in my correspondence mentioned my prison experience. He wrote back and said that Peggy Johns was still alive: "She's a sturdy old lady." I tell you, I was thrilled when I heard this. I got her address and wrote her right away. "Dearest Ernestine," she wrote back. But she wasn't so impressed with me when she saw me in person. To me she looked like a *grande dame*. The writer left us and I went with her to the bars in the village.

We just walked around from one bar to another. In one of them I noticed that every time a young girl came in she'd go over and kiss Peggy on the cheek. I thought it was so delightful to see that sort of thing—nobody ever did that to me.

Then I met an old, old boyfriend of mine. It was after so many years, I had been just a young girl when I knew him. She was disgusted with me. She did invite me to come and visit, though. I never did. We weren't impressed with each other.

I don't recall any of the other women that I met in Washington, except Alice Paul. My impression of her was of a very serious and dedicated woman. Most of the women were liberal-conservative. They were not radicals; their vision was limited to voting rights. That doesn't mean there were no radicals in the group—there were—but they were not effective and they would not waste their time there. Like Peggy Johns, who was a socialist or an anarchist or a radical. It was really a conservative group of women. Many of them came from fine, rich families with very good minds and a willingness to fight for their ideas; to endure prison and the food and to even starve if they couldn't eat the food. One woman was terribly sick when she was taken out of there. She came from a wealthy family, and going to prison was a real sacrifice for her. Two of those women had husbands or fathers who were senators or representatives in the Congress.

I sure felt awfully sorry for those women. After all, I came from a poor family. They weren't poor like I was, and they could be very choosy about their food, and very demanding. But this was the first time I confronted worms, and these were outstanding because there were so many of them. You know, for about thirty years afterwards, I couldn't eat oatmeal or soup in a restaurant. It just sickened me, just the mere thought of it. And to this day, I keep searching for things in it. This is the lasting effect that jail had on me.

Also, after I came out of prison I had much more awareness of feminism and suffragette-ism than I did before then. Before then, it wasn't that I didn't hear about it, but I didn't become overheated about it. But when I went back to New York I had no thoughts of continuing involvement. I mean I would engage in any parade or big affair they had. It's funny. You see, this is where some of my own revolutionary zeal ceases to be revolutionary. The denial of the vote struck me as very undemocratic. There was such a lack of democracy regarding women that I should think I would have fought in it—that I would have continued in that organization. And yet I didn't. The trouble was that I was in a political group, but most of them were writers or artists of one kind or another. So, really, my interests were fragmented.

SITTING ON THE FENCE, BETWEEN ANARCHISM AND SOCIALISM

After I returned to New York I heard from this Katherine Hodges again. She felt that she was responsible for my being arrested and being sent to jail for thirty days. Jails had a very bad reputation for anyone, especially for women. If you were a jailbird, you were a fallen woman. She felt guilty for having sent me to Washington. She asked if I would like to come West. I don't think the idea had ever occurred to me, but I wasn't doing anything, and again, I was very adventurous. I wrote and told her I'd love it but didn't have any money. She paid my fare.

So I packed up and went West. Of course, my mother was very heartbroken about it—which is normal for mothers, to be heartbroken. I stopped in a number of places. I stopped in this place where this old girlfriend of mine was, and visited with her for a few days and then went on and stopped in Butte, Montana. Katherine had asked me to stop there and get her a pint of whiskey. The State of Washington was bone-dry, and I didn't even know it was illegal.

Here I was—they were examining the bags in the train and

I didn't even know. When I heard about it, I told somebody next to me, "My God, what am I going to do? I didn't know it was illegal because I was just told to get a bottle of whiskey, and I'm bringing it." He said, "Stick it at the bottom, they won't go that far. You're too young to be suspected." So I stuck the bottle at the bottom of my case. That was quite an experience—to learn about bone-dry states. Anyway, I arrived there in Everett, Washington, in April 1918. I had a public stenography business there, but I didn't do too well with it. Katherine Hodges set me up in the office with everything, typewriter, papers, etc. I think I managed to pay the rent in that office, but I don't think I really made any money. I was not qualified, really, either as a typist or stenographer. I didn't finish my course and I hadn't really worked except in Brunswick, New Jersey. I wasn't making any money and was living off the Hodges and I didn't like that very well.

A friend of Katherine's came to Everett to visit and suggested that he might be able to get me a job in Seattle. He was a secretary of one of the AFL unions. So I went to Seattle, and as I recall, I got a job with the Electrical Workers. Through the job with the union, I entered the Labor Temple. I used to go every week and sit in the balcony that was set aside for nonmembers or nondelegates. It was a fascinating experience. I was a member of the office employees' union which, at that time was called the Bookkeepers Union. So I knew what was going on in the labor movement through my interest in the Labor Temple and through the union members that I met.

I didn't last long in that office. I wasn't much of a worker, and my inexperience was a barrier. Just as I was getting used to the work, my boss thought he couldn't keep me. So that was the end. It's strange, looking back on my life, I never was much of a worker. I was doing stenographic work for the unions, not organizational work as such. When the particular union I was working for had an organizing drive, I would help out. That's all. I really didn't know how, but I also think I was lazy. If it was interesting enough, I would do it. You don't become trained that way, though. You really have to become a plodder to be a craftswoman in organizational work—which I didn't do.

Shortly after I arrived in Seattle, I met quite a large group—the radical elite, the anarchists, the socialists, the radicals without any association. It was a very lively period. I was young, I was fascinated by it. It was something like some of my years in New York City. I became a member of YPSL (Young People's Socialist League), but I was also attending the Wobbly (IWW) socials and classes and going up there to the headquarters and meeting people and talking to them.

The IWW was a very large section in Seattle, next to the largest IWW in the country (Chicago was the largest). It was not only the lumberjacks, but electrical workers, too. I remember Local 110, 210, 510, 310, 410. I think 510 were the harvest workers. They all used to eventually land in Seattle, and the first place they went was to the hall, and then they'd probably join the fellows in the saloon on Skid Road. I recall dimly that the hall itself had just one small room for an office. The other offices were down in a basement across the street from the hall; the various locals each had their own little cubicles there.

I didn't work for the IWW in Seattle. My involvement was primarily at the socials. They used to have big picnics, and there were lots of women there, perhaps a third or half were women—the wives or the mothers or the sisters of the Wobblies. Like in our working force, there was always a division of labor in the IWW. Without the women, I don't know what those men would have done. The women did all the cooking and the serving and the washing of the dishes and the men did all the talking and eating. There used to be a long table at one end of the hall and all the food and the coffee urn was put there. Time after time they had to refill the coffee urn, make more coffee. They were the kitchen slaves.

The IWW had an old-fashioned attitude toward women. I remember a young girl, her last name was Pharr. She was the singer of the group; she used to lead the Wobblies in song and became quite an angel among them. They were not used to meeting respectable women, and to them she was not merely respectable, but something that dropped out of heaven; they just worshiped her. They thought they would defile her if they touched her.

At the socials they always had speakers, so I got quite an education. But I had my political differences with them. They were very limited in their political views; they were very much against what they called politics. Their only knowledge of politics is what they called capitalist politics. They couldn't understand political policies as being part of their own organization. It was all economic. That's one reason that I didn't stay with them too long after I joined. They simply weren't offering me anything educationally or intellectually.

So my affiliation was mainly with this mixed group of people. They were really dilletantes, though, as far as activity was concerned. They were intellectuals. The most interesting person was one they called Heine Abrams. He was quite a character in Seattle—a homosexual, but also a political person with all the knowledge of machinations and chicanery of political life. He was born too late. He should have been born much sooner to have been a buffoon in the court of some king.

It was an interesting group and was educational for me. Many in the group had friends at the Home Colony,* and I'd go along with them to the colony. As I became acquainted with people there, I'd go alone. I came to know a number of people there. They were basically anarchists, but they weren't getting along too well together. They were quarelling over power, electrical power. Instead of having one source for the whole village, they each put in their own. So I had my first disillusionment with anarchism; I thought that communally it might not work as it should.

There were many women in this group of mine, and I'm sure that feminism was one of the issues we discussed. The

---

* A rather large anarchist community which was located in the country several hours from Seattle.

men, though, found it either not practical to denigrate us or were in agreement. I cannot recall arguments, but then there were no very profound discussions. It was just taken for granted. Also, the issue then was suffrage, not full emancipation. I considered full emancipation as part of my entire philosophical struggle against discrimination, so that wherever discrimination existed, I opposed it. There wouldn't be any specific part more than another that I would oppose. I was opposed to the First World War. I was opposed to police brutality—because there was a great deal of it at that time. I even had an experience with the police, but it wasn't a matter of police brutality.

I was picked up one day by the police in the post office. You know how they tap you on the shoulders. I looked up and they said, "You're wanted, upstairs." It was the FBI, I think. I was trembling in my boots, and bewildered. They asked me all kinds of questions. They were certain that I was an Ernestine Evans who was a radical or journalist in France. They were sure I was her and that she'd come back to the U.S. They wanted to arrest me. It took all my wits to explain that I didn't know any Ernestine Evans. My name was Ernestine Hara and I had never been outside the country, except before I first came to the United States. They asked me about a German acquaintance of mine who had just given me a book of poetry. They kept me there for an hour, questioning and questioning me. Finally they let me go, they thought I was innocent. But that's been my experience with the police; I have and I have not been innocent. They let me go because of my youth and my helplessness. Actually, I had to even put on the helplessness business. You'd think I would have been scared to death, and I was. But I really had more courage than I realized. Even to this day, I'm scared of a policeman.

I'd been in Seattle awhile, going to the IWW Hall, when one day I met A. L. Emerson and he fell in love with me on the spot—which was very sad for both of us because I didn't fall in love with him. Archer Lyle Emerson was a grand-cousin of Ralph Waldo Emerson. I don't know how long he had been

in Seattle. I should have had more of a history of his life than
I had. The story he told me was that he was a newspaperman
in his hometown in Michigan but that his vision became quite
poor and he had to quit that work. He went into manual
labor and joined the IWW and became a secretary of the
Electrical Workers Section, 310.

He told me afterwards that as soon as he saw me he thought,
Now there's the woman I want to marry. And he didn't even
know my name. So he rushed me and we were married. My
attitudes toward marriage had actually been pretty anarchistic.
I believed in free love and in trial marriages. But I felt that
ultimately I'd get married because that was the thing to do
and it certainly didn't contradict my free-love ideas. Besides I
thought that marriage would give me the stability that I
couldn't seem to get on my own. So after a month or so, we
married. It wasn't a good relationship, though. I was fond of
him, but I just don't think I loved him. Also I was naïve on
the one hand, and much too sophisticated for him, on the
other.

From the beginning of our marriage, the police were after
Emerson. They wanted information, but they couldn't get
hold of it; you have to have an excuse for raiding an office
(this was the time of the Palmer raids). They knew what he
was. And then I was more or less of an infamous person in
Seattle; I was connected with some anarchists and other se-
ditious characters. This was after the police had picked me up
and taken me for questioning.

We were constantly badgered by the police, coming there,
knocking on the doors. I think they had a metal ring—you
could always tell it was the police. They'd look around. I tell
you, I just wanted to shoot them, because they had such gall.
They'd look in the closet, and if they'd see any papers they'd
take them out. They'd go through books to see if anything was
hidden in them. Then they'd look through the drawers.

I had a habit of writing and not mailing letters. I had just
read something on what to use as a contraceptive and was
writing about it to my sister-in-law in Michigan who had just

written asking me some questions. Well, this policeman got hold of that letter and it dawned on me that the dissemination of that information made me subject to arrest. The city was viciously anti-birth control, and there were even statutes on the books that people publicly advocating or even writing about birth control were subject to arrest. Even so, we all had the knowledge and we spoke openly about it and there were pamphlets on the subject.

I could have been arrested. So I decided I would talk so much that he wouldn't be able to get the gist of the letter. And though he read it from the first page to the last, he never did catch on. If he had been a bright policeman, I could have been arrested and been given quite a stiff sentence.

On one occasion, shortly after our marriage, we were coming home to our apartment and found two policemen waiting for us. They had a warrant for Emerson's arrest. They actually had a warrant! I was a little bit of a thing and frightened—but not too much. I didn't like the idea of beginning married life in that manner—beginning or ending any life in that manner. Anyway, they arrested him. But before they took him off, he had already given me the high sign about the keys to the Wobbly post office box. He had them on the rafter. This was a real Western apartment with wide beams across the top of the ceiling. I don't know how the heck I got up there, but as soon as the police left, I took the keys down.

I then immediately called some of my friends and told them what happened and they got a lawyer. The only thing they could arrest him on was a book they found, right on top of the bookcase. It was the records of the Young People's Socialist League (YPSL). They thought they had something wonderful on him that would get him at least two years in jail. But I was the recording secretary for YPSL, not Emerson. When the case came up in court, the charge was sedition. The defense lawyer got up and told the judge that the sedition charge was against a young social group, that they were completely innocuous, they were not demonstrating, they were just merely getting together and discussing and having a good old social time. Furthermore, Emerson was not a member and could not possibly have been the recording secretary. The judge got disgusted and threw the case out of court.

But the police weren't too happy about that. It wasn't a month later that they arrested him on Skid Road. Two policemen, one on each side of him, walked along with him and they planted some nude pictures in his pocket. They were pictures of me that had been taken in Provincetown. They were lovely pictures as far as the sand dunes were concerned. I have nothing to say about myself.

I couldn't understand how the police got those pictures. I looked through the trunk and realized that they had taken the negatives. They took out all kinds of junk—poetry, stories that I wrote, even musical compositions.

They couldn't arrest him on anything, they couldn't even arrest him on the basis of the pictures. The lawyer even proved that he didn't know about the pictures, that it was his wife's trunk. But they wanted something on him, so they held him over for trial. The bail was only three hundred dollars, but we had a heck of a time getting it. One of his friends lent us the money and then we got it from his sister. While we were getting the bail money he was serving time at the county workhouse—this was during the Seattle general strike of February 1919.

Once he was out on bail, he said, "I cannot afford to get arrested again. They'll give me years." So we skipped bail. We changed our names. They all did that, and in those days the police weren't as spread out as they are now, there was no CIA. So we went to Tacoma, where he got a job. I don't recall if I was working or not. After only a few months, we went to Elbee, a small village of only about four hundred people, about fourteen or sixteen miles from Mount Ranier. We got a place on some woman's farm right by a stream. We put up a tent and built an oven for cooking.

This woman, who was a drug addict and an ex-madame from Butte or someplace, suggested that while we were there it would be a good idea to make some whiskey. So we got started in the moonshine business. I can't say we made a living out of it, but living was very cheap. One time a deputy sheriff showed up and my husband had to rush into the woods and dump a whole ten gallons.

We were there just during the summer. When fall and winter came it got too cold and wet, so we went into town and rented a couple of rooms in what had once been a hotel. He took a job as a lumberjack. During this period Anna Louise Strong took an interest in us and helped us. After all, Emerson was a bigshot in the IWW, was arrested on false charges, and framed. She took care of the mail for us; sent it to us in different envelopes with our new names. She did that for the whole period we were away from Seattle, about one and a half years.

We came back to Seattle and we didn't get along. He was rabidly jealous. It was an impossible situation. We were breaking up and going back together and breaking up again. Finally, he left Seattle in 1923 or the end of 1922. There was nothing to hold me, I was a free-lancer, so I could go anyplace. I thought of going back to New York, but I did it in slow steps. I went to Butte, Montana, first where an old IWW friend of mine, Alicia Rosenbaum, was living with her husband. I got a housekeeping room in the hotel where they were staying and took a job with the IWW, which was just up the street. That's when I joined. I had not been a member, even after marrying Emerson. In Seattle I had been a member of the Bookkeepers and Stenographers. But in the IWW, you joined the local for which you worked. So you might say that it was an economic necessity. In that sense, I wasn't really an ideological member.

After about a year there I became restless and moved on to Chicago. There, I got a job in the IWW headquarters. Something like thirty people were working in that office. I took shorthand, typed, made entries. By this time I was already experienced. They used me as a stenographer during a conference, or perhaps it was the committee meeting before the 1924 convention. There were political arguments between the two factions in the IWW. As I recall, it was between the sympathizers of the Soviet Union and the hard-boiled antipolitical faction. It was a bitter conference, I can remember that, though I didn't understand all their arguments. I wasn't a dyed-in-the-wool IWW. I criticized the antipolitical stance, even in those days.

Even so, the IWW more or less infected my political views. Even today, I'm very sympathetic to it. It's a dying organization, but that doesn't mean it may not rise again—perhaps in a different form, a form which includes political activity. After the breakup of the IWW in the mid-1920s I was, as a friend said, sitting on a fence between anarchism and socialism. I was not active in either movement. I was connected with those people, but not active.

When I went to New York later in 1924 or 1925, I took a job with a committee of the Communist Party, believe it or not. A job opened up with a motion-picture distributing company. They distributed Russian films throughout the U.S. I met a number of Communists and attended a great number of their classes. They were educated in those days, not like the uneducated Communists they are today. I learned quite a bit, but I didn't like their authoritarianism. It just seemed to be contrary to my concept of what a socialist society should be. In New York they were trying to colonize certain industries, trying to influence the politics in certain unions. They tried to have me do the same thing. I discussed it with some of my anarchist friends, my nonaligned political friends, and they told me to refuse. I turned it down.

Then, that summer, I went to Madison and took a summer session in German and history, ancient history. I was there about eight weeks and then returned to Seattle. Once you live on the West Coast you can't stand the East Coast anymore. I couldn't stand the extreme cold, the winters there, and the thunderstorms and heat in the summer. So I went back to Seattle and I've been on the West Coast ever since.

I stayed in Seattle one or two years, but wasn't active in anything. Then I moved to San Francisco and remarried in 1928. We went up to Seattle to get married and we celebrated the marriage in Vancouver, British Columbia, for a weekend. When we returned to San Francisco, we moved to Sausalito. My husband was a printer and he was not a political person, so I just lived quietly with him. I worked during those years, but not in union offices. Although I was leading a kind of domestic life, I don't think I ever had a desire for children. I like children very much, especially babies, but I had no desire for my own. Perhaps that was due to an attitude about bringing children into this kind of world. I'm glad that it happened that way, because I've seen too much unhappiness in families.

Those years were the dead years of my life; politically they were dead. I was still a feminist and had arguments on feminism. My husband accepted my views, or at least he never argued. He couldn't argue. He was a much simpler person than I. He was not a proper husband for me. Again, I married badly in that sense. I didn't have an intellectual companion. Perhaps that kept me inactive, because it's very tough to combine a political life with a marriage unless both partners are active. The only time I rose to have any kind of political opinion was during the Moscow trials. I knew a great deal about them and I had an anarchist friend who used to be an editor of a Seattle paper during the years I lived there. In spite of my disappointment in what happened after the Russian Revolution and my disagreement with Soviet politics, I had a habit of seeing both sides. I mentioned this to my anarchist friend, and he took me by the scruff of my neck and threw me out of his house.

Even during those dead years I was still a political person with an interest in politics. I read the paper every day but I didn't read anything basic; I hadn't read Marx or Lenin or Trotsky.

THIRTY YEARS OF
UNION ACTIVITY

My husband died in 1936, and about six months later I returned to New York. While there, I joined the Office Employees Union—the new one, the CIO one. After about a year and a half I came back. It was natural for me to return to San Francisco. That's where my husband and I lived, and I had been away from Seattle for a number of years. I transferred my membership in the Office Employees Union to San Francisco. That was during the depression still, and work was very scarce. I applied to WPA and worked all together on three projects: the first was registering stolen guns for the police; then a writers project; and last, a music project. Then I was kicked out and told to get a private job, so I got a job with the unions. I worked for the Bakers Union, the Marine Cooks and Stewards, and several others.

I became active in the Office Employees Union and wrote articles for the paper. Sometimes I was commended by the Communists, other times I was commended by the anti-Communists. My political education really began at that time. There were a number of Trotskyites in the local who got interested in me and began to try to recruit me into the Socialist Workers Party. Although I didn't join it until about two years later, they became the focus of my social and political life. I realized how ignorant I was about history and I had to read constantly, to learn constantly. They were puzzled that for all my intellectualism, on the one hand, I was ignorant. Although I didn't dare admit it then, I was quite ashamed of my ignorance.

But I learned from the top down, and they were impressed with my ability to absorb quite a new idea within a very short period of time.

Within the SWP (Socialist Workers Party) the issues were really political and on an extremely high level. It was simply inconceivable how high the level was! Don't forget it was a break between a man like Max Schactman and Trotsky, when Trotsky was still alive, or between Jim Cannon and Max Schactman. You have to really know your theories, otherwise you can't discuss it. And, of course, the Soviet Union was the major problem in the SWP, and the one issue that really split the party. Unfortunately, as I saw it then and still see it today, neither side really understood the issues, except perhaps Max Schactman. The rank-and-file members didn't understand; they just formed their alliances on the basis of loyalty to one side or another.

As for feminism, that wasn't really an issue. After all, Socialists were supposed to have a notion of equality between all people and naturally that equality would extend to women as well; they certainly believed in equality for women in industry and politics. They claimed that so long as you live in a capitalist country you're not going to get that equality. Except that we couldn't turn the society overnight into a socialist one, so therefore you have to fight for it individually, or piecemeal. Whenever I did have an argument it was short and not bitter. It was usually about whether or not women had the intellectual ability to absorb knowledge to the same degree as men.

All during those years I worked out of the Office Employees Union. They had contracts with all the union offices in San Francisco. In the early forties I worked for the waterfront union. They were sending men to a maritime school, but first they had to have an affidavit that they were not sailing during the 1934 and 1936 strikes. They would be sent to me to be interviewed, and to be given a card. I had a very interesting experience because some of these boys would be Southerners and they'd say, "I hope there are no goddamned niggers on those boats." I would say, "Brother, you're going to be awfully unhappy, because there are niggers on those boats, and you're going to take it or get off the ships. You won't be happy on any ship. Those niggers are members of a union!"

I worked for the ILGWU (International Ladies Garment Workers Union) for a while, but I couldn't take it. They were always complaining about their jobs, about their secretary, about Jenny Matyas.* Finally, I quit. Then I worked for the Operating Engineers. It was a lovely job. Even though it was a temporary job, I ended up working there eight months and could

---

* Vice president of the ILGWU who worked in the San Francisco office of the union.

have worked there permanently. That was the job I left to come down to L.A. in 1948.

I really worked at the wrong end of the union. I should have been working out in the field, organizing, because I talked to many girls, and every time I talked to them they changed their views. A lot of them regarded me as their speaker.

But I was active in the union—at least vocally. When I joined, the union had already broken away from the AFL and gone into the CIO. They organized pretty heavily, especially some big industries. Then we had trouble with the Communists. That was the beginning of my knowledge of how the Communists really operated. And I must admit they were successful. I begrudged them their success. They were so powerful, and [Harry] Bridges used to come down to the meetings and tell us to toe the line, or else. We had to make a choice: toe the line, or else. So we were forced to make overtures to the AFL, to return to it. Those who were Communists and sympathetic to Communist members stayed in the CIO and were taken over by the Warehousemen.

We walked off with all the furniture, the money, all the records. We felt quite justified in doing that because we really represented most of the members in the local. At the time there were, at the most, eight hundred members in the local and we took two thirds or more. We lost several hundred members after the split in 1938. We didn't lose them to the CIO; they were lost altogether when their contracts expired. The worst of it was that at the first meeting after the split the state chairman of the AFL spoke to us. He started to lay down the line. He might just as well have said "Toe the line, or else." He sounded like Bridges. You can imagine how we felt—from the frying pan into the fire. We were really glum about the whole business, but another officer—who was either an anarchist or a socialist—saw our attitudes and got up and said, "I don't think we ought to put such demands on a new local. They're repenting their struggle with us. Our attitude should be more tolerant."

I remained active in that union and was a sergeant at arms for a few years, and to any degree that I understood the arguments within the local, I would take a position—always the liberal side. I was too radical for them. One of the problems I had was arguing with some of the employers, union employers, too. They were breaking some of the clauses in our contract. Unfortunately, the business agent didn't like my arguments. So I asked her, "What on earth did you do when you were not a business agent and were working in union offices where they were breaking clauses?" "I kept my mouth shut." It was the most outrageous answer that I ever received! Then our business agent kept calling our union a business. I couldn't accept that. I argued with her very severely saying, "A union is not a business, it is a beneficial association organized to benefit its members and if you don't benefit the members, then you are not a union—nor a business." She used to get very angry with me. In fact, she wanted to expel me. She wanted to expel four of us. There was a reviewing committee and they talked to each one of us and they couldn't see any reason to expel us; we had not broken any union regulations. It was mainly our political ideas. One of these ideas was to expel the business agent! It was really quite an exciting period.

We had a lot of excitement in the union up there, and down here in L.A., too. I got very tired of the San Francisco climate. I was getting two or three colds a year. The rains were tremendous, the fog was intolerable and the winds were ungodly. I came to L.A. for a visit in 1948 and kind of liked it. I met a lot of people, a lot of Wobblies, especially. So I decided to move down here. I went to live with Mary Gallagher for several months. She had been very active in the Tom Mooney defense and in the [support for the] sharecroppers many years ago.

I continued to work in the unions, except once when I was in private business. I stayed active in the Office Employees Union until I withdrew from it when I retired in 1965. I was tired of working. But I had no business to stop my activities. I'm really against retirement in a political sense. Boy, I've never been so tired of my retirement as I am now!

FEMINISM: THE LONG VIEW

A few years ago, in about 1969, I became involved in the current women's movement. Earlier, people had tried to persuade me to join the League of Women Voters, but I just couldn't do it. It felt foreign to me. I just couldn't understand what I call capitalist politics. (I have enough arguments within my own socialist group! They are forever critical of the capitalist system, but still at each election, they'd vote for the same people. Voting for McGovern, of all candidates!)

I went with a friend from the Socialist Party to the NOW (National Organization for Women) meeting. I became known right away, the first time I went. I spoke to the young woman at the desk who was giving out literature and name tags and told her, "You know, I spent thirty days in jail for the vote." This is how I connected the National Organization for Women —as a continuation of the voting struggle.

It took a long time for the information about my jail term to really penetrate the membership. I looked too young to have been in that fight. Finally, they went to the library and picked up a book. I was the only Ernestine. It's awfully hard to find a picture of a twenty-one-year-old, but I happen to remember what kind of a hat I wore. In 1970, when we had that big march and celebration, they asked me to speak there about my experiences.

My activity, though, was limited to going to meetings. The meetings were at a restaurant on Eighth and Vermont, in the back, in a large banquet room. Most of those girls have cars and they can go here and there, without having to exercise their feet. On the other hand, my feet hurt badly and I have no car. If I go to a meeting, I have to go out in the dark and the city has become dangerous in the dark. It's dangerous enough in the day. Also my eyes are not very good. So I can't go to the headquarters and spend some hours there answering the telephone and meeting people.

There used to be more women of my age in NOW than

there are now. The women of my age seemed to become disgusted with the sexual concentration. At that time there was more concentration on it. They had a play about it. This woman, who must have been in her seventies, got up and said, "Can't you girls think of anything else? This whole meeting has been devoted to sex and I think that's filthy." Boy, you can't imagine what it did to us. We tried to pacify her. It's one of the things I've fought against my whole life. I thought, My God, is it possible that people would come to a NOW meeting and still hold those views? I think, really, she considered it an extraneous subject, which it isn't. They recognize we've been sexually maligned as well as mistreated. We want the right to understand sex and then to use our own option as to whether we want extramarital relationships or premarital relationships. We want to at least be given an education on birth control and venereal disease.

I'm more committed to NOW than to the women's liberation movement. I've met some Communists in the women's liberation movement, and I'll tell you, because of my past experiences, I've gotten frightened of them. Also, women's liberation started out, in my opinion, badly, though they're recovering from it now. They started out badly in the sense that they focused on issues that were not the important ones. To me there are very basic discriminatory issues that we have to fight. Whether you wear a bra or don't wear a bra is immaterial to me. It's healthier to wear a bra than to let the breasts move up and down, which may cause a breakage of some of the muscles if you're too heavy.

There are certain things like that. And then, also the freedom of using four-letter words. I have no objection to them except that they're misused. They are meaningless. We have some very good words in the dictionaries that mean much more than those four-letter words. I've had a certain objection to them all my life for the reason that they're used without discrimination.

I feel the goal of the current women's movement is to get

all the clauses within the ERA passed. It'll be a piecemeal struggle, absolutely piecemeal. You have to fight for each thing separately. It may take hundreds of years, but we have to fight. Wage discrimination will be one of the hardest of all the battles. Aside from the fact of negotiating wages, unions will have the hardest fight. Really, the differential between male and female wages is much too great to tolerate. So many women are aware of it and just take it for granted; that's the division of the sexes.

Of course, to me, the worst of anything to which I have great objection is the intellectual inequality between the sexes. I mean, the belief that the male brain is more equipped to think than the female brain. You meet so many men and so many women; you find them both ignorant and you're not equipped to talk to either of them. They are not equipped to carry on a conversation with anyone who's had some education. I'm talking generally, now, of the average public.

But I see changes. I see changes especially since the women's rebellion six years ago. Before then, the only fight was in the unions, and that was almost solely on economic issues. But when you live through periods, you don't see the changes unless they're violent. Actually, the feminist movement today started out violently and has been violent throughout. I don't mean they fought physically, but they did fight intellectually. Also, their persistence in changing the status of women and changing their image in society is very sharp today—to an extent where men cannot ignore it any longer. It's comparable to the fight for woman's suffrage in 1917 and 1918. The persistence is quite comparable to that, but the issues are much broader.

Otherwise, you can't compare the two. That was simply one issue, the voting right. To me, the voting right was only a minor right. I was something of an anarchist and I had no faith in capitalist society. What did it matter whether I voted or not? What did it matter whether a man voted or not? That's why it wasn't a major issue with me. In fact, I wasn't even in favor of citizenship. The only thought I had in mind was that voting didn't help the working people, that all that would happen was to add so many more votes, but that nevertheless it had the illusion of equality. It really was an illusion.

I think that what happened is that they put so much importance in the vote for women that when they got the vote, they felt like they had a victory, a tremendous victory. Well, it was a tremendous victory, but it was a one-issue victory, and that one issue was not enough. Through the votes they should have had all kinds of civil codes changed. For instance, in the economy of our country, women are so underpaid in similar work with men that it's a disgrace. You can't think of it in any other way than as a disgrace. I can't think of a stronger word.

Today, so many needs have arisen, like child care. Where both parents work, the child has to be left someplace. There is no satisfaction in hiring somebody to take care of the children; those children could be spoiled that way. Actually, having contact with others their own age is preferable. So you need child care. Whether parents can afford the child care has been the principal issue. Today what we've discovered is that many women are the sole supporters of the children. They have to have a child care center where they can leave the children and pay a nominal sum for them to be taken care of while they're working. This is one issue. This is the economic issue.

There is also the social and the personal issue. The parents are actually enslaved to their children. It's not good for either the children or the parents. They're in bondage. The moment they have a child, they're in bondage. They have to redefine the word "responsibility." To what degree are they forced to be responsible? Should they be responsible? Both these issues, the degree and whether they should or should not be responsible, is part of the bondage system that parents have been forced into for as long as the human race existed. It was easier in tribal days when all the parents took care of all the children. The children were the responsibility of a whole group. Today they are the responsibility of—it's not even a group—two people, instead of thirty or fifty.

None of these issues were really pursued after the vote, except for the ERA. But the fact that Alice Paul, for so many years, fought for the ERA just shows she didn't have much support. That party organization of hers should have spread throughout the country and should have really been the national organization that was organized only about six years ago.

This is what women have failed to understand. The vote was nothing. Even the men had it. The men misused the vote and the women misused the vote. This is one of the misfortunes of a democracy—people can't judge, have no way of judging, what would be to their benefit and what turns out to be to their loss.

This is the way I have always thought—in these terms. My group of anarchists and Wobblies and Socialists, the women especially, thought as I did. To an extent the men did, but to a large extent they felt superior to the female sex. Women were still not in the forefront as writers or as artists or as philosophers or as teachers. Women themselves wouldn't go to the forefront. There were very few women like George Eliot or Gertrude Stein.

There are very few such women. They were unusual in a sense. We mistakenly say they are like men. We say that because we have no other comparison. We compare one existence to another and arrive at some conclusion. That is why the saying is "She's just like a man." But actually, she's not like a man. She's just a human being with certain talents and aspirations and development. In that sense, both women and men have them.

But a woman has to fight for the specific needs of herself as a human being, not as a sexual object. Whatever she gains, men should also gain. If she gains something that men do not have, men are entitled to the same gain. For instance, the protective right for women in industry. Men are entitled to it, and have always been entitled to it.

Freedom for women was an essential necessity every year of my life, but it was a wider issue than just one specific one like the voting rights, like the same pay for the same work, and so on. It meant getting rid, most of all, of men's attitude that women were inferior creatures—even while they leered at them and wanted them.

But I think men's attitudes are different now than they were back then. They realize that women have been discriminated against in jobs and education. Even the attitude men have that women have no brains and should stay in the kitchen. There is, amongst the more intelligent men, a change. Whatever we know has been instilled in us by our parents and by society: schools, newspapers, streets, organizations we belong to. And it's been extremely prejudicial. But the realization that prejudice is a very bad form of thinking has struck men as well as women.

Men are also in bondage, though they may think they are superior to women, not only economically and politically, but socially. You're in bondage if you are not free to make certain decisions or if you are brainwashed all of the time. We are brainwashed all the time, even the most intelligent of us.

But mind you, it'll always be a minority of each sex that will fight for social gain, never a majority. The majority will win by default. And they will benefit. Like with the vote. Women think they always had the vote, they don't know. It's part of our history, but we don't know the history. That history isn't taught in school.

But women have been very timid about their rights for many years. It was surprising that the states went so far as to give them the vote in 1920. The men, I think, didn't want a continuation of the female struggle for voting rights. They feel the same way about the equal rights amendment.

It becomes corrosive, this idea of equality. All right, so you have equality, now what else do you want? And this is only the beginning of the struggle for women! Now they have to fight for equality in specific areas. It's going to be a fight for as long as they live.

For as long as society exists, women are going to fight for their rights.

SUFFRAGE WINS IN SENATE; NOW GOES TO STATES

Constitutional Amendment is Passed, 56 to 25, or Two More Than Two-thirds.

WOMEN MAY VOTE IN 1920

Leaders Start Fight to Get Ratification by Three-fourths of States in Time

DEBATE PRECEDES VOTE

Wadsworth Explains His Attitudes in Opposition— Resolution Signed with Ceremony

Special to The New York Times
WASHINGTON, June 4.— After a long and persistent fight advocates of woman suffrage won a victory in the Senate to- day when that body, by a vote of 56 to 25, adopted the Susan Anthony amendment to the Con- stitution. The suffrage sup- porters had two more than the necessary two-thirds vote of Sen- ators present. . . .

The amendment, having al- ready been passed by the House, where the vote was 304 to 89, now goes to the States for rati- fication, where it will be passed upon in the form in which it has been adopted by Congress, as fol- lows:

"Article—. Section 1.—The right of citizens of the United States to vote shall not be denied or abridged by the United States or by any State on account of sex.

"Section 2.—Congress shall have power, by appropriate legis- lation, to enforce the provisions of this article" . . .

Suffragists thronged the Sen- ate galleries in anticipation of the final vote, and when the out- come was announced by Presi- dent Pro Tem. Cummins they broke into deafening applause. For two minutes the demonstra- tion went on, Senator Cummins making no effort to check it.

CHRONOLOGY

1776 The New Jersey State Constitution grants votes to *all* inhabitants, twenty-one and over, with property valued at fifty pounds or more.

1787 The Constitutional Convention places the determination of voting qualifications in the hands of the states. The qualifications, determined by sex, race, age and property holding, effectively excludes women in all states except New Jersey.

1806 New Jersey, as a result of a surprise election outcome largely influenced by the women's vote, restricts suffrage to white males. The denial of the elective franchise to American women becomes universal.

1840 Lucretia Mott and Elizabeth Cady Stanton, along with other women, are denied their seats (as delegate and observer, respectively) to the World Anti-Slavery Convention in London due to their sex. This incident leads to a recognition of the need for women to have a convention of their own, and is ultimately responsible for the founding of the women's rights movement in the United States.

1848 Lucretia Mott, Elizabeth Cady Stanton, Jane Hunt, Martha Wright and Mary McClintock issue a public notice for a meeting at Seneca Falls, New York, to be held on July 19, 20, "to discuss the social, civic and religious rights of women."

The Declaration of Sentiments and a set of resolutions is adopted at Seneca Falls and signed by 68 women and 32 men. The first formal demand for women's right to vote is made in the United States.

A women's rights convention is held later in the year at Rochester, New York, signaling the rise of state organizations devoted to the cause of women's rights, including suffrage.

A state women's rights convention is held in Salem, Ohio, which bars men from participation.

1850   Women's rights leaders, including Lucy Stone, Lucretia Mott and Abby Kelley, meet during the Boston Negro Rights Convention and plan the First National Women's Rights Convention, to be held in Worcester, Massachusetts, October 23.

One thousand people attend the First National Women's Rights Convention, including abolitionists, temperance workers, Quakers, and women from cities and farms. This marks the first of the yearly conventions held until 1860.

A resolution is passed that women be entitled to the right to vote and that the word "male" be stricken from state constitutions. Out of the convention a National Central Committee is organized, the first of its kind, to produce literature, promote woman's rights and help to plan other conventions.

Susan B. Anthony joins the ranks of the women's rights crusaders.

1851–   Suffrage leaders continue to devote their energies to both the
1860   cause of women's rights and the abolition of slavery, often appearing before legislatures in efforts to reform the laws unfavorable to women.

At the Women's Rights Convention in Akron, Ohio, in 1851, Sojourner Truth, an ex-slave, helps to save the meeting from men who threaten to break it up. In response to the attacks on women by several clergymen, she rose to give her now-famous "Ain't I a woman" rebuttal.

Yearly women's rights conventions are held until the Civil War diverts the energies of all the suffrage figures to a total concentration on the anti-slavery fight.

The Fourteenth Amendment is drafted, and with it the word "male" is introduced into the federal constitution for the first time. Abolitionists argue with suffragists that extending the franchise to women at this time would hurt the cause of the blacks.

1866   Suffragists make a direct request to Congress, with petitions bearing 10,000 signatures, for an amendment prohibiting disenfranchisement on the grounds of sex. The majority hold firm about not striking the word "male" from the Fourteenth Amendment.

The first debate on woman's suffrage is held in Congress in connection with a move to extend the vote in Washington, D.C.

The first Women's Rights Convention since the Civil War is held on May 1. A disagreement is brewing within the suffragist ranks over the Fourteenth Amendment (with its "male only" clauses). The convention resolves itself into the American Equal Rights Association, with Lucretia Mott as president, and pledges to work for suffrage for both women and Negroes.

Susan B. Anthony and Elizabeth Cady Stanton continue to battle against the "male only" Fourteenth Amendment, to the point of opposing its ratification—a position which causes them to lose some of their supporters.

1867   Kansas puts two proposed amendments on the ballot: to grant suffrage to women and to Negroes. This marks the first time that woman's suffrage is put to a direct vote. Both measures lose.

1868   The Fourteenth Amendment is ratified.

1869   The Fifteenth Amendment is proposed, prohibiting denial or abridgment of rights on the basis of race, color or condition of previous servitude. Woman's rights leaders receive little support in their efforts to include "sex" in the wording of the Fifteenth Amendment.

The Equal Rights Association breaks up over a disagreement in philosophy and tactics. Susan B. Anthony and Elizabeth Cady Stanton feel women were betrayed by the male abolitionists (who refused to push for the exclusion of "male" from the Fourteenth Amendment or the inclusion of "sex" in the Fifteenth Amendment). They form the National Woman's Suffrage Association (NWSA), exclusively for women, to dedicate their energies to a fight for a federal amendment granting woman's suffrage and to the broader issues of women's rights.

Lucy Stone, a few months later, forms the American Woman's Suffrage Association (AWSA). This group includes men, is dedicated to securing suffrage through state battles rather than through a federal amendment and is generally more conservative and single-issue-oriented than the Stanton-Anthony group, NWSA.

Women win the right to vote in Wyoming, following the granting of territorial status. This represents the first enfranchisement of women (since the women of New Jersey lost their rights) in the United States.

1870   The Territory of Utah grants woman's suffrage (a right they will later lose under the Edmunds-Tucker Act of Congress in 1887).

Victoria Woodhull appears before the House Judiciary Committee, being the first woman to speak in the Capitol.

1871   The Anti-Suffrage Society is formed, composed of wives of prominent men, including many Civil War generals.

1872   Victoria Woodhull becomes the first woman to run for President, on her own ticket, with Frederick Douglass as the vice-presidential candidate.

Susan B. Anthony registers to vote in an effort to force a court decision (which might then obviate the need for a constitutional amendment) on woman's suffrage. She is tried, convicted and fined $100, which she refuses to pay.

1875   Virginia Minor sues the registrar's office in St. Louis for denying her the right to vote, in an attempt to test the Fourteenth Amendment. She loses her case.

1876   Lucretia Mott, Susan B. Anthony and Elizabeth Cady Stanton open offices during the Centennial in Philadelphia. They issue a Woman's Declaration of 1876 and disrupt the official program to present their declaration.

1877   Suffragists petition the Senate for the Sixteenth Amendment to grant woman's suffrage (the Anthony amendment, ultimately the Nineteenth).

1878   Senator Aaron Sargent of California introduces the Sixteenth Amendment. Elizabeth Cady Stanton appears at the hearings held by the Senate Committee on Privileges and Elections. The committee reports against the proposed amendment.

1882   Select committees of both houses of Congress are appointed, and both report favorably on the suffrage amendment.

1886   The woman's suffrage amendment is called up on the Senate floor.

1887   January 25, the first vote on woman suffrage is taken and the measure is defeated two to one.

1890   The two major suffrage organizations, the National Woman Suffrage Association (NWSA) and the American Woman Suffrage Association (AWSA) merge, becoming the National American Suffrage Association (NAWSA). Because of the failure to secure the passage of a federal amendment, they pledge themselves to state-by-state fights.

The South Dakota campaign for woman's suffrage is lost.

1893   Colorado votes for woman's suffrage following an energetic campaign by Carrie Chapman Catt and other suffrage figures. This represents the first time that male voters decide by direct choice to grant woman's suffrage.

1894   Petitions with 600,000 signatures are presented in an effort to convince a New York State Constitutional Convention to submit a woman's suffrage amendment to the voters. The campaign fails.

Lucy Stone, one of the pioneers of women's rights, dies. Her daughter, Alice Stone Blackwell, continues her work.

Efforts fail in Kansas to extend woman's suffrage (limited to municipal and school district elections) to general suffrage.

1895   Carrie Chapman Catt presents a plan of reorganization to the NAWSA Convention and revitalizes the suffrage struggle.

The first victory under the new organization is won in Utah, where woman's suffrage is reinstated after nine years.

1896   Idaho grants woman's suffrage.

1900   Susan B. Anthony turns the leadership of the NAWSA over to Carrie Chapman Catt.

1902   Elizabeth Cady Stanton, the philosopher of the women's rights movement, dies.

1904   Carrie Chapman Catt resigns due to ill health, and Anna Howard Shaw becomes the president of the NAWSA.

1906   Susan B. Anthony, the early organizational force behind the suffrage movement, dies.

1908   Harriet Stanton Blatch, daughter of Elizabeth Cady Stanton, returns from England fresh with ideas from the British suffrage movement. She founds the Women's Political Union in New York and introduces new strategy (street speaking, parades, etc.) which helps to change the tone of the national suffrage movement.

1910   The first suffrage parade in New York is held.

The fourteen-year lull is broken with the granting of woman's suffrage in the State of Washington.

1911   A huge campaign in California is successful in winning the vote for women in that state.

Three thousand suffrage supporters join the New York parade.

Emmeline Pankhurst, the militant British suffrage figure, speaks at the NAWSA Convention.

1912   The Progressive Party, under the leadership of Teddy Roosevelt, favors woman's suffrage.

A parade to Pennsylvania Avenue is held in Washington, D.C., to present the annual petition for the woman's suffrage amendment to Congress.

A major suffrage parade is organized in New York City. Ten thousand march.

Oregon, Arizona and Kansas grant woman's suffrage.

1913   The Alaskan Territory grants woman's suffrage. Illinois grants limited suffrage (in municipal and presidential elections). This represents the first victory east of the Mississippi River.

Alice Paul and Lucy Burns return from London where they both had participated in the militant suffrage struggle. They form the Congressional Union as an auxiliary of the National American Woman Suffrage Association (NAWSA) and set up offices in Washington, D.C., to launch a renewed campaign for a federal amendment.

A parade of 8,000 women is held the day preceding Woodrow Wilson's presidential inauguration. The Washington, D.C., police deny the suffragists police protection, and after attacks by mobs the Secretary of War calls out troops from Fort Meyer.

A delegation from the Congressional Union visits Woodrow Wilson to ask him to include woman's suffrage in his message to a special session of Congress. He is uncooperative.

Suffragists march to the Capitol to present petitions.

The Susan B. Anthony amendment is reintroduced in the House and Senate. The Senate reports favorably on the amendment, but all action is blocked in the House.

1914   Nevada adopts woman's suffrage.

A vote is taken in the Senate on the suffrage amendment, the first vote since 1887. (The vote is 35–34.) The amendment is stalled by a tie vote in the Rules Committee of the House.

The Democratic caucus declares that suffrage is a state issue. Since Woodrow Wilson states he can only follow his party, the Congressional Union moves to direct political action, holding the Democratic Party, as the party in power, responsible for the continued disenfranchisement of women.

1915   A transcontinental tour by suffragists yields over a half million signatures on petitions to Congress.

The House, for the first time in history, votes on national woman's suffrage. The measure is defeated 204–174.

Forty thousand march in a New York suffrage parade, the largest parade of any kind ever seen in New York.

Woman's suffrage measures are defeated in New Jersey, New York, Massachusetts and Pennsylvania.

1916   Alice Paul and the members of the Congressional Union break away from the NAWSA over a disagreement on tactics, and the National Woman's Party (NWP) is formed.

Both the NAWSA and the NWP march on the Republican Convention and succeed in having woman's suffrage adopted in the Republican platform for the first time. The Republican presidential candidate, Charles Evans Hughes, comes out in favor of a constitutional amendment.

The suffragists converge on the Democratic Convention but are unsuccessful. The platform of the Democratic Party and the presidential candidate, Woodrow Wilson both favor action by individual states only. The National Woman's Party, in response, opens a political war against Woodrow Wilson.

1917   Three hundred militant suffragists, including Harriet Stanton Blatch and Alice Paul, meet to plan action in Washington. A decision is made to post "sentinels of liberty" at the White House.

January 10, pickets appear in front of the White House and remain stationed there permanently, with hourly changes of shift. On Inauguration Day, 1,000 suffragists join the regular pickets.

In June the arrests of the White House pickets begin. 218 suffragists are eventually illegally arrested for obstruction of traffic.

Beginning in August the pickets begin to draw 30- and 60-day sentences. They first institute a work strike at the Occoquan Workhouse, and in September a number of the jailed suffragists begin a hunger strike. They are subjected to forcible feeding and threatened with transfer to an insane asylum.

The House finally sets up a Woman Suffrage Committee, taking the Susan B. Anthony amendment out of the control of the hostile House Judiciary Committee.

North Dakota, Indiana, Rhode Island, Nebraska and Michigan grant women the right to vote for President. Arkansas grants women's participation in primary elections.

Constitutional victories are won in South Dakota and Oklahoma. New York finally approves woman's suffrage.

1918   In January President Wilson finally publicly declares his support for woman's suffrage—just one day before the House vote. The amendment passes the House by exactly two-thirds majority, 272–136.

The suffragists are released from prison by order of the President. The Washington, D.C., appeals court later rules they were illegally arrested, convicted and imprisoned.

The suffrage amendment is kept from coming to a vote in the Senate. The National Woman's Party (NWP) transfers its pickets to the Senate, and continues to put pressure on Wilson to secure his assistance in passage in the Senate.

Wilson appears at the Senate in October to appeal for immediate passage of the suffrage amendment as a war measure. It is defeated in the Senate by 2 votes short of the two-thirds majority.

1919   The suffrage amendment is brought to a vote again in the Senate, and is still one vote short of the two-thirds majority.

Beginning January 1919, a perpetual fire is built in an urn in direct line with the front door of the White House. Every time President Wilson delivers a speech about democracy, the NWP tolls a bell and burns his words. The watchfire for freedom burns day and night, with women on guard all night. The urn is broken and scattered, but the women rebuild the fire.

The President brings his pressure to bear on the Democratic members of the Senate, and the final vote is secured.

The woman's suffrage amendment, the Nineteenth Amendment to the Constitution, is passed on June 4, 1919. It is the same as the amendment originally authored by Susan B. Anthony and first introduced in 1878.

1920   On August 18, 1920, after a year's struggle to secure ratification by two-thirds of the states, Tennessee becomes the thirty-sixth state to ratify the amendment. Official word is received in Washington, and the amendment is signed into law on August 26, 1920.

SELECTED BIBLIOGRAPHY

WOMEN IN THE EARLY TWENTIETH CENTURY

Boone, Gladys, *The Women's Trade Union League in Great Britain and the U.S.A.* New York: Columbia University Press, 1942.

Breckenridge, Sophonisba, *Women in the 20th Century: A Study of their Political, Social and Economic Activities.* New York: McGraw-Hill, 1933.

Brown, Esther, *Nursing as a Profession.* New York: Russell Sage, 1940.

Buhle, Mary Jo, "Women and the Socialist Party, 1901–1914," in Edith Altbach (ed.), *From Feminism to Liberation.* Cambridge, Mass.: Schenkman, 1971.

———, Ann Gordon, and Nancy Schromm, "Women in American Society: An Historical Contribution," *Radical America*, Vol. 5, 1971, pp. 3–66.

Davies, Margery, "Woman's Place Is at the Typewriter: The Femi nization of the Clerical Labor Force," *Radical America*, Vol. 8, 1974, pp. 1–28.

Degler, Carl, *Out of Our Past: The Forces That Shaped Modern America.* New York: Harper & Row, 1970.

Dennett, Mary Ware, *Birth Control Laws.* New York: Graton Press, 1926.

Dorr, Rheta Childe, *A Woman of Fifty.* New York: Funk & Wagnalls, 1924.

———, *What Eight Million Women Want* (reprint edition). Boston: Kraus, 1971.

Faulkner, Harold, *The Quest for Social Justice, 1898–1914.* New York: Macmillan, 1931.

Gordon, Michael (ed.), *The American Family in Social Historical Perspective.* New York: St. Martin's Press, 1973.

McGovern, James R., "The American Woman's Pre-World War I

Freedom in Manners and Morals," *Journal of American History,* Vol. 55, 1968, pp. 315–318.

Nathan, Maude, *The Story of an Epoch-Making Movement.* Garden City, N.Y.: Doubleday, Page & Co., 1926.

Ryan, Mary P., *Womanhood in America: From Colonial Times to the Present.* New York: New Viewpoints, 1975.

Sanger, Margaret, *Woman and the New Race.* New York: Truth Publishing, 1920.

Scott, Anne Firor, *The American Woman, Who Was She?* Englewood Cliffs, N.J.: Prentice-Hall, 1971.

Slosson, Preston, *The Great Crusade and After, 1914–1928.* New York: Macmillan, 1930.

Smuts, Robert W., *Women and Work in America.* New York: Columbia University Press, 1959.

Sochen, June, *Movers and Shakers.* New York: Quadrangle, 1973.

———, *The New Woman in Greenwich Village, 1910–1920.* New York: Quadrangle Books, 1972.

Women's Bureau, "The Occupational Progress of Women, 1910–1930," Bulletin No. 104.

"Women in the Modern World," *Annals of the American Academy of Political and Social Science,* Vol. 143, 1929.

WOMAN'S SUFFRAGE

Blatch, Harriet Stanton, and Alma Lutz, *Challenging Years: Memoirs of Harriet Stanton Blatch.* New York: Putnam & Sons, 1940.

Catt, Carrie Chapman, and Nettie Rogers Shuler, *Woman Suffrage and Politics: The Inner Story of the Suffrage Movement.* New York: Scribner's, 1923.

Flexner, Eleanor, *Century of Struggle: The Woman's Rights Movement in the United States.* New York: Atheneum, 1968.

Irwin, Inez Haynes, *Up Hill with Banners Flying: Story of the National Woman's Party.* Penobscot, Me.: Travesty, 1964.

Kraditor, Aileen, *The Ideas of the Woman Suffrage Movement, 1890–1920.* New York: Columbia University Press, 1965.

O'Neill, William L., *Everyone Was Brave: The Rise and Fall of Feminism in America.* Chicago: Quadrangle, 1969.

Park, Maud Wood, *Front Door Lobby.* Boston: Beacon Press, 1960.

Sinclair, Andrew, *The Emancipation of American Women.* New York: Harper, 1960.

Stevens, Doris, *Jailed for Freedom.* New York: Boni & Liveright, 1920.

WOMEN IN THE 1920s

Chafe, William H., *The American Woman, Her Changing Social, Economic and Political Roles, 1920–1970.* New York: Oxford University Press, 1972.

Freedman, Estelle, "The New Woman: Changing Views of Women in the 1920's," *Journal of American History*, Vol. 61, 1974, pp. 372–393.

Gordon, Linda, "The Politics of Population: Birth Control and the Eugenics Movement," *Radical America*, Vol. 8, 1974, pp. 61–98.

Gruberg, Martin, *Women in American Politics: An Assessment and Sourcebook.* Oshkosh, Wis.: Academia, 1968.

Kennedy, David, *Birth Control in America.* New Haven: Yale University Press, 1970.

Lemons, J. Stanley, *The Woman Citizen: Social Feminism in the 1920's.* Urbana: University of Illinois Press, 1973.

Lynd, Helen and Robert, *Middletown: A Study of Contemporary American Culture.* New York: Harcourt, Brace and Jovanovich, 1929.

Yellis, Kenneth, "Prosperity's Child: Some Thoughts on the Flapper," *American Quarterly*, Vol. 21, 1969, pp. 44–64.

ABOUT THE EDITOR

SHERNA GLUCK is a feminist lecturer and researcher. She is a co-founder and director of the Feminist History Research Project and has designed a women's studies course which she taught at UCLA. She lives in Topanga Canyon, California, and is active in the women's liberation movement in Los Angeles.

VINTAGE WORKS OF SCIENCE
AND PSYCHOLOGY

VINTAGE CRITICISM,
LITERATURE, MUSIC, AND ART

VINTAGE POLITICAL SCIENCE
AND SOCIAL CRITICISM